Claudia Olk
Virginia Woolf and the Aesthetics of Vision

Buchreihe der ANGLIA/
ANGLIA Book Series

Edited by
Lucia Kornexl, Ursula Lenker, Martin Middeke,
Gabriele Rippl, Hubert Zapf

Advisory Board
Laurel Brinton, Philip Durkin, Olga Fischer, Susan Irvine,
Andrew James Johnston, Christopher A. Jones, Terttu Nevalainen,
Derek Attridge, Elisabeth Bronfen, Ursula K. Heise, Verena Lobsien,
Laura Marcus, J. Hillis Miller, Martin Puchner

Volume 45

Claudia Olk

Virginia Woolf and the Aesthetics of Vision

DE GRUYTER

For an overview of all books published in this series, please see
http://www.degruyter.com/view/serial/36292

ISBN 978-3-11-055391-8
e-ISBN 978-3-11-034023-5
ISSN 0340-5435

Library of Congress Cataloging-in-Publication Data
A CIP catalog record for this book has been applied for at the Library of Congress.

Bibliographic information published by the Deutsche Nationalbibliothek
The Deutsche Nationalbibliothek lists this publication in the Deutsche Nationalbibliografie;
detailed bibliographic data are available in the Internet at http://dnb.dnb.de.

© 2017 Walter de Gruyter GmbH, Berlin/Boston
This volume is text- and page-identical with the hardback published in 2014.
Printing: CPI books GmbH, Leck

♾ Printed on acid-free paper
Printed in Germany

www.degruyter.com

Acknowledgements

It is a pleasure to acknowledge the generous help of many friends, colleagues, and the crucial role played by many institutions in the preparation of this book. First of all I would like to thank Verena Olejniczak Lobsien for encouraging this project and for her inspirational guidance during its Habilitation phase. I am also very grateful to my two external referees Renate Brosch and Bernfried Nugel for all their helpful advice.

I would like to express my gratitude to the Studienstiftung des deutschen Volkes, the Stifterverband für die deutsche Wissenschaft, Dr. Meyer-Struckmann-Stiftung, the Alexander von Humboldt-Foundation, and the Fulbright Association, who granted me scholarships that were of immense help to my research.

Furthermore, I would like to thank the board of the Anglia Series at de Gruyter/Niemeyer, who supported the book, and my editor Dr. Ulrike Krauß for her expertise and steadfast commitment. For their scrupulous copy-editing I am indebted to Jennifer Bode and Marlene Dirschauer.

At the International Virginia Woolf Society I found a helpful audience and would like to thank them for providing me with the occasion to present earlier versions of single chapters at their annual conferences.

My special thanks go to the many colleagues and friends with whom I was fortunate to discuss this project: Christoph Bode, David Bradshaw, Jeri Johnson, Andrew James Johnston, Renate Hof, the late Carole Huffmann, Ulrike Kappler, my mentor the late Gert Mattenklott, Christian Nitschke, Manfred Pfister, Jürgen Schlaeger, Sarah Stanton and Helen Watanabe O'Kelly.

Claudia Olk

Contents

Acknowledgements —— V

List of Abbreviations —— IX

Introduction —— 1
    Modernism and vision —— 3
    Aesthetic vision and visual culture —— 7
    Woolf studies and vision —— 11

1   **Aesthetic Vision and Experience —— 18**
1.1   The semantics of seeing in Woolf's essays —— 26
1.2   Immediacy and abstraction in *The Voyage Out* —— 32
1.3   The transformation of vision: *To the Lighthouse* and the immanence of art —— 36
1.3.1   Immanence and ideal in Woolf's reading of Platonism —— 36
1.3.2   The dynamics of the image in *To the Lighthouse* —— 42
1.3.3   Light, love and perfection: Platonic *eros* and the dynamics of narrative in *To the Lighthouse* —— 49

2   **Modalities of the Gaze: Windows, Mirrors, and the Veil —— 54**
2.1   The window and the novel as narrative space —— 54
2.1.1   The mediated gaze in *The Voyage Out* —— 58
2.1.2   The multiplicity of symbolic form in *Jacob's Room* —— 65
2.1.3   The dialectics of perspective: windows in *Mrs. Dalloway* —— 72
2.2   "The veil of words" and the poetics of the diaphanous —— 78
2.2.1   The diaphanous in Modernist aesthetics —— 78
2.2.2   Twilight and fog: vague and fading vision —— 84
2.2.3   Seeing through tears —— 86
2.3   The looking glass and the reflection of difference —— 91
2.3.1   Beyond the looking glass: the surface and "the other side of life" —— 92
2.3.2   Water and glass in *Between the Acts* —— 99

3   **The Temporality of Aesthetic Vision —— 109**
3.1   Modernist temporalities of the view —— 109
3.2   Beginnings: the sketch and the scene —— 116
3.3   *Jacob's Room* and the space of time —— 126

3.4	"Was that the end?" – *Between the Acts* and the paradox of vision in time —— **134**	
3.4.1	Vision and silence —— **140**	
3.4.2	The rhythm of vision in time —— **146**	

4 The Poetry of Aesthetic Vision in *The Waves* —— 155
4.1   Visibility and form in the *Interludes* —— **157**
4.2   The "little language" and the private view —— **165**

Conclusion —— 184

Bibliography —— 189
   Texts and Editions —— **189**
   Secondary Sources —— **190**

List of Abbreviations

Works by Virginia Woolf

AROO	*A Room of One's Own*
AWD	*A Writer's Diary*
BA	*Between the Acts*
BERG	The Berg Collection of English and American Literature, New York Public Library, Astor, Lenox and Tilden Foundations.
CSFVW	*The Complete Shorter Fiction of Virginia Woolf*
D I-V	*The Diary of Virginia Woolf*
DM	*The Death of the Moth*
E I-VI	*The Essays of Virginia Woolf*
CDB	*The Captain's Death Bed and other Stories*
CE I-IV	*Collected Essays of Virginia Woolf*
CR I-II	*The Common Reader*
GR	*Granite and Rainbow*
JR	*Jacob's Room*
L I-VI	*The Letters of Virginia Woolf*
MB	*Moments of Being*
MD	*Mrs Dalloway*
ND	*Night and Day*
O	*Orlando*
TL	*To the Lighthouse*
TVO	*The Voyage Out*
TY	*The Years*
W	*The Waves*

Works by other Writers

HoD	Joseph Conrad, *Heart of Darkness*
MAC	William Shakespeare, *Macbeth*
MND	William Shakespeare, *A Midsummer Night's Dream*
Remembrance	Marcel Proust, *Remembrance of Things Past*
U	James Joyce, *Ulysses*
VD	Roger Fry, *Vision and Design*

Introduction

> I believe that the main thing in beginning a novel is to feel, not that you can write it, but that it exists on the far side of a gulf, which words can't cross: that it's to be pulled through only in a breathless anguish. Now when I sit down to an article, I have a net of words which will come down on the idea certainly in an hour or so. But a novel, as I saw, to be good should seem, before one writes it, something unwriteable: but only visible.[1]

In this letter to Vita Sackville West, Virginia Woolf describes the conception of a novel out of a sense of the impossible, the "unwriteable: but only visible". Like the artist Lily Briscoe in *To the Lighthouse*, Woolf playfully investigates into the novel as "the thing itself before it has been made anything" (*TL*, 193), suggesting that both the artist's and the writer's vision resist received representational modes. The novel rather unfolds as the result of a transitional process between vision and language, in which the unwritten and the unmade for which no 'net of words' or conventions is readily at hand, gains aesthetic presence. Woolf's Modernist writings reinvent themselves out of this sense of the impossible that is born out of the fruitful insight that reality is ultimately unrepresentable. Vision, as this example presents it, is a productive principle of narrative. The visual is not only pertinent to Woolf's process of composition, but her novels create a kind of vision that is proper to the text itself – a vision that reflects on the experience of seeing and renegotiates the relation between the reader and the text.

The category of vision is not only central to Modernist writing, but it also plays a significant role in the unfolding discourse of Modernism itself. The constellation of paradigms subsumed under the epithet 'Modernism' implies a sense of historical transition, or even crisis, and in its presentation of vision, Modernist discourse distinguishes itself in significant ways from its predecessors. The received sense of a Modernist break with realism, its pervasive interest in the workings of the individual mind, and its generic reclassifications of the novel also intimately affected the role of vision, which gained a conceptual rather than natural status.[2] The Modernist preoccupation with processes of seeing, with visibility and the aesthetic object implies both a critique of conventionalised ways of perception and an affirmation of the immanent potential of the text to bring forth new kinds of aesthetic perception which initiate a dialogue between the text and the reader in which aesthetics generates, mediates and reflects on perceptual cognition.

---

[1] *L* III, 529.
[2] Cf. Malcolm Bradbury and James McFarlane (eds.), *Modernism. A Guide to European Literature 1890–1930* (London: Penguin, 1991).

Whereas realist texts become legible within a positivist epistemology, Modernist texts depart from any such mimetic faith. The period is therefore characterised by and sometimes even seen as synonymous with its many experiments in narrative technique. The loss of confidence in the equation of seeing and believing, and the concomitant destabilising of an overall reliance on visual representation as a truthful rendition of reality produces new forms of visual relations as they are presented in the works of Virginia Woolf, and her many contemporary writers.

From Joseph Conrad's self-imposed task to "make you hear, to make you feel, it is before all to make you *see*. That is all and it is everything"[3] to Virginia Woolf's statement in "Mr. Bennett and Mrs. Brown" that human character changed 'in or around 1910', the year of the Post-Impressionist Exhibition, Modernist writers have always pointed to their interests in the visual, both in the arts and in narrative. The present study is concerned with such forms and functions of aesthetic vision created in Modernist prose, and it pursues the central question why and how experimental texts turn towards phenomena of the visual. In focusing on the fictional and critical works of Virginia Woolf, it seeks to define and to reveal the aesthetic implications of this turn towards the visual. It explores what is at issue when narrative attempts to emulate the effects attributed to vision without imitating them.

Woolf certainly lived and worked in an environment thriving with artistic creativity and providing fertile ground for developing her criticism and her fiction.[4] However, even if scholarship has recently argued that "Woolf's responses to modern visual cultures are what make her a modernist writer",[5] I do not merely wish to limit Woolf's aesthetics to one of response to contemporary influences, but rather seek to explore how Woolf's art emerges as a creative reworking of these influences.

Woolf's way of analysing her creative processes has left us with a rich and complex account of her aesthetics of production. The interpretations therefore draw on a large number of published and unpublished letters, diaries and memoirs that provide a wealth of subtle variations and even contradictions, and they assert the pervasiveness of Woolf's writerly concern with vision. In situating Woolf's critical and fictional works at the intersection of the discourses on vision and aesthetics, this study, however, attempts to shift the emphasis in the ongoing

---

[3] Joseph Conrad, *The Nigger of the 'Narcissus'* (London: Dent, 1964), x.
[4] Maggie Humm, "Virginia Woolf and the Arts", *The Edinburgh Companion to Virginia Woolf and the Arts*, ed. by Maggy Humm (Edinburgh: Edinburgh UP, 2010), 1–4.
[5] Maggy Humm, "Virginia Woolf and visual culture", *The Cambridge Companion to Virginia Woolf*, ed. by Susan Sellers 2nd edition (Cambridge: Cambridge UP, 2010), 214.

discussion of vision from the cultural to the aesthetic. Rather than stating influences, tracing motifs, or presenting formal comparisons of aesthetic technique, the purpose of this study is to explore the dimensions of aesthetic vision as they are presented in both Woolf's literary aesthetics and her fiction, and to show that there is an immanent reflection of vision in Woolf's works.

The category of aesthetic vision pursued in this study is not only central to contemporary theories of art and aesthetic experience, but has also received critical attention in structuralism, semiotics, phenomenology and hermeneutics. Aesthetic vision will both be considered as a narrative strategy in which the text engages with perceptual processes, and as a function of this engagement for the experience of reading. Woolf's narrative presentation of "vision" will be understood metaphorically within a spectrum of possibilities inevitably delimited by the text. Metaphor will not merely be taken as a literary device, but as a means of creating aesthetic vision in providing a new correlation between objects and perspectives, as Woolf describes it with reference to Proust in "Phases of Fiction": "a different view of the same object in terms of metaphor" (*CE* II, 98). Where necessary, the single chapters of this study will draw on relevant research in narratology, phenomenology, theories of aesthetic experience and contemporary discourses on vision, time and art. It will examine contexts, traditions and counter-traditions that resist or redefine established notions of perception in literature. Through the investigation of key dimensions of aesthetic vision as they are reflected in Woolf's fictional and critical works, I seek to provide new perspectives on literary texts as well as contexts for a reassessment of what occurs in Modernism's relationship to vision.

Modernism and vision

The history of criticism dealing with Modernism and vision is particularly long. In fact, it would be difficult to find a consideration of Modernist art without some kind of appraisal of the Modernist fascination with the visual, or, more generally, with the Modernist concern with seeing in a "modern" way. From abstraction in painting to Imagism in poetry, Modernism has always been taken as obsessed with the visual. As a challenge to conventional vision, Modernist art has likewise been traditionally depicted as anti-representation, personal, subjective vision, the refutation of any kind of objective perspective, and putting to the test the eye of the spectator in visual experiments.

In response to the copious extent of approaches dealing with specific problems of visual culture, and the visual in Modernism, I will provide an overview over the main strands of criticism, and briefly consider their relevance for this study, rather than exhaustively rehearse all the significant approaches on visual culture, as this would indeed require a study on its own.

The rise of new sceptical philosophical discourses of vision in the first half of the twentieth century has brought about what Martin Jay has called a "crisis in ocularcentrism",[6] and there are mainly two ways in which recent scholarship has approached Modernism's relation to the visual. The first tendency is represented by diachronic approaches professed in the works of Jonathan Crary and David Levin,[7] that locate the visual in earlier historical periods, and trace its various ways of emerging in intellectual and technical history. The second tendency, which manifests itself in Jay's works, is marked by the cultural historian's interest to establish the centrality of the visual in certain historical contexts and periods.

David Levin regards the history of vision as reflected in the history of philosophy and examines "the history of vision as a history of the discursive construction of vision within, and consequently by, the history of philosophy".[8] In turn, he is interested in the impact of a rhetoric of vision on the history of philosophy. Levin's diachronic studies scrutinise the Western philosophical tradition in which thinking has been conceived of in terms of seeing, and they trace Modernism back to the paradigm of vision as it was engendered by enlightenment rationality.[9] If, as Levin claims, the gaze of the philosopher is guided by the light of reason, one of his major hypotheses is that "philosophical accounts of vision are actually rational reconstructions of sight".[10]

Starting from the shift in philosophical and epistemological thought in the first decades of the twentieth century in which language is given a decisive role in the philosophical paradigm of knowledge,[11] Levin both inspects the language of vision which interrelates the discourses of vision, knowledge and truth, and the tenets implicit in a philosophical critique of vision. Since vision for Levin not only refers to sight and perception but also carries an ethical dimension, it at the same time encompasses the speculative notion of what life and the world could

---

[6] Martin Jay, "The Rise of Hermeneutics and the Crisis of Ocularcentrism", *Poetics Today*, 9 (1988), 307–326.
[7] Jonathan Crary, *Techniques of the Observer* (Cambridge, Mass.: MIT Press, 1991); Martin Jay, *Downcast Eyes. The Denigration of Vision in Twentieth-Century French Thought* (Berkeley: U of California Press, 1993).
[8] David M. Levin (ed.), *Sites of Vision. The Discursive Construction of Sight in the History of Philosophy* (Cambridge, Mass.: MIT Press, 1997), 1f.
[9] See also: David M. Levin, *The Philosopher's Gaze: Modernity in the Shadow of Enlightenment* (Berkeley: U of California Press, 1999).
[10] Levin, *Sites of Vision*, 8.
[11] Richard Rorty, *Philosophy and the Mirror of Nature* (Princeton: Princeton UP, 1979), 63.

be like, and entails a profound questioning of any ordinary vision and prevailing habits of perception.

Concomitant to the revaluation of vision as potentially liberating, it has become a common critical view that Modernism was challenged by an emerging mass culture and the new forms of visual technology that Walter Benjamin described in "The Work of Art in the Age of Technical Reproduction", and that were further developed by the cultural criticism of the first Frankfurt school.[12] Criticism has been long alert to the close link between discourses of vision and those of power. Many studies thus go back to Michel Foucault's method of treating vision in a predominantly political and historical context, and his analyses of power structures that determine what is visible and what remains invisible. Michel Foucault prominently uses the *panopticum* as an example to describe how the vantage point of a hidden observer constituted one of the visual paradigms connected to institutionalised practices of surveillance.[13] Drawing on Foucault, Martin Jay "analyzes scopic regimes of modernity" and contextualises Foucault's analysis when he explores the social field of the gaze in twentieth-century French thought.[14]

Although "power" is not the only lens through which discourses of vision can be seen and analysed, the issues raised by Foucault and others have become crucial when, for instance, one evaluates the importance of media in the construction of the social world. Media studies nowadays occasionally uses the term "viscourses" for the investigation of how meaning is controlled and solidified by the media in general, how the individual's perception of reality is affected by them, and how their exposure to certain kinds of media in turn constitutes their beliefs about social reality.[15]

The Modernist preoccupation with the visible was compounded and also complicated by the technological advances in photography and film that challenged the nature of mimesis and the role of the artist. As Jonathan Crary has shown, the historical development of instruments that expand the scope of vision coincides with the instrumentalisation of visual perception as a whole, since tech-

---

12 Johanna Drucker, *Theorizing Modernism. Visual Art and the Critical Tradition* (New York: Columbia UP, 1994), 3–5; Walter Benjamin, "Das Kunstwerk im Zeitalter seiner technischen Reproduzierbarkeit", *Gesammelte Schriften*, 1.2. hrsg. von Rolf Tiedemann und Hermann Schweppenhäuser (Frankfurt am Main: Suhrkamp, 1972), 435–508.
13 Michel Foucault, *Überwachen und Strafen* (Frankfurt am Main: Suhrkamp, 1976), 254ff.
14 Martin Jay, "Scopic Regimes of Modernity", *Vision and Visuality*, ed. by Hal Foster (Seattle: Bay, 1988), 2–28; *Downcast Eyes: The Denigration of Vision in Twentieth-Century French Thought*, chapter 3.
15 Lisa Parks, *Cultures in Orbit: Satellites and the Televisual* (Durham: Duke UP, 2005).

nology was believed to enable a greater and more perfect knowledge of nature. According to Crary, Descartes' rationalism and its dependence on vision-centered paradigms are among the founding principles of the rationalist tradition with its reliance upon visual representations. Descartes was fascinated with lenses that expand human vision and bring the imperceptible and the previously invisible into the domain of human perception. His meditation on vision in *La Dioptrique* (1637) connects the perfectibility of human knowledge with the extension of human perception through artificial organs. They expand the horizon of perception while obliterating its experimental, all-too-human character. This distancing of the "all-too-human" from perception is indicative of Descartes' hypothesis of the split between the mind and the body. This distancing is also what makes him, in Martin Jay's formulation, "a quintessentially visual philosopher, who tacitly adopted the position of a perspectivalist painter using a camera obscura to reproduce the observed world".[16] Crary, Jay and Fredric Jameson all heuristically invoke the Cartesian spectator as a figure for neutrality which preceded narrative realism.[17] As Crary's study has shown, the accelerated impact of visual technologies produced distinct kinds of observers and visual relationships, and provided the basis for a change in thinking about the relation between vision and reality in Modernism. The works of Karen Jacobs and Sara Danius likewise trace the influence of technology and perceptual figurations of machines in selected novels by Mann, Proust and Joyce.[18] Jacobs' study investigates the relationship between technology and aesthetics and analyses the impact of photography and the cinema on sensory experience and perceptual habits. Danius regards the thematic inclusion of technology in Modernist novels as particularly apt to "represent the immediacy of lived experience",[19] and argues both for an increased internalisation of the technological into the sensuous and the incorporation of perceptual technologies into Modernist aesthetics.

Although the notion of the novel and the media as rival expressive forms vying for cultural authority at the beginning of the twentieth century is still popular, this study does not seek to prolong a narrative of an anxiety of influence. It also refrains from yielding to the impetus to exclusively polarise between

---

[16] Jay, *Downcast Eyes*, 69. Richard Rorty offers an analysis of the disembodied observer. *Philosophy and the Mirror of Nature*.
[17] Fredric Jameson locates modernism at the intersection of the Cartesian spectator and narrative realism. *Signatures of the Visible* (New York: Routledge, 1990), 158.
[18] Sara Danius, *The Senses of Modernism. Technology, Perception, and Aesthetics* (Ithaca: Cornell UP, 2002); Karen Jacobs, *The Eye's Mind. Literary Modernism and Visual Culture* (Ithaca: Cornell UP, 2001).
[19] Ibid., 191–192.

experimental and realist fiction, which would address aesthetic vision merely as a subversion of tradition. In contrast to the conventional reading of the Modernist novel as a visual wonderland or Modernist poetics as some kind of Modernity-induced *ut pictura poesis*, I examine literary uses of visual tropes, metaphors, and meanings in the light of aesthetic, philosophical, and narrative considerations of the power that vision has wielded over depictions of reality and knowledge.

While numerous previous studies have focused on the primacy of the visual in Modernism, and on the relationship between literature, technology and the visual arts, none inquires into aesthetic vision as it is presented and also invented by the narrative text. This study will not be concerned with vision as a vehicle of the dominant social ideology or a subversive articulation of competing discourses, but with vision and its potentialities as a metaphor, a process, and a formal and structural means of creating narrative reality and perceptual cognition in literature.

Rather than withering beneath the rapid growth of new visual technologies and media, the present study argues, Modernist texts confront conventional strategies of narration and representation inherent in mainstream discourses and they renegotiate the relation between perception and the text as an aesthetic object. Vision therefore becomes not only a thematic concern in literary works, but an aesthetic reflection on the experimental possibilities of narrative.

Aesthetic vision and visual culture

Whereas visual culture has come into swift prominence in the last decades as an area of study through attention to visual paradigms in philosophy, science, cultural studies, and critical theory, there are still very few studies that look at the convergences between discourses on vision, visual culture and the visual as a thematic and structural concern of literary texts.[20] These mainly focused on the relation between text and image, on ekphrastic strategies, and the formation of the gaze in relation to narrative perspective.[21]

---

20 Cf. for instance: Volker Mergenthaler, *Sehen schreiben – Schreiben sehen. Literatur und visuelle Wahrnehmung im Zusammenspiel* (Tübingen: Niemeyer, 2002); Gabriele Rippl, *Beschreibungs-Kunst – Zur intermedialen Poetik angloamerikanischer Ikon-Texte (1880–2000)*, (München: Fink, 2005).
21 From the 1980s onwards the discussion of ekphrasis as a narrative means of visualisation gained renewed attention. For a comprehensive survey cf.: Renate Brosch, "Verbalizing the Visual: Ekphrasis as a Commentary on Modes of Representation", *Mediale Performanzen: Historische Konzepte und Perspektiven*, hrsg. von Jutta Eming; Annette Jael Lehmann and Irmgard Maassen

As Renate Brosch has shown in her analysis of the centrality of visual perception in the late works of Henry James, the modernisation of the gaze manifests itself in crises of seeing which result in changes in perception and perspective, an altered role of the spectator, and an increasingly dematerialised narrative reality. James' late novels present dynamic negotiations of the image and depart from an objectivist and positivist way of seeing.

Vision has become a predominant topic of criticism in the humanities and many thinkers on the subject have discerned a "pictorial turn" in theory reminiscent of the "linguistic turn" in the philosophy of language earlier in the century. Studies in the field of visual culture have raised and disseminated crucial questions about the role of vision, and of cultural practices and modes of production connected to it. The opening of traditional fields of research and a recurrent concern with the practice of vision have remobilised interdisciplinary thinking about visuality, and led to a general reconceptualisation of vision and the image in different disciplines.

Critical consensus for some time now has been moving towards the idea that inter- as well as transdisciplinarity are not only highly significant as an institutionalised practice, but also enhance the immanent discourses and methodologies of single disciplines. W.J.T. Mitchell as one of the initiators of the study of visual culture was therefore interested in the development of visual culture as 'an indiscipline causing turbulence'.[22] Mitchell defines visual culture as "the study of the social construction of visual experience", and he speaks about the "convergence of disciplines of art history, literary and media studies, and cultural studies" around the "pictorial turn".[23] Mitchell's early and not unjustifiably euphoric outlook on visual culture as the interdiscipline *par excellence* has meanwhile given way to more modest estimations, that have led himself to consider the term visual culture as "a more problematic rather than a well defined theoretical object".[24]

In his later works, Mitchell is concerned with the evolution of images which he does not merely regard as passive reproductions, but as agents in actively shaping relations of power.[25] In this vein, numerous approaches are based on

---

(Freiburg i.Br.: Rombach, 2002), 103–123. See also: James Heffernan. *Space, Time, Image, Sign: Essays on Literature and the Visual Arts* (Frankfurt am Main et al.: Lang, 1987); ---. *Museum of Words: The Poetics of Ekphrasis from Homer to Ashbery* (Chicago: U of Chicago Press, 1993); Peter Wagner (Ed.), *Icons – Texts – Iconotexts. Essays on Ekphrasis and Intermediality* (Berlin et al.: de Gruyter, 1996).
22 W.J.T. Mitchell, "Interdisciplinarity and Visual Culture", *Art Bulletin*, 77 (1995), 542.
23 Ibid., 540.
24 Ibid., 542.
25 W.J.T. Mitchell, "Über die Evolution von Bildern", *Der zweite Blick: Bildgeschichte und Bildreflexion*, hrsg. von Hans Belting und Dietmar Kamper (München: Fink, 2000), 43–55.

the analysis of the visual as a phenomenon of quotidian life in which they, not without uneasiness, diagnose a visual turn that manifests itself in the expansion of images and a general dominance of seeing: "In this swirl of imagery, seeing is much more than believing. It is not just a part of everyday life, it is everyday life".[26]

The surge of publications in the late 1990s, however, has also encouraged a number of oversimplifications and reductive views. The hopes initially invested into a globalised, all encompassing theory of visual culture, have hitherto remained unfulfilled. Visuality has not yet become the master discourse of transgression, and neither has visual culture proved to be the hybrid interdiscipline it was designed to be. Although critics like Nicholas Mirzoeff depart from the idea of disciplinarity and regard visual culture as "a tactic, not an academic discipline",[27] the difficulties in creating a common theoretical and terminological ground have remained and they have revealed the traditional and persistent differences between the disciplines, so that today there are almost as many visual cultures as there are fields of study.

One of Mitchell's definitions of visual culture as "anything that can be visually read" corresponds to an integrative conception of the image[28] that includes artistic, optical, perceptual, mental and verbal images, and is based on a dialogical relationship between text and image. Mitchell's classification of the image serves as a wide umbrella for a heterogeneous collection of approaches towards the visual. It provides a general terminological basis from which to describe analogies between literature, art and mechanically produced images, and his definition of the image can be applied to the analysis of images in literary texts. His conception of the visual, however, is rather too broad a term to have any explanatory power for structural and metaphorical processes of vision in narrative, or to provide a feasible methodology for the analysis of the presentation of perception. Nevertheless, it emphasises the dynamics inherent in processes of image formation that bring about new interactions and forms of reception. Visual culture, as contemporary theory defines it, is more concerned with the event, the visual object, and the manifestations of the visual in every sphere of social life than with processes of seeing, and the relation between vision and literature.[29]

---

26 Nicholas Mirzoeff, *An Introduction to Visual Culture* (London, New York: Routledge, 1999), 1. For a sociological perspective on visual culture see: Christopher Jenks, *Visual Culture* (London, New York: Routledge, 1995).
27 Ibid., 4.
28 W.J.T. Mitchell, *Iconology. Image, Text, Ideology* (Chicago: U of Chicago Press, 1987), 10.
29 Mitchell defines visual culture as a "new social/political/communicational order that employs mass spectacle and technologies of visual and auditory stimulation in radically new

The scope of the present study is in many ways consistent with that of visual culture broadly defined, and its purpose is not to mitigate the achievements in the field, but it argues that considering the aesthetic functions of vision – a move allowed by stepping away from the dominant narratives of visual culture – helps to uncover the fuller range of vision as a subject and as a textual strategy in the experimental novel.

Modernist texts turn towards the visible, towards the phenomenal to experiment with new ways of aesthetic experience, and an altered way of seeing. In order to arrive at a notion of vision and of the image that is more differentiated and thereby applicable to the literary text, it is necessary to revisit the studies of Gottfried Boehm and Hans Belting, who, in the aftermath of Edmund Husserl and Maurice Merleau-Ponty, emphasise the anthropological foundation of a phenomenological conception of the image.[30] Like Mitchell, Belting argues in favour of a reciprocal relation between the production of mental and physical images.[31] Belting starts from the twofold epistemological assumption that the experience of reality can be configured into images, and that it can also become a productive agent in the medial construction of reality. In a similar vein, Boehm maintains that images do not exhaust themselves in their materiality, but are marked by an iconic difference between the image and what it represents.[32] Images are governed by an iconic paradox in that they create something that without them would not exist.[33] Their presence conveys an absence, and they present what is absent as present. Images therefore create and appear as something other than

---

ways". "What is Visual Culture?", *Meaning in the Visual Arts: Views from the Outside*, ed. by Irving Lavin (Princeton: Institute for Advanced Study, 1995), 207. Cf. also Mirzoeff's definition: "Visual culture is concerned with visual events in which information, meaning, or pleasure is sought by the consumer in an interface with visual technology". *Introduction to Visual Culture*, 3.
30 Hans Belting, "Vorwort zu einer Anthropologie des Bildes", *Der zweite Blick: Bildgeschichte und Bildreflexion*, hrsg. von Hans Belting und Dietmar Kamper (München: Fink, 2000), 7–11. *Bildanthropologie* (München: Fink, 2001), 11. In an early article Gottfried Boehm defines the dual notion of presence and presentation inherent in his theory of the image. "Im Horizont der Zeit. Heideggers Werkbegriff und die Kunst der Moderne", *Kunst und Technik. Gedächtnisschrift zum 100. Geburtstag von Martin Heidegger*, hrsg. von Walter Biemel und Friedrich-Wilhelm v. Herrmann (Frankfurt am Main: Klostermann, 1989), 278. *Figur und Figuration: Studien zu Wahrnehmung und Wissen*, hrsg. von Gottfried Boehm, Gabriele Brandstetter und Achatz von Müll (Paderborn: Fink, 2006).
31 The perception of images, according to Belting, is a symbolic action. Hans Belting, *Bildanthropologie* (München: Fink, 2001), 11.
32 "Die Wiederkehr der Bilder", *Was ist ein Bild?*, hrsg. von Gottfried Boehm (München: Fink, 1994), 30–31.
33 Lambert Wiesing, *Phänomene im Bild* (München: Fink, 2000), 10. Levin, *Sites of Vision*, 20.

themselves, as Boehm describes it: "they establish negation as a condition of possibility".[34] They suggest evidence and immediacy where there is no immediacy. Images make visible the invisible, but at the same time, they conceal what they represent.

Even though it would make a neat critical narrative if Woolf had emerged as a forerunner of contemporary discourses on visual culture, I resist the inevitable anachronism that any uncritical application of present-day theories on Woolf's works would entail. Virginia Woolf's many uses of vision in narrative were doubtlessly informed by contemporary contexts and discourses, her works, however, not only retain and refine processes of seeing, but they present an aesthetics of vision in which the text guides the reader towards how to 'see' it.

Woolf studies and vision

Woolf was part of an extraordinary and intimate environment of painters and artists. Hence Woolf scholarship has been continuously preoccupied with questions about vision and the visible as they emerge in her novels, which, however, makes it all the more surprising that there is still no study extant that treats the narrative and aesthetic functions of vision in her works. Whereas the books of Elfi Bettinger, Klaus Schwank, and Peter te Boekhorst are concerned with the function of motifs, metaphors, leitmotifs, and symbolic patterns,[35] Marianna Torgovnick's monograph was among the first interdisciplinary studies to examine thematic analogues between contemporary painting and the novels of Henry James, D. H. Lawrence, and Virginia Woolf. Torgovnick takes Woolf's Bloomsbury involvement in Impressionism and Post-Impressionism as a point of departure from which to analyse the role of painting in selected novels. The many books and articles by Willi Erzgräber, Sue Roe, Christopher Reed, and Jesse Matz are

---

34 *Beschreibungskunst, Kunstbeschreibung: Ekphrasis von der Antike bis zur Gegenwart*, ed. by Gottfried Boehm and Helmut Pfotenhauer (München: Fink, 1995).
35 Peter te Boekhorst, *Das literarische Leitmotiv und seine Funktionen in Romanen von Aldous Huxley, Virginia Woolf and James Joyce* (Frankfurt am Main: Lang, 1987); Elfi Bettinger, *Das umkämpfte Bild. Zur Metapher bei Virginia Woolf* (Stuttgart, Weimar: Metzler, 1993); Klaus Schwank, *Bildstruktur und Romanstruktur bei Virginia Woolf. Untersuchungen zum Problem der Symbolkonstitution in Jacob's Room, Mrs. Dalloway und To the Lighthouse* (Heidelberg: Winter, 1975). For a detailed account on the reception of Woolf in Germany see: Vera and Ansgar Nünning, "The German Reception and Criticism of Virginia Woolf", *The Reception of Virginia Woolf in Europe*, ed. by Mary Ann Caws and Nicola Luckhurst (London, New York: Continuum, 2002), 68–102.

likewise concerned with the particular impact of contemporary art and art theory on the novel, and they identify parallels in compositional technique, colour symbolism and narrative structure.[36]

The reciprocal relation between the text and the visual arts is a continuous concern in the monographs and collections by Diane Gillespie and Leslie Hankins.[37] Gillespie's pioneering book *The Sisters' Arts* offers a comparative approach to the study of the visual and the verbal arts in Modernism. She acknowledges the aesthetic significance of the art of Vanessa Bell for Virginia Woolf, and illuminates Woolf's writings through the prism of the professional relationship between the sisters. The contributions in *The Multiple Muses of Virginia Woolf*, and *Virginia Woolf and the Arts* acknowledge the dissolution of the boundaries between the novel and other media and study Bloomsbury's involvement in art and the media. The groundbreaking works of Leslie Hankins, Pamela Caughie, Jane Dunn, and Maggie Humm revaluate Vanessa Bell's and Virginia Woolf's visual experiments with regard to the contemporary art and media scene.[38]

In her study on *Virginia Woolf's Aesthetics*, Vera Nünning examines and identifies principles of unity, order and wholeness in Woolf's essays and reasserts her position in contemporary aesthetics.[39] The intellectual formation of Woolf's

---

[36] Cf. for instance: Willi Erzgräber, "Nachimpressionistische Anschauungen über Kompositionstechnik und Farbsymbolik in Virginia Woolfs Roman *To the Lighthouse*", *Miscellanea Anglo-Americana: Festschrift für Helmut Viebrock*, hrsg. von Kuno Schumann, Armin Paul Frank und Wilhelm Hortmann (München: Pressler, 1974), 148–183; Sue Roe, "The Impact of Post-Impressionism", *The Cambridge Companion to Virginia Woolf*, ed. by Sue Roe and Susan Sellers (Cambridge: CUP, 2000), 164–191; Christopher Reed, "Through Formalism: Feminism and Virginia Woolf's Relation to Bloomsbury Aesthetics", *The Multiple Muses of Virginia Woolf*, 11–36. Jesse Matz, *Literary Impressionism and Modernist Aesthetics* (Cambridge: CUP, 2001).

[37] Diane Gillespie, *The Sisters' Arts: The Writing and Painting of Virginia Woolf and Vanessa Bell* (New York: Syracuse UP, 1988); Diane Gillespie and Leslie Hankins (eds.), *Virginia Woolf and the Arts* (New York: Pace UP, 1997); ---. *The Multiple Muses of Virginia Woolf* (Columbia: U of Missouri Press, 1993); Marianna Torgovnick, *The Visual Arts, Pictorialism and the Novel* (Princeton: Princeton UP, 1985); Allen McLaurin, *Virginia Woolf. The Echoes Enslaved* (Cambridge: CUP, 1973), Meisel, *The Absent Father: Virginia Woolf and Walter Pater* (New Haven: Yale UP, 1980).

[38] Leslie Hankins, "'Across the Screen of my Brain': Virginia Woolf's 'The Cinema' and Film Forums of the Twenties", *The Multiple Muses of Virginia Woolf*, 148–180; Jane Dunn, *A Very Close Conspiracy: Vanessa Bell and Virginia Woolf* (Boston: Little Brown, 1990); Pamela Caughie, *Virginia Woolf in the Age of Mechanical Reproduction* (New York: Garland, 2000); Maggie Humm, *Modernist Women and Visual Cultures: Virginia Woolf, Vanessa Bell, Photography and Cinema* (New Brunswick: Rutgers UP, 2003).

[39] Vera Nünning, *Die Ästhetik Virginia Woolfs: eine Rekonstruktion ihrer philosophischen und ästhetischen Grundanschauungen auf der Basis ihrer nichtfiktionalen Schriften* (Frankfurt am Main: Lang, 1990).

writing is reconsidered in Ann Banfield's study. Banfield demonstrates the centrality of Formalism and Impressionism to Woolf's art, and examines Bloomsbury aesthetics against the background of contemporary epistemology, early analytic philosophy, and the art criticism of Roger Fry.[40] Instead of focusing exclusively on philosophy and Bloomsbury art, Jane Goldman's monograph on the *Feminist Aesthetics of Virginia Woolf* offers a materialist and historical reading.[41] Goldman relocates Woolf's concern with the visible into the context of avant-garde aesthetics and politics. She connects the Post-Impressionist Exhibition of 1910 and the solar eclipse of 1927 as significant historical moments that shaped Woolf's understanding of light and colour and claims that Woolf uses the colours of suffrage banners to produce a feminist aesthetics. Emily Dalgarno's investigation into Woolf and the visible world applies a Lacanian reading of the mirror stage to Woolf's works. She examines vision and optics as forms of power and intends to show that vision in Woolf's works was transformed by the notion that light creates the subject as object.[42]

Among the studies which explore the use of perception in Woolf's works, T.E. Apter's book is among the first to be concerned with processes of seeing in her novels and states that "the strength of her writing, and the originality of her writing, reside in her presentation of a reality that is created and sustained by the perceiver; and this reality is far more substantial, coherent and complex than the novelist was able to explain in her critical essays, letters or diaries".[43] Apter shifts the emphasis from the biographical to the psychological and epistemological implications of symbolism. Her study presents a chronological reading of Woolf's novels to propose a logic of vision, that adheres to the notion of a development of her fiction in terms of a tragic plot in which *To the Lighthouse* and *The Waves* present "culminations", and where "[t]he final two novels reveal a destruction of what has been so painstakingly established: the world is not transformed by vision".[44]

Like Apter, Harvena Richter and Stella McNichol also focus on the emotional and experimental potential of perception in selected novels where, for instance in *To the Lighthouse*, "the experimental core of the work inheres in the processes of perception which the author conveys in her exploration of the human conscious-

---

[40] Ann Banfield, *The Phantom Table. Woolf, Fry, Russell and the Epistemology of Modernism* (Cambridge: CUP, 2001).
[41] Jane Goldman, *The Feminist Aesthetics of Virginia Woolf. Modernism, Post-Impressionism, and the Politics of the Visual* (Cambridge: CUP, 1998).
[42] Emily Dalgarno, *Virginia Woolf and the Visible World* (Cambridge: CUP, 2001).
[43] T.E. Apter, *Virginia Woolf. A Study of her Novels* (London: Macmillan, 1979), 1.
[44] Ibid., 5.

ness".[45] Verena Olejniczak inquires into Woolf's novels from a receptionist perspective and identifies textual structures and modes of presentation that establish a communication with the reader and both evoke and undermine expectations about conventional narrative techniques.[46] Gudrun Rogge-Wiest draws on Olejniczak, as well as on Richter's and Apter's approaches to perception, and analyses the function of narrative perspective in selected novels.[47] Rogge-Wiest offers a narratological and constructivist investigation into perception, which she defines in opposition to mere reception. Holly Henry in her monograph on the aesthetics of astronomy in Woolf likewise asserts that "through deploying a multiplicity of perspectives Woolf forged new and alternative possibilities for her modernist art, and for inhabiting the world".[48] The role of nature in Woolf's works and her ways of seeing and recording life are at the centre of Christina Alt's study that analyses Woolf's overall "movement away from a taxonomic aesthetic and towards an aesthetic of observation and protection".[49]

Even though Woolf's works were credited as particularly innovative when it comes to experimenting with perception, and given the abundance of studies on visuality, there are no systematic studies extant which consider the significance of aesthetic experience and vision, or link the aesthetic dimensions of vision to its literary presentation. The general aim of the present study is to develop an approach that makes it possible to reveal and to define the specific modality of aesthetic vision in the works of Virginia Woolf.

What Woolf calls "vision" not only refers to the literary presentation of perception, but also to the processes inherent in the creative imagination. An "Aesthetics of Vision" hence seeks to extend and enhance modes of perception and signification. It refers to the structural, functional, formal, discursive, and increasingly reflexive differentiations of processes of seeing in the novel. As a narrative practice it self-consciously presents the kind of seeing it describes. I argue that Woolf's preoccupation with processes of vision, with visibility and the aesthetic object implies both a critique of conventionalised ways of seeing and an

---

[45] Stella McNichol, *Virginia Woolf and the Poetry of Fiction* (London, New York: Routledge, 1990), 117–118.
[46] Verena Olejniczak, *Wirkungsstrukturen in ausgewählten Texten T.S. Eliots und Virginia Woolfs: Eine Untersuchung zur Lesewirkung moderner englischer Literatur* (Hildesheim: Olms, 1987).
[47] Gudrun Rogge-Wiest, *Wahrnehmung und Perspektivik in ausgewählten Romanen Virginia Woolfs* (Frankfurt am Main, et al.: Lang, 1999).
[48] Holly Henry, *Virginia Woolf and the Discourse of Science. The Aesthetics of Astronomy* (CUP, 2003), 92.
[49] Christina Alt, *Virginia Woolf and the Study of Nature* (Cambridge: CUP, 2010), 180.

affirmation of the potential of the text to redefine the link between perception and reading which significantly influenced reception theory.

Aesthetic vision will be regarded as a new mode of seeing, highly conscious of itself as a subjective process, which rather challenges the drive towards perceptual and representational accuracy that underscores numerous forms of twentieth century vision, and is evident across a wide range of technological, philosophical, and aesthetic discourses. I argue that Woolf considered vision as a site where the narrative presentation and the thing represented converge in a process in which the narrative becomes what it is about. This study intends to show that Woolf engages with visual perception, not as a transparent perceptual continuum between the observer and the observed, but rather as a mode of production. It does so through an engagement with four related developments:

1. Aesthetic vision and experience
2. Modalities of the gaze
3. The temporality of aesthetic vision
4. The poetry of aesthetic vision

In its methodology, this study departs from the received critical practice of analyzing one novel after the other, which would mean to superimpose teleology on Woolf's œuvre. Although the four main chapters of this study constitute a structure for studying aesthetic vision, they do not do so in a hierarchical fashion. Each chapter focuses its discussion on a significant issue of aesthetic vision, and moves out from a specific problematic offered by the complexities and nuances of vision and the visual. Rather than merely fanning out perspectives, the single chapters of my study are connected by the assumption that aesthetic vision is a dynamic function of the text and mediates between immediate experience and abstraction, between transparency and opacity, between presence and absence, and between subject and object.

The internal coherence of the four chapters depends on a central aspect of vision and is built by the notion of aesthetic vision as a generative category in narrative fiction, and a reflection on experience. The line of argument starts from the analysis of the experience of seeing, and moves out to its textual transformations in which modalities of the gaze, and spatio-temporal constellations create distancing devices. The reflection of poetic potentiality marks a return towards aesthetic vision as a generative principle, which provides an altered view on the reader as aesthetic subject.

The first chapter examines the significance of vision in Virginia Woolf's literary criticism within the context of phenomenology and theories of aesthetic experience. Apart from addressing Woolf's essays, it also spans contemporary criticism that has contributed to shape today's understanding of literary transitions in Modernism and beyond. The chapter analyses the act of seeing in selected novels such as *Mrs. Dalloway, The Voyage Out,* and *To the Lighthouse,* and it is concerned with the relation between empirical sight and idealist vision. It focuses on the narrative function of vision as it is dealt with in the presentation of perceptual constellations that range between the phenomenal, the concrete and quotidian and the abstract and immaterial. Vision is both a subjective constitution of meaning and a failure to bring about meaningful relations.

The second chapter treats aesthetic vision as a means of dealing with perceptual boundaries and thresholds. It investigates into the notion of surfaces and examines windows, mirrors, and the veil as material analogues to fiction. It conceptualises them in what Ernst Cassirer in his *Philosophy of Symbolic Forms* has defined as "Anschauungsformen". Glass and fabric are treated as symbolic materiality which reflects on the materiality of the text. The chapter considers the immaterial potential of the mirror for fictional projection in Woolf's short stories, in *Orlando* and in *The Waves*. It analyses the window as an imaginative trajectory in *To the Lighthouse*, the ambiguities of the window in *Mrs. Dalloway*, and the metaphorical and meta-narrative function of broken glass in *The Voyage Out* and *Between the Acts*. A final sub-chapter looks at the 'veil of words' or the 'veil in the text' as it is prominently discussed in contemporary literary discourse and as part of Woolf's critical reflections. The last part of this chapter hence analyses the notions of the diaphanous, the semi-transparent, as well as blurred vision and seeing through tears in *The Waves, The Voyage Out, The Years* and *Jacob's Room*. I argue that in Woolf's criticism and in her novels, the notion of the diaphanous reflects the relations between seeing and aesthetics. It is both a critique of conventionalised vision, and an image for the imaginary.

The third chapter analyses the link between aesthetic vision and the experience of time. It focuses on ways in which Woolf's fiction creates temporality through narrative modes of perception. A first part is concerned with minimalist forms such as the sketch, the scene, and the interlude in which temporality and vision are entwined. It looks at *A Sketch of the Past* to analyse the rhetorical function of beginnings and a-chronic strategies in which the text stages its own anteriority. A second part is concerned with narrative processes of creating presence through anachronism, achronicity and anticipation that become particularly prevalent in spatio-temporal constructions of aesthetic vision in *Jacob's Room* and *To the Lighthouse*. A final part focuses on the role of vision in *Between the Acts* and its creation of paradoxical temporality in configurations between the revelatory stasis of a moment of being and the linear unfolding of narrative.

Chapter four is concerned with the relation between aesthetic vision in narrative and the experience of reading. It examines the ways in which Woolf's essays conceptualise the interaction between reader and text in terms of vision, and reveals the notion of privacy as a mode of perception. In focusing on *The Waves*, this chapter analyses how the novel reflects on the impetus to represent and to read a character in fiction, and, at the same time, expresses the impossibility of the very attempt. Aesthetic vision in *The Waves* is treated as a counter-movement to representation which includes the reader in the creation of the aesthetic object. It both evokes and reframes existing discourses on the visible and transforms the experience of reading.

It is the aim of my study to show that vision becomes a significant semantic and structuring principle of Woolf's novels as well as one of their organising paradoxes. That Woolf should use vision as her field in which to present the ambiguity of vision is no coincidence, and in addressing these main paradoxes and dialectical constellations in Woolf's criticism and her fictional works, this study explores the connections between seeing and language which are part of the foundations of Modernist literary aesthetics.

1 Aesthetic Vision and Experience

> the reading of these books seems to perform a curious couching operation on the senses; one sees more intensely afterwards; the world seems bared of its covering and given an intenser life (*AROO*, 6, 114).

Reading, as Virginia Woolf describes it in *A Room of One's Own* alters one's way of looking at 'the world'. The act of reading a literary text like "*Lear* or the *Recherche*" inspires a different sense of reality, one which is livelier and more intense, and leaves the reader in a state of heightened perceptual sensitivity.[1] The kind of seeing Woolf refers to is not merely an expression for optical sight, but it creates an aesthetic experience that results from the reader's interaction with the work of art.[2]

Processes of seeing and the affinity between vision and literature were a vital interest of Virginia Woolf, and her fictional and critical works explore the nature as well as the narrative scope of vision.[3] Woolf's aesthetic interest in the connection between forms of narrative presentation of vision and the ways in which it affects the reading process can be viewed against a more general Modernist turn towards the phenomenal, towards subjective experience and towards a renewed concern for the link between aesthetic experience and the

---

[1] This new kind of seeing in Woolf's aesthetics can be read against Viktor Šklovskij's formalist conception of perception, which includes both the notion of estrangement and the creation of new kinds of seeing through the engagement with a work of art. Woolf was not familiar with Šklovskij's theory, but, as Meghan Fox explains, "intuits the value of this literary technique, using it often within her own work and indirectly defending its necessity in a postwar era of stagnation and barbarity". "'The Vision must be perpetually remade': An Examination of Ethical and Aesthetic Revisions in *To the Lighthouse*", *Woolf Editing/Editing Woolf. Selected Papers from the Eighteenth Annual Conference on Virginia Woolf*, ed. by Eleanor McNees and Sara Veglahn (Clemson: Clemson University Digital Press, 2009), 18. Renate Lachmann, "Die 'Verfremdung' und das 'Neue Sehen' bei Viktor Šklovskij", *Poetica*, 3 (1970), 226–249. The notion of aesthetic perception as a heightened form of ordinary perception is pertinent to aesthetic theory from Walter Pater's conclusion to the *Renaissance* to contemporary approaches such as the one proposed by Martin Seel. "Über die Reichweite Ästhetischer Erfahrung – Fünf Thesen", *Ästhetische Erfahrung im Zeichen der Entgrenzung der Künste. Epistemische, ästhetische und religiöse Formen von Erfahrung im Vergleich*, hrsg. von Gert Mattenklott (Hamburg: Meiner, 2004), 73.
[2] The term aesthetic experience as it is used in this study is indebted to Hans Robert Jauss' description of the structural properties of aesthetic experience, which consists in the twofold relation of distance to and identification with empirical experience. Hans Robert Jauss, *Ästhetische Erfahrung und literarische Hermeneutik* (Frankfurt am Main: Suhrkamp, 1982), 37–44.
[3] Harvena Richter, *Virginia Woolf: The Inward Voyage* (Princeton: Princeton UP, 1976); Apter, *Virginia Woolf. A Study of her Novels*.

visual. The emergence of aesthetic experience as an issue of critical debate went along with the rise of an experimental aesthetics. Roger Fry considers looking at a work of art as distinct from the everyday experience of seeing: "The vision with which we regard such objects is quite distinct from the practical vision of our instinctive life", he writes in "The Artist's Vision", and continues to define aesthetic vision as "the vision with which we contemplate works of art".[4] In a similar vein, T.S. Eliot reflects on aesthetic experience,[5] when, in "Tradition and the Individual Talent", he distinguishes between ordinary experience and the kind of experience brought about by art: "The effect of a work of art upon the person who enjoys it is an experience different from any experience not of art".[6] The discourse of aesthetics is defined by a constitutive dialectics and is doubly-encoded in the specific and concrete on the one hand, and the abstract and general on the other. Aesthetics is therefore not to be limited to the fine arts alone or to an exclusive theory of *aisthesis*, but it provides a theory of the senses and includes the production, presentation, and reception of a work of art.[7] Modernist aesthetics as it is viewed in this study marks both a return towards experience, and a new conception of it. The programmatic break with convention professed by Modernists and the ensuing necessity to renegotiate their link to tradition materialises in aesthetic discourse,[8] and is crucial to their understanding of vision.

---

4 Roger Fry, "The Artist's Vision", *Vision and Design*, ed. by J.B. Bullen (New York: Dover, 1981), 34–35.
5 In "The Metaphysical Poets" Eliot coins the term "dissociation of sensibility". According to Eliot, the Metaphysical Poets, and among them John Donne in particular, had still possessed a "direct sensuous apprehension of thought", and "a mechanism of sensibility which could devour any kind of experience", which waned under the influence of Dryden and Milton. T.S. Eliot, "The Metaphysical Poets", *Selected Essays by T.S. Eliot* (London: Faber & Faber, 1932), 287–288.
6 T.S. Eliot, "Tradition and the Individual Talent", *The Sacred Wood. Essays on Poetry and Criticism* (London: Methuen, 1957), 54.
7 Cf. Christoph Menke, "Wahrnehmung, Tätigkeit, Selbstreflexion: Zu Genese und Dialektik der Ästhetik", *Falsche Gegensätze. Zeitgenössische Positionen zur philosophischen Ästhetik*, hrsg. von Andrea Kern und Ruth Sonderegger (Frankfurt am Main: Suhrkamp, 2002), 25: "Das Sinnliche wird in der Ästhetik nicht nur neu bewertet, nämlich als eine Weise gegenstandsadäquaten Auffassens, sondern auch neu beschrieben: als eine eigene Weise subjektiver Tätigkeit".
8 This programmatic vein of self-definition in Modernist discourse manifests itself in Ezra Pound's emphasis on continuous renovation in his credo "Make it new", or the various constellations between tradition and the individual in the works of Eliot, Woolf and Joyce.

In Woolf's works, the presentation of vision[9] is structural and metaphorical rather than mimetic.[10] Aesthetic vision, the kind of seeing that is created by the literary text, reflects on the experience of seeing and describes a dynamic interaction between the viewer and the object of vision. Metaphors of vision create relations between the subject and the object of vision, which mutually shape each other and are no longer merely active or passive components of vision. Metaphors of vision gain semantic and semiotic qualities, and Woolf uses the terms 'seeing' and 'vision' to describe both the creative imagination, and the aesthetic perception of the phenomenal world.

In *A Room of One's Own*, Woolf adopts this phenomenological stance towards vision, when she urges the novelists of the future to see "the sky, too, and the trees or whatever it may be in themselves" (*AROO*, 111) and extends this idea to verbal artifacts, 'things' created by language: "things in themselves: the sentence in itself beautiful: multitudinous seas; daffodils that come before the swallow dares" (*D* IV, 126). Vision presents experience, reflects on it, and potentially transforms it. It models the relation between the perceiving subject and the object perceived and attains an intermediate aesthetic status. Hermione Lee emphasises the crucial link between the narrative presentation of vision, experience and aesthetic creation: "In every novel we find a consistent and energetic presentation of perception and experience, which invites analogies between the conditions under which her characters feel and live, and their creator's idea of the nature of fiction".[11] The individual, segmented, but also complementary and dialectical ways in which the characters in Woolf's works perceive the world they inhabit create the overall narrative reality of her novels.[12] James Hafley describes the synthetic function of vision in Woolf's aesthetics which combines experience and the imaginative reflection on it: "she sought and found a new way of looking at life – an original perspective, a vision of experience".[13]

---

9 Woolf uses the term vision both in relation to perception and the imagination. The present study will do likewise. The terms aesthetic vision and aesthetic perception will be used as synonyms.
10 Hans Blumenberg has shown that metaphors not only endow the world with structure, but also constitute a layer of thought beyond the limited scope of both terminology and experience. Hans Blumenberg, *Paradigmen zu einer Metaphorologie* (Frankfurt am Main: Suhrkamp, 1998).
11 Hermione Lee, *The Novels of Virginia Woolf* (London: Methuen, 1977), 23.
12 Mark Hussey emphasises the importance of individualised experience: "Virginia Woolf's art tells us not about an external, objective Reality, but about our *experience* of the world. One of the most salient points she has to make is that the experience of being in the world is different for everyone and is endless, a process of constant creativity". Mark Hussey, *The Singing of the Real World. The Philosophy of Virginia Woolf's Fiction* (Columbus: Ohio State UP, 1986), xiii.
13 James Hafley, *The Glass Roof. Virginia Woolf as Novelist* (Berkeley and Los Angeles: U of Cali-

Vision is therefore not only a narrative strategy to present the world of Woolf's novels, but it also becomes a dimension of reception, and serves to mediate between the characters' perception and the readers' imagination. Hans Robert Jauss describes this interplay between sense perception, identificatory reception, and aesthetic experience:

> Ästhetische Erfahrung geht indes nicht im erkennenden Sehen (*aisthetis*) und sehendem Wiedererkennen (*anamnesis*) auf: der Sehende kann vom Dargestellten selbst affiziert werden, sich mit den handelnden Personen identifizieren, den so erregten eigenen Leidenschaften freien Lauf lassen und sich mit ihrer Entladung auf lustvolle Weise erleichtert fühlen, als sei ihm eine Heilung (*katharsis*) zuteil geworden.[14]

The analogy between vision and reception defines aesthetic vision both as a configuration created by the narrative structures, perspectives and images of the text, and as an activity on the part of the reader.[15] Reception theory has substantially contributed to the inclusion of vision into the discourse of aesthetic experience,[16] and to some extent Woolf's works articulate models of aesthetic vision which originate in phenomenology and have developed into classical receptionist paradigms. According to Wolfgang Iser the work of art contains generative structures, which determine its potentially infinite reception. In *The Act of Reading*, he draws a hermeneutic and structural parallel between reading and actual experience:

> Reading has the same structure as experience, to the extent that our entanglement has the effect of pushing our various criteria of orientation back into the past, thus suspending their validity for the new present. This does not mean, however, that these criteria or our previous experiences disappear altogether. On the contrary our past still remains our experience, but what happens now is that it begins to interact with the as yet unfamiliar presence of the text. This remains unfamiliar so long as our previous experiences are precisely as they had

---

fornia Press, 1954), 2. It is not merely coincidental, therefore, that Woolf's early concept of "Moments of Vision" presents formal analogues to her later reminiscences collected in *Moments of Being*. Virginia Woolf, "Moments of Vision", TLS, No. 853 (London, 1918), 243.

14 "Aesthetic experience is not merely a kind of seeing that understands what it sees and one that recognizes what it sees. The person who sees can be affected by what is presented, he can identify with the characters and freely indulge in passions and their release as if he himself had undergone some kind of cure (*katharsis*)" (Transl. C.O.). Hans Robert Jauss, *Ästhetische Erfahrung und literarische Hermeneutik*, 73.

15 Jauss defines aesthetic production, presentation, and reception all as performative modes of aesthetic experience. Ibid., 103–191.

16 Georg Bensch, *Vom Kunstwerk zum ästhetischen Objekt. Zur Geschichte der phänomenologischen Ästhetik* (München: Fink, 1994), 8. Georg Bensch traces the history of phenomenological aesthetics and reveals the affinity of reception theory and phenomenology as it has been professed by the School of Constance.

been before we began our reading. But in the course of the reading, these experiences will also change, for the acquisition of experience is not a matter of adding on --- it is a restructuring of what we already possess.[17]

Woolf describes the relation between writer and reader as the result of a similar process in which the presentation of perceptions and recognisable objects precedes the reader's participation in the creative imagination.

> The writer must get into touch with his reader by putting before him something which he recognizes, which therefore stimulates his imagination, and makes him willing to cooperate in the far more difficult business of intimacy. And it is of the highest importance that this common meeting place should be reached easily, almost instinctively, in the dark, with one's eyes shut (*CE* I, 331).

In Woolf's novels and criticism the pragmatic dimension of seeing and visual experience is neither abandoned, nor categorically separated from aesthetic experience. Woolf's metaphorical treatment of modes of vision, her differentiation between empirical and imaginative seeing, the parallels she draws between seeing and being, as well as the way in which she directs her approach towards a presumptive horizon create numerous methodological analogues to phenomenology.

The discourse of vision in Modernist texts is governed by the tension that emerges between the phenomenal and the ideal. Modernist texts are rooted in the ordinary world of experience, but, at the same time, they create aesthetic experience beyond objective empiricism. Vision as perception is situated within the world of quotidian experience, and yet, as aesthetic vision and imagination, it is liberated from the constraints and discursive pressures of that experience. Even though many Modernist texts take their narrative point of departure in the presentation of an everyday reality and present common ways of perception, they challenge empiricist and realist approaches to vision. Lucio Ruotolo stresses the correspondence between phenomenology and Woolf's discarding of Edwardian conventions:

> Virginia Woolf's closing advice that English literature will reach a new greatness only 'if we are determined never, never to desert Mrs. Brown' – like the axiom of phenomenology, '*Zu den Sachen selbst!*' – [...] urges her contemporaries to tunnel with her into the depth of life and character, in search of what Husserl termed the 'genesis of meaning' (*Sinngenesis*).[18]

---

[17] Wolfgang Iser, *The Act of Reading: A Theory of Aesthetic Response* (Baltimore: Johns Hopkins UP, 1978), 132.
[18] Lucio Ruotolo, *Six Existential Heroes. The Politics of Faith* (Cambridge, Mass.: Harvard UP, 1973), 17–18.

The visual paradigm in phenomenology describes a similar contrastive as well as complementary relation between vision and experience: "The phenomenologist describes visual perception only in order to recapitulate certain of its features in a strictly non-perceptual register, and the descriptions of perception themselves already reflect this theoretical itinerary."[19] In phenomenology perceptual experience is linked to an intentional consciousness, and the phenomenological analysis of perception takes its starting point in the experience of the perceiving subject.[20] It is not so much concerned with any essentialist meaning of a work of art, but with the way in which the subject can experience it. Perception, as Husserl explains it, is a process of interpretive approximation. It is inherently dynamic, relational,[21] and even contradictory because it is always directed towards something which itself it is not and attempts to include it.[22]

Husserl's phenomenological method was further developed by Roman Ingarden, who conceptualises the literary text as an aesthetic object that is constantly evolving and needs to be described in terms of its capacity to generate aesthetic experience.[23] For Ingarden aesthetic experience is founded on the subject's immersion into the immanent structures of the work of art, and the aesthetic object holds potentialities, which are to be actualised by the experiencing subject. In his landmark lecture on "Das ästhetische Erlebnis", he attributes a

---

19 Mary C. Rawlinson, "Perspectives and Horizons: Husserl on Seeing and Truth", *Sites of Vision. The Discursive Construction of Sight in the History of Philosophy*, 266.
20 In the aftermath of Husserl's theory, Maurice Merleau-Ponty as one of Husserl's most prominent followers bases his phenomenology of perception on the experience of the body in space and time. Likewise, he regards phenomenology as a structural movement which is analogous to the productivity of Modernist writers: "Si la phénoménologie a été un mouvement avant d'être une doctrine ou un système, ce n'est ni hazard, ni imposture. Elle est laborieuse, comme l'œuvre de Balzac, celle de Proust, celle de Valéry ou celle de Cézanne, – par le même genre d'attention et d'étonnement, par la même exigence de conscience, par la même volonté de saisir le sens du monde ou de l'histoire à l'état naissant. Elle se confond sous ce rapport avec l'effort de la pensée moderne". *Phénoménologie de la perception* (Paris: Gallimard, 1945), xvi.
21 On Husserl's categories of dynamic and relational moments cf. Kevin Mulligan, "Perception", *The Cambridge Companion to Husserl*, ed. by B. Smith and D.W. Smith (Cambridge: CUP, 1995), 176–177.
22 Edmund Husserl, *Analysen zur passiven Synthesis. Aus Vorlesungs- und Forschungsmanuskripten 1918–1926*, Husserliana Bd. IX, hrsg. von M. Fleischer (Den Haag: Nijoff, 1966), 3–4.
23 Roman Ingarden, *Das literarische Kunstwerk* (Tübingen: Niemeyer: 2. Aufl., 1960). Ingarden's approach is situated between an exclusively contextual reading and a strictly formalist analysis. He conducts an ontological analysis of the work of art and addresses both structural and existential problems. Ingarden's methodology emphasises the polyphony of a literary text and his analysis reveals its multiple layers.

potential to works of art that brings about a fundamental change of perspective for the recipient. He uses the term "original aesthetic emotion" ("ästhetische Ursprungsemotion") to describe the kind of emotional and creative reception that is activated by the work of art.[24] Ingarden focuses on the transformative potential of perception and emphasises the role of aesthetic perception as a prerequisite for the formation of the aesthetic object,[25] a process in which the reader's imagination is evoked through the presentation of perception in the text.

Contemporary approaches turn towards aesthetic perception as a specialised field of aesthetic experience. Martin Seel's conception of aesthetic experience is indebted to both phenomenology and reception theory. Seel's notion of aesthetics as appearance (φαίνεσθαι)[26] is intrinsically phenomenological, and also bears resemblance to Heidegger's ontological categories where he describes being as revealing itself in the mode of something which is incommensurate with itself.[27] Seel is concerned with the ways in which the aesthetic object presents itself, and he relates the immanent qualities of the work of art to how it appears to the recipient:

---

[24] Roman Ingarden, "Das ästhetische Erlebnis", *Erlebnis, Kunstwerk und Wert. Vorträge zur Ästhetik 1937–1967* (Tübingen: Niemeyer, 1969), 3.

[25] See also: Manfred Smuda, *Der Gegenstand in der bildenden Kunst und Literatur. Typologische Untersuchungen zur Theorie des ästhetischen Gegenstands* (München: Fink, 1979), 7. Eckhard Lobsien further explains the relation between aesthetic perception and the aesthetic object in literary texts, and traces the development of phenomenology in France as it is presented in the works of Sartre and Dufrenne. Eckhard Lobsien, "Bildlichkeit, Imagination, Wissen: Zur Phänomenologie der Vorstellungsbildung in literarischen Texten". *Bildlichkeit. Internationale Beiträge zur Poetik*, hrsg. von Volker Bohn (Frankfurt am Main: Suhrkamp, 1990), 89–114; Georg Bensch, *Vom Kunstwerk zum ästhetischen Objekt*, 101–155.

[26] Martin Seel proposes that aesthetic perception and the aesthetic object are interdependent. Although his conception of aesthetic perception is not exclusively concerned with the realm of the visual alone, the present study will align with his definition of aesthetic perception: "Etwas um seines Erscheinens willen in seinem Erscheinen zu vernehmen – das ist ein Schwerpunkt aller ästhetischen Wahrnehmung". Martin Seel, *Ästhetik des Erscheinens* (Frankfurt am Main: Suhrkamp, 2003), 38.

[27] In *Sein und Zeit*, Heidegger defines "Erscheinen" within a phenomenological context: "Erscheinung als Erscheinung 'von etwas' besagt demnach gerade *nicht*: sich selbst zeigen, sondern das Sichmelden von etwas, das sich nicht zeigt, durch etwas, was sich zeigt. Erscheinen ist ein Sich-nicht-zeigen. [...] Obzwar 'Erscheinen' nicht und nie ist ein Sichzeigen im Sinne von Phänomen, so ist doch Erscheinen nur möglich *auf dem Grunde des Sichzeigens* von etwas. Aber dieses das Erscheinen mit ermöglichende Sichzeigen ist nicht das Erscheinen selbst. Erscheinen ist das Sich-*melden* durch etwas, was sich zeigt." *Sein und Zeit* (Tübingen: Niemeyer, 1986), 29.

Der Weg zur Weltpräsentation, falls diese vorhanden ist, führt über die Selbstpräsentation des Werks, seines Materials, seiner internen Konfigurationen, seiner Perspektiven usf. *Kunstwerke sind Wahrnehmungsereignisse einer besonderen Art, eben weil sie Darbietungsereignisse einer besonderen Art sind.*[28]

Seel's definition of aesthetic perception as a special kind of attention to the ways in which the work of art appears to the perceiving subject can be related to the question how vision is presented in the narrative strategies of the text, and how it affects the reception process.

Vision in literature presents, produces and critically reflects on perception. In proceeding from the analysis of the metaphorical presentation of subjective perceptual experience, this chapter will focus on the structural processes of vision which constitute the text as an aesthetic object, and are directed towards a change in the recipient's perception.[29]

Woolf's œuvre is of particular interest because it reassesses the relation between aesthetic production, presentation, and reception. Her critical and literary works put to the test received notions of vision and inquire into the status of the visual, its semantic, metaphorical and epistemological qualities, in order to produce new and altered ways of seeing, which not only affect the 'common reader', but involve the author, the characters, and the critic alike.[30]

---

28 "The presentation of the world is achieved by way of the self-presentation of the work of art, its material, its internal configurations, its perspectives etc. Works of art are special events of perception because they are special events of presentation." (Transl. C.O.) Martin Seel, "Über die Reichweite ästhetischer Erfahrung", 76–77.

29 On the basis of his phenomenological conception of aesthetics, Georg Bensch defines aesthetic experience as "ein Prozeß, in dessen Verlauf das Kunstwerk, und zwar gerade dadurch, daß das rezipierende Subjekt in eigentümlicher Weise auf es gerichtet ist, zum ästhetischen Objekt heranreift, als welches es selbst wiederum Gegenstand ist eines sich ästhetisch entwickelnden Bewußtseins". *Vom Kunstwerk zum ästhetischen Objekt*, 9.

30 The importance of the implied reader for Woolf has been stressed by Mark Goldman, who characterises Woolf's aesthetic position as aiming "to arrive at a more balanced or complex view of the common reader as literary critic" (276). Goldman regards Woolf's conception of the reader as one who balances creativity and criticism: "He must 'train his taste' not only to read creatively, with insight and imagination, but to read critically; to evaluate a work in terms of its internal laws and against the great tradition which was the final standard for Virginia Woolf" (278). Mark Goldman, "Virginia Woolf and the Critic as Reader", *PMLA*, 80 (1965), 275–284. Harvena Richter, in *The Inward Voyage*, likewise refers to the "collaborative role of the reader" (234). She defines reader-participation in terms of identification: "The contribution of the eye, all the facets of the perceptive process – from the angle of vision through which Mrs. Woolf makes the reader view the object, to the creation of the image itself through a complexity of physical and psychical phases – are perhaps the most consciously realized means by which the reader participates" (240–241).

Whereas Fry argues in favour of a distanced and defamiliarised gaze, Woolf includes and embraces sensations. She analyses and explores possibilities as well as limitations of perception in order to create an altered relation between language and vision, between reality and narrative representation, one that lies beyond conventional conceptions of imitation and representation.

1.1 The semantics of seeing in Woolf's essays

Woolf's aesthetics relies on the interplay between empirical sight and imaginative insight, and it creates a structural dynamics of aesthetic vision which both evokes and refutes the visible as a referent. In "Modern Fiction" she programmatically outlines a model of the process of aesthetic vision that centres on the correspondence between the ephemeral multiplicity of impressions and the order of the pattern:

> The mind receives a myriad impressions – trivial, fantastic, evanescent, or engraved with the sharpness of steel. [...] Let us record the atoms as they fall upon the mind in the order in which they fall, let us trace the pattern, however disconnected and incoherent in appearance, which each sight or incident scores upon the consciousness. Let us not take it for granted that life exists more fully in what is commonly thought big than in what is commonly thought small.[31]

Woolf does not merely describe a hierarchical relation between the concrete and the abstract, but indicates a dialectical movement of thought, which mediates between the whole, the pattern or design, and the small and particular. In "Life and the Novelist", she likewise distinguishes the array of impressions the mind receives from the more complex process of cognitive structuring: "Of these two processes, the first – to receive impressions – is undoubtedly the easier, the simpler, and the pleasanter" (*CE* II, 132). Woolf's argument creates an analogy between the processes of aesthetic production and reception, and she maintains that an "abundance of sensation", a "fineness of perception", and a "boldness of the imagination" (*AROO*, 140; *CE* II, 3) are indispensable qualities of both the writer and the critic.

Woolf has drawn a close analogy between the processes of production and reception in the imperative rendered in "How Should one Read a Book": "Do not try to dictate to your author, try to become him. Be his fellow-worker and accomplice" (*CE* II, 2).
31 Virginia Woolf, "Modern Fiction", *CR* 1st series (New York: Harcourt & Brace, 1984 [1925]), 150.

Although Woolf reminds herself in one of her last diary entries to "mark Henry James's sentence: Observe perpetually" (*D* V, 357), she departs from any exclusively empirical equation of life and the novel. Woolf mocks a conventional realist rendering of an abundance of details and facts as the "hand-to-mouth method" (*CE* II, 134) of the "materialists" (*CE* I, 332).[32] She generally characterises the type of authors who adhere to the realistic mode in "Phases of Fiction" as "truth-tellers" whose style appeals particularly to the eye: "What they describe happens actually before our eyes. We get from their novels the same sort of refreshment and delight that we get from seeing something actually happen in the street below" (*GR*, 95).

In her essay "Life and the Novelist", she does not suggest that the novelist renounce life,[33] but rather illustrates his exposure to incessant impressions: "He can no more cease to receive impressions than a fish in mid-ocean can cease to let the water rush through his gills" (*CE* II, 131). The essay then emphasises the necessity for the writer to eventually retreat from the immediacy of impressions, and, in doing so, to transform the commonplace notion of 'life':[34]

> in that solitary room, whose door the critics are for ever trying to unlock, processes of the strangest kind are gone through. Life is subjected to a thousand disciplines and exercises. It is curbed; it is killed. It is mixed with this, stiffened with that, brought into contrast with something else (*CE* II, 131).

Aesthetic vision is not a one-way process, but depends on the interaction between the 'eye of the mind' and the 'eye of the body'. In a passage from "Street Haunting", Woolf describes the paradoxical stance of the observer, who is only able to open his innermost "enormous eye" to the outside when he finds himself inside a private room freed from the encrustations of conventional vision.

---

32 "The novelist who is a slave to life and concocts his books out of the froth of the moment is doing something difficult [...] But his work passes as the year 1921 passes, as fox-trots pass, and in three years' time looks as dowdy and dull as any other fashion which has served its turn and gone its way" (*CE* II, 136).
33 "On the other hand, to retire to one's study in fear of life is equally fatal. [...] He must expose himself to life; he must risk the danger of being led away and tricked by her deceitfulness; he must seize her treasure from her and let her trash run to waste. But at a certain moment he must leave the company and withdraw, alone, to that mysterious room" (*CE* II, 136).
34 T.E. Apter distinguishes between the 'creative perceiver' and the one "who sees only what is publicly known and publicly accepted, [and] kills the world as he observes it." *Virginia Woolf. A Study of her Novels*, 51–52. Alex Zwerdling, who seeks to counter the familiar notion of Woolf as modeled on Tennyson's "Lady of Shalott", reclusive and isolated from the world in "the ivory tower of Bloomsbury", vindicates Woolf's interest in external reality. *Virginia Woolf and the Real World* (Berkeley, Los Angeles, London: U of California Press, 1986), 14.

> But when the door shuts on us, all that vanishes. The shell-like covering which our souls have excreted to house themselves, to make for themselves a shape distinct from others, is broken, and there is left of all these wrinkles and roughnesses a central oyster of perceptiveness, an enormous eye (*CE* IV, 156).

In the same way as reality lies within the subject, the 'vision of life', which the text presents to the reader is the result of a symbolic reduction and selection from the variety of impressions. The concentration on the interior goes hand in hand with what Woolf describes as 'the writer's task' to refocus the impressions received and to integrate them into a synecdochal representation to make the reader see the particulars:

> For it is true of every object – coat or human being – that the more one looks the more there is to see. The writer's task is to take one thing and let it stand for twenty: a task of danger and difficulty; but only so is the reader relieved of the swarm and confusion of life and branded effectively with the particular aspect which the writer wishes him to see (*CE* II, 135).

The work of art gains a reality on its own, and in *Moments of Being* Woolf reflects on this unique reality of fiction, which is produced by language, goes beyond appearances and creates a momentary aesthetic whole: "a token of some real thing behind appearances; and I make it real by putting it into words. It is only by putting it into words that I make it whole" (*MB*, 72). Woolf does not readily jettison the link to the world of sensuous perception, but she asserts that language creates even livelier visions than ordinary sight, and leaves an even stronger impact on the reader than any factual description of reality with its claims towards objectivity ever could. Here Woolf's exploration of the link between aesthetic vision and the imagination resembles Joseph Addison's stance in "Pleasures of the Imagination": "As we look on any Object, our Idea of it is, perhaps, made up of two or three simple Ideas; but when the Poet represents it, he may either give us a more complex Idea of it, or only raise in us such Ideas as are most apt to affect the Imagination".[35]

Woolf discusses the relation between the immediate and the abstract within the context of painting and describes a movement parallel to the relation between Impressionism and Post-Impressionism.[36] Like Woolf, Fry in "An Essay in Aesthetics" generally refutes the notion of art as imitation (*VD*, 12). In

---

[35] Joseph Addison, "Pleasures of the Imagination", *The Spectator*, 416 (1712), ed. by G. Gregory Smith, vol 3 (New York: Everyman, w.Y.), 76.
[36] The inspiration Woolf gained from theories and techniques of 'Post-Impressionism' is widely documented. See for instance: Sue Roe, "The Impact of Post-Impressionism", *The Cambridge Companion to Virginia Woolf*; Marianna Torgovnick, *The Visual Arts. Pictorialism and the Novel*

his inaugural lecture at the University of Leeds on "Roger Fry", Quentin Bell states that "these painters whom Fry himself christened the 'Post-Impressionists' were able to restore the artist to his old position as a designer and not a mere observer".[37] In *Vision and Design*, Fry distinguishes between different kinds of perception, and speaks of "a double life; one the actual life, the other the imaginative life" (*VD*, 13). In his analysis of Impressionism he voices the general need to discriminate between ordinary ways of seeing and a distinctly artistic vision: "they upheld, more categorically than ever before, the complete detachment of the artistic vision from the values imposed on vision by everyday life" (*VD*, 7). Fry criticises conventional habits of looking at art from a rather elitist stance, and emphasises the incapacity of the "ordinary eye" to engage in art criticism:

> [t]he effects thus explored were completely unfamiliar to the ordinary man, whose vision is limited to the mere recognition of objects with a view to the uses of everyday life. He was forced, in looking at their pictures, to accept as artistic representation something very remote from all his previous expectations, and thereby he also acquired in time a new tolerance in his judgments on works of art (*VD*, 7).

Fry considers artistic vision and aesthetic judgments as cultural techniques which are not naturally bestowed on the viewer, but have to be acquired through training and experience. He equates the development of painting from Impressionism to Post-Impressionism with the altered role of the viewer who likewise proceeds from vision to design.

Woolf also frequently draws on the analogy between painting and writing to illustrate different ways of seeing. In her essay on Walter Sickert, she provides a humorous evolutionist analogue to the transformational process from empirical to aesthetic vision. In her example, she parallels the retinal capacity of archaic insects, who epitomise the unquestioned and reciprocated link between seeing and being ("those insects, said still to be found in the primeval forests of South America, in whom the eye is so developed that they are all eye, the body a tuft of feather, serving merely to connect the two great chambers of vision")[38], to the viewing situation of a first-time visitor of an art gallery: "On first entering a picture gallery, whose stillness, warmth and seclusion from the perils of the street

---

(Princeton: Princeton UP 1985); Bernard Denvir, *Post-Impressionism* (London: Thames and Hudson, 1992); Diane Gillespie, *The Sisters' Arts*.
37 Quentin Bell, *"Roger Fry", Inaugural Lecture Delivered in the University of Leeds 2nd December 1963* (Leeds: Leeds UP, 1964), 11.
38 Virginia Woolf, *Walter Sickert. A Conversation* (London: The Hogarth Press, 1934), 7. BERG.

reproduce the conditions of the primeval forest, it often seems as if we reverted to the insect stage of our long life".[39]

In both cases, an almost prelapsarian, innocent, disinterested, and undifferentiated vision provides the first stage of forming a relation to the external world. In the course of the evolution, however, this kind of original vision cannot be preserved, and vision becomes one among many other physical features, which had to be adjusted to the altered demands of the world: "And it is many ages now since we lost 'the microscopic eye'. Ages ago we left the forest and went into the world, and the eye shriveled and the ear grew, and the liver and the intestines and the tongue and the hands and feet".[40] Towards the end of her essay she speaks of the task of the novelist to "make the reader see" and to emulate visual impressions without merely reproducing them.

> For though they must part in the end, painting and writing have much to tell each other; they have much in common. The novelist after all wants to make us see. [...] The novelist is always saying to himself how can I bring the sun to my page? How can I show the night and the moon rising? And he must often think that to describe a scene is the worst way to show it. It must be done with one word or with one word in skilful contrast with another. [...] They speak at once, striking two notes to make one chord, stimulating the eye of the mind and of the body.[41]

In "The Death of the Moth" Woolf likewise distinguishes between the "eyes of the body" and the "eyes of the mind" to illustrate the contrast between a surface view and one that reaches beneath it: "The eye is not a miner, not a diver, not a seeker after buried treasure. It floats us smoothly down a stream; resting, pausing, the brain sleeps perhaps as it looks" (*DM*, 20).

She most prominently elaborates on the distinction between "eye" and "brain" in her essay "The Cinema/The Movies and Reality", one of the first British essays on the techniques and effects of contemporary cinema.[42] Woolf again uses the image of the eye and the brain that, as Maggie Humm writes, "matches Freud's model of the unconscious, that is the representation of visual thinking as an archaic consciousness".[43] Woolf was fascinated by the technological reproduction of images in photography and film and imagines the transformative

---

39 Ibid., 8.
40 Ibid., 10.
41 Ibid., 22.
42 Humm, "Virginia Woolf and the Arts", *The Edinburgh Companion to Virginia Woolf and the Arts*, 10.
43 Humm, "Virginia Woolf and visual culture", *The Cambridge Companion to Virginia Woolf*, 222.

potential of montage techniques that create synthesising effects and endow what is seen with a different kind of reality:

> Together they look at the King, the boat, the horse, and the brain sees at once that they have taken on a quality which does not belong to the simple photograph of real life. They have become not more beautiful, in the sense in which pictures are beautiful, but shall we call it (our vocabulary is miserably insufficient) more real, or real with a different reality from that which we perceive in daily life? (*E* 4, 349)

Woolf does not conceive of film as a mimetic medium, but "argues that the power of cinema lies in its anti-mimetic power and that spectators experience a dynamic visual process which releases buried memories and dreams".[44] Her criticism of mimetic realism that exclusively appeals to the eye is also a criticism of mere receptivity and the passive gaze. In "Life and the Novelist" she compares the effect of reading a realist novel to watching a film: "All this representation of the movement of life has sapped our imaginative power. We have sat receptive and watched, with our eyes rather than with our minds, as we do at the cinema, what passes on the screen in front of us" (*CE* II, 134).

Woolf relates 'eye' and 'brain' when she analyses the narrative techniques of other writers. In "The Russian Point of View" she takes the style of Tolstoy as a model for a connection between the two. In his characters, Tolstoy manages to reconcile appearance and essence and he possesses both the talent to present impressions, and the ability to go beyond them:

> And what his infallible eye reports of a cough or a trick of the hands his infallible brain refers to something hidden in the character, so that we know his people, not only by the way they love and their views on politics and the immortality of the soul, but also by the way they sneeze and choke (*CR* I, 181).

Woolf distinguishes between different kinds of seeing as ways of creating meaning. She describes the tension between experiential and imaginative modes of perception to express the need to see something in several ways at once. This integrative vision corresponds to what she describes in "Modern Fiction" as a synthesis of significant impression and aesthetic form, in which the "proper stuff of fiction" would consist of "every feeling, every thought, every quality of brain and spirit".[45]

---

44 Ibid., 223.
45 Richter, *The Inward Voyage*, 9.

1.2 Immediacy and abstraction in *The Voyage Out*

Virginia Woolf's presentation of different kinds of vision and modes of seeing has been regarded as a constant and central part of her aesthetics.[46] The connection between seeing and being in the world, and the semantics pertaining to different kinds of vision exceeds mere problems of multiperspective narrative.

In Woolf's aesthetics, as this study approaches it, the question about the nature and scope of vision is inherently a question about the composition and reception of fictional reality. Woolf's novels distinguish between different kinds of seeing, and create narrative reality through the ways in which characters relate to their surroundings. They offer a taxonomy of ways of seeing and juxtapose unmediated kinds of vision of everyday phenomena with more abstract and theoretical views. Most of Woolf's characters hence live in two worlds, the ordinary immediate reality and the imaginary world of their thoughts, and they assert that seeing involves both sense perception and imaginary abstraction.

The alternation between immediacy and distance is prominent in *To the Lighthouse* and it is dealt with in the opposition of Mrs. Ramsay's pragmatic, short-sighted view that reveals her phenomenological closeness to ordinary life, and Mr. Ramsay's "long-sighted eyes" (*TL*, 207) and his intellectual vision:

> Indeed he seemed to her sometimes made differently from other people, born blind, deaf, and dumb, to the ordinary things, but to the extraordinary things, with an eye like an eagle's. His understanding often astonished her. But did he notice the flowers? No. Did he notice the view? No (*TL*, 70).

The Voyage Out in its portrayals of the characters' views likewise negotiates between immediacy and distance. At the beginning of the *The Voyage Out*, Helen Ambrose works on a piece of embroidery which frames a pictorial view of the South American tropics. Drawing on the conventional colonial notions of exotic fertility, abundance of food, and bellicose natives, Helen's preconceived idea of her destination materialises into her meticulous needlework, and is complemented by her reading of G.E. Moore's non-idealist *Principia Ethica*, while she is working on her design. The framed view of Helen's embroidery precedes her

---

[46] Sue Roe advocates a strong bond between Woolf's writing and Post-Impressionism: "In the meantime, she wove it into her writing, finding, as her writing developed, increasingly more experimental and more complex ways of incorporating into her writing style a synaesthesia which began, for her, with the challenge she set herself to see writing initially, at some vital level, as a visual medium". Roe, "The Impact of Post-Impressionism", *The Cambridge Companion to Virginia Woolf*, 167.

encounter with the tropical destination and balances the view *en miniature*, the imaginative design with the larger philosophical vision of reality, matter, and nature[47]:

> Mrs. Ambrose would have found it very dull. As it was, she had her embroidery frame set up on deck, with a little table by her side on which lay open a black volume of philosophy. She chose a thread from the vari-coloured tangle that lay in her lap, and sewed red into the bark of a tree, or yellow into the river torrent. She was working at a great design of a tropical river running through a tropical forest, where spotted deer would eventually browse upon masses of fruit, bananas, oranges and giant pomegranates, while a troop of naked natives whirled darts into the air. Between the stitches she looked to one side and read a sentence about the Reality of the Matter, or the Nature of Good (*TVO*, 25).

Whereas Helen's view alternates between her coloured embroidery and her reading of the black volume, Rachel, at first, as if in meditation, fixes her gaze on perceptual details: "Her eyes were fixed so steadily upon a ball on the rail of the ship that she would have been startled and annoyed if anything had chanced to obscure it for a second" (*TVO*, 27). Rachel is immersed in gazing at a static object, and seeing for her is both a way of isolating an object, and isolating herself from the world in the process.

> By these means Rachel reached that stage in thinking, if thinking it can be called, when the eyes are intent upon a ball or a knob and the lips cease to move. [...] To feel anything strongly was to create an abyss between oneself and others who feel strongly perhaps but differently (*TVO*, 28–29).

From the beginning of the novel, Rachel's sense of not belonging to the world of the others is expressed in her way of seeing. Her youthfully-coded viewpoint is characterised by its desire towards immediacy and the failure to reach it. Rachel tries to get close to the core of the phenomena she sees. She adopts a selective and materialist view on her environment and refuses to acknowledge the reality of abstractions:

> 'I believe in the bed, in the photographs, in the pot, in the balcony, in the sun, in Mrs. Flushing,' she remarked, still speaking recklessly, with something at the back of her mind forcing her to say the things that one usually does not say. 'But I don't believe in God, I don't believe in Mr. Bax, I don't believe in the hospital nurse. I don't believe – ' She took up a photograph and, looking at it, did not finish her sentence (*TVO*, 236).

---

[47] A similar, ironic view on art as a woman's past-time activity is rendered when Mrs. Elliot describes her hobby-horse: "'I sketch a great deal,' said Mrs. Elliot, 'but that isn't really an occupation. It's so disconcerting to find girls just beginning doing better than one does oneself! And nature's difficult – very difficult!'" (*TVO*, 105).

Looking at something, for Rachel, becomes an attempt to communicate without words.[48] Instead of articulating her thoughts, she tries to absorb perceptual details, and seeks to reach another person beneath them: "Falling silent she looked at her visitor, her shoes, her stockings, the combs in her hair, all the details of her dress in short, as though by seizing every detail she might be closer to the life within" (*TVO*, 237–238). Rachel, however, does not achieve to get closer to life, and remains mostly a passive observer of it (*TVO*, 11). She merely registers impressions and is unable to transform them into thought or language. Rachel communicates what comes to her mind on impulse, and she speaks in a kind of impressionistic language of unfinished, or monosyllabic sentences, stammers (*TVO*, 28), or conveys her observations in spontaneous exclamations such as: "'It blows – it blows!'" (*TVO*, 11). On the ship Rachel does not take part in the conversations at table ("Rachel was rather too still as a hostess" (*TVO*, 10)), and her means of expressing herself in society are limited to phatic remarks and trained politeness. She is often at a lack for words, and cannot verbalise theoretical matters: "Rachel had other questions on the tip of her tongue; or rather one enormous question, which she did not in the least know how to put into words" (*TVO*, 48).

Rachel's attempt of relating to the world in an unmediated way marks her viewpoint as ingenuous and juvenile. Her receptiveness is expressed in her eyes, which "were unreflecting as water" (*TVO*, 14). Her aunt Helen notices in Rachel's way of communicating "a hesitation in speaking, or rather a tendency to use the wrong words, [which] made her seem more than normally incompetent for her years" (*TVO*, 13). According to Helen, Rachel lacks character and refinement: "There was nothing to take hold of in girls – nothing hard, permanent, satisfactory" (*TVO*, 13), and the isolated way in which she was brought up implies a critique of Victorian standards in the education of young women, which preserved Rachel's "fine natural indolence" (*TVO*, 26).

In the character of Rachel Vinrace Virginia Woolf creates a parallel to Daisy Miller in Henry James' novella. Daisy, like Rachel, dies of malaria while on a journey which was initially meant to educate her. *The Voyage Out* can therefore be read as a reversal of the classical *Bildungsroman*. Unlike a *Bildungsroman* which describes the production of a self, *The Voyage Out* conveys Rachel's inner stasis through both her way of looking and speaking. Although Rachel intermittently

---

[48] Edward Bishop regards vision in *The Voyage Out* as a strategy in which the text seeks to recapture narrative reality through visual metaphors: "Woolf continues the struggle begun in *The Voyage Out* to restore language to its metaphorical intensity – to transform words from pellets of information into channels for perception – and thereby to net that elusive reality that is just on the far side of language". Edward Bishop, *Virginia Woolf* (London: Macmillan, 1991), 31.

experiences a moment of vision as insight, she neither develops in character nor in language, but remains awkwardly inarticulate:

> The vision of her own personality, of herself as a real everlasting thing, different from anything else, unmergeable, like the sea or the wind, flashed into Rachel's mind, and she became profoundly excited at the thought of living. 'I can be m-m-myself,' she stammered (*TVO*, 75).

Rachel is at odds with her emotions and does not reach clarity about them. She relates to the world outside by selective perception in which ordinary sights gain importance to her:

> [s]he walked without seeing. [...] So she might have walked until she had lost all knowledge of her way, had it not been for the interruption of a tree, which, although it did not grow across her path, stopped her as effectively as if the branches had struck her in the face. It was an ordinary tree, but to her it appeared so strange that it might have been the only tree in the world. [...] Having seen a sight that would last her for a lifetime, and for a lifetime would preserve that second, the tree once more sank into the ordinary ranks of trees (*TVO*, 159–160).

Rachel desires to be exposed to the immediate presence of momentary reality, rather than seeking explanations for the state of the world, or looking for abstractions. The objects of her vision stand for themselves, and do not correspond to any internal reflection. Although she observes in detail what is in front of her, she is unable to describe what she sees: "'What are you looking at?' he asked. She was a little startled, but answered directly, 'Human beings'" (*TVO*, 123). Since both abstract questions and views at large increase her insecurity, Rachel becomes absorbed in visually dissecting the phenomena to delineate her own small world: "it pleased her to scrutinise this inch of the soil of South America so minutely that she noticed every grain of earth and made it into a world where she was endowed with the supreme power" (*TVO*, 129).

For Rachel, sight, like music, becomes a substitute for language and a way of expressing herself. Music makes it possible for her to convey the simultaneity of expression and form, and when Terence Hewet tells her that he wants to become a writer, she advises him to rather become a composer, because she thinks that, in contrast to language, music creates an all-encompassing impact: "It says all there is to say at once" (*TVO*, 195–196). Rachel's encounters with Hewet, who wants to write a novel about silence, are characterised by their attempts at communicating without words. In contrast to the others, Hewet is fascinated by Rachel's remoteness and her elliptic utterances: "The broken sentences had an extraordinary beauty and detachment in Hewet's ears, and a kind of mystery too, as though they were spoken by people in their sleep" (*TVO*, 171).

Rachel attaches her gaze to appearances and reads them in a silent language of vision without reaching beneath them. The turning point of the novel, marked by the journey on the river and the time Rachel and Terence spend together in the jungle is likewise characterised by silence.

> 'You love me?' Terence asked at length, breaking the silence painfully. To speak or to be silent was equally an effort, for when they were silent they were keenly conscious of each other's presence, and yet words were either too trivial or too large. She murmured inarticulatedly, ending, 'And you?' (*TVO*, 265).

Rachel lacks the ability to create a link between the phenomenon and the concept, between vision and understanding. For her the conceptions of love, happiness, and marriage remain abstractions, since she cannot reconcile her received ideas with any actual experience or emotion. She remains within the world of appearances until her illness further detaches her from it. The beginning of her illness, in which she gradually falls into a dreamlike trance, is presented in her increasingly unfocused and impersonal vision: "The eyes of Rachel saw nothing. Yellow and green shapes did, it is true, pass before them, but she only knew that one was large and another small; she did not know that they were trees" (*TVO*, 262). The link between Rachel and the world outside her that had been created by vision is severed at the end of the novel, when she is no longer able to connect with her surroundings. Rachel's youthful death, similar to that of Daisy Miller, preserves her remoteness from the world of the novel, like the figurative "virgin land behind a veil" (*TVO*, 79), and expresses the inevitability of failure in her attempts to relate to it.

1.3 The transformation of vision: *To the Lighthouse* and the immanence of art

1.3.1 Immanence and ideal in Woolf's reading of Platonism

The constellation between the phenomenal and the ideal, the finite and the infinite, the world of visible appearances and the unvisual world beneath and beyond it finds a remarkable parallel in Platonist thought. Woolf's texts not only reflect motifs and metaphors emerging from Platonic philosophy, but Platonism's dominant analytical tension between immanence and ideal creates a central paradox for Modernist writing. Modernist aesthetics hence remains dependent on the very tradition from which it seeks to liberate itself. In Joyce's *Ulysses* Plato and Aristotle paradigmatically stand for the Scylla and Charybdis between which experimental writing situates itself, and the artist Stephen Dedalus ironically asks himself 'which of the two would have banished him from his commonwealth'.[49] Whereas Joyce's artist as Modernist needs both extremes to define himself, Woolf, as I would like to suggest, transforms the analytical division between the phenomenal and the ideal into an immanent aesthetics of the text. As she describes it in *Moments of Being*, the disappearance of the Platonic horizon is constitutive for the creation of a work of art.

> From this I reach what I might call a philosophy; at any rate it is a constant idea of mine; that behind the cotton wool is hidden a pattern; that we – I mean all human beings – are connected with this; that the whole world is a work of art; that we are parts of the work of art. *Hamlet* or a Beethoven quartet is the truth about this vast mass that we call the world. But there is no Shakespeare, there is no Beethoven; certainly and emphatically there is no God; we are the words; we are the music; we are the thing itself. And I see this when I have a shock (*MB*, 72).

Woolf's anti-Platonic statement marks a denial of the search for reference outside the text. Woolf goes beyond the dualism of form and substance, and in her aesthetics truth and reality manifest themselves in art and do not exist independent from it in a static and remote world of ideas. Likewise, processes of signification are not simply transcendentally provided for, but they are continuously created through the narrative images and structures of the text.

Woolf's aesthetics combines the conception of holistic unity, "the whole", with that of form, "the pattern". Her resistance to the aesthetic ontology of Platonism can both be understood as a refutation of metaphysics, and as an integration of the ideal transcendence into the aesthetic immanence of the text, "the thing itself". She describes an anti-Platonic conception of art, and yet bases it on the Platonic and Neoplatonist conception of form as unity. The constellation between the singular phenomenon and the general, the finite and the potentially infinite continuity of being, the world of visible appearances and the idea of an invisible world beyond it, which is characteristic for Woolf's aesthetics, stands within an ambivalent analogy to Platonist and Neoplatonist thought.

Woolf, unlike T.S. Eliot or W.B. Yeats, questioned metaphysical foundations and her interests in Greek literature were mainly philological. She was a passionate reader of the Platonic dialogues and classical texts in general. "Reading Antigone. How powerful that spell is still – Greek [...] an emotion different from any other. I will read Plotinus, Herodotus, Homer I think" (*D* IV, 257). To her, Greek tragedy is capable of creating synaesthetic experience: "it is this art which plays

---

[49] "Upon my word it makes my blood boil to hear anyone compare Aristotle with Plato. Which of the two, Stephen asked, would have banished me from his commonwealth?" (*U*, 9, 80–83).

upon us in so many ways at once and brings us to an exultation of mind which can only be reached when all the powers are called upon to contribute their energy to the whole" (*CE* I, 10).

In 1925 when she started working on *To the Lighthouse*, Woolf published her essay "On not knowing Greek", where she stresses the inevitable otherness of Greek literature and the inability of any reader to ever claim to 'know' Greek:

> it is vain and foolish to talk of knowing Greek, since in our ignorance we should be at the bottom of any class of schoolboys, since we do not know how the words sounded, or where precisely we ought to laugh, or how the actors acted, and between this foreign people and ourselves there is not only difference of race and tongue but a tremendous breach of tradition (*CE* I, 1).

Classical literature provided Woolf with a new angle from which to reflect on tradition and against which to measure her own works and those of her contemporaries.[50] To Woolf it is the very unattainability and cultural hermeticism of classical works[51] that conveys a sense of purity and originality, and inspires the reader's imaginative quest:

> Does not the whole of Greece heap itself behind every line of its literature? They admit us to a vision of the earth unravaged, the sea unpolluted, the maturity, tried but unbroken, of mankind. Every word is reinforced by a vigour which pours out of olive-tree and temple and the bodies of the young. The nightingale has only to be named by Sophocles and she sings; the grove has only to be called ἄβατον, 'untrodden', and we imagine the twisted branches and the purple violets. Back and back we are drawn to steep ourselves in what, perhaps, is only an image of the reality, not the reality itself, a summer's day imagined in the heart of a northern winter. Chief among these sources of glamour and perhaps misunderstanding is the language. We can never hope to get the whole fling of a sentence in Greek as we do in English (*CE* I, 11).

Woolf's own quest for classical works is in itself both Platonic and Romantic. The vision of "unravaged" serenity recalls the "unravish'd bride of quietness" of John Keats' "Ode to a Grecian Urn". Like Keats' urn, Woolf's notion of Greece is endowed with the idea of remote and hermetic wholeness. She attests to literature the quality to convey a sense of this wholeness, and describes the particular

---

[50] Rowena Fowler analyses the references to Greece in Woolf's autobiographical writings, and traces ways in which Woolf might have absorbed "Greek models of form and genre". Fowler also mentions Woolf's first and now lost Greek essay "Magic Greek". "Moments and Metamorphoses: Virginia Woolf's Greece", *Comparative Literature*, 51 (1999), 215–242.

[51] "But the Greeks remain in a fastness of their own. Fate has been kind there too. She has preserved them from vulgarity" (*CE* I, 1).

power of words to appeal to the imagination. The uniqueness of Greek literature relies on a semantic and semiotic surplus of language that causes a Platonic mimesis of appearance, "an image of reality, not the reality itself". Reading Greek literature becomes both a pursuit of wholeness, and the insight into the impossibility to ever attain it.

As Rowena Fowler remarks, "Woolf felt both attraction and suspicion" towards the Dialogues of Plato,[52] because they were connected to her own study of Greek and the education of her brothers at Cambridge.[53] Particularly in her early novels, the reading of Plato is a recurrent topic. The ironic display of learnedness through the knowledge of ancient texts is pervasive in the portrayal of Cambridge in *Jacob's Room*: "If any light burns above Cambridge, it must be from three such rooms; Greek burns here; science there; philosophy on the ground floor" (*JR*, 49). Jacob himself worships Greek literature and philosophy not only because it conveys the light of reason, but because of its setting of standards for civilisation and its quality to outlast other literatures: "The Greeks – yes, that was what they talked about – how when all's said and done, when one's rinsed one's mouth with every literature in the world, including Chinese and Russian (but these Slavs aren't civilized), it's the flavour of Greek that remains" (*JR*, 101).[54] It is through Jacob's enthusiastic and immature perspective that the novel stages and parodies a received notion of Platonism by setting up dualisms. The main opposition which governs Jacob's stance towards Greek is that between the original and derivative, inferior copies of it. Jacob's affinity for Greek bestows on him a feeling of intellectual superiority: "'Probably,' said Jacob, 'we are the only people in the world who know what the Greeks meant'" (*JR*, 102).

The passion for Plato polarises the characters in *The Voyage Out*, and *Mrs. Dalloway*. For the young Clarissa Dalloway in *Mrs. Dalloway*, reading Plato, along with reading Morris and Shelley, inspires a romantic kind of social critique and forms part of her lively and spirited encounters with Sally Seton:

> There they sat, hour after hour, talking in her bedroom at the top of the house, talking about life, how they were to reform the world. They meant to found a society to abolish private property, and actually had a letter written, though not sent out. The ideas were Sally's, of

---

52 Fowler, "Moments and Metamorphoses", 227.
53 Woolf attended performances of Greek plays in Cambridge in 1900 and 1903. Ibid., 229.
54 Among Jacob's general lament about the degeneration of civilisation, a latent criticism about Aristotelianism can be detected in the portrayal of a waiter during Jacob's journey in Greece: "The whole civilization was being condemned. The waiter was quite indifferent to that too. Aristotle, a dirty man, carnivorously interested in the body of the only guest now occupying the only armchair" (*JR*, 190).

course – but very soon she was just as excited – read Plato in bed before breakfast; read Morris; read Shelley by the hour (*MD*, 36).

In *The Voyage Out*, the works of Plato, in addition to those of Sophocles and Homer, pertain to the novel's intertextual network with its focus on classical Greek literature. The knowledge of Greek, however, is reserved to men. Women either show enthusiasm about learning Greek, like the mundane Clarissa Dalloway – "'I'd give ten years of my life to know Greek,' she said, [...] For an instant she saw herself in her drawing-room in Browne Street with a Plato open on her knees – Plato in the original Greek" (*TVO*, 37) – , or, like Mrs. Flushing, express their aversion against it: "'I'd rather break stones in the road'" (*TVO*, 183). In Woolf's later novels, classical texts do not so much gain referential or thematic relevance, but rather emerge on the structural level of aesthetic figurations.

The works of Walter Pater provided the most prominent conduit between Woolf and Plato.[55] Not only did Pater's *Plato and Platonism* belong to the Stephens' library,[56] but Woolf was herself an avid reader of Plato.[57] The link between Woolf and Plato provided by Pater is revealing, and what is particularly remarkable about Pater's reading of Plato is that he did not conventionally conceive of Platonic philosophy in terms of intellectual abstraction, but that he emphasises Plato's affinity to the visible world:

> Platonism is in one sense an emphatic witness to the unseen, the transcendental, the non-experienced, the beauty, for instance, which is not for the bodily eye. [...] Austere as he seems, and on well-considered principle really is, his temperance or austerity, aesthetically so winning, is attained only by the chastisement, the control, of a variously interested, a richly sensuous nature. Yes, the visible world, so pre-eminently worth eye-sight at Athens just then, really existed for him: exists still – there's the point! – is active still everywhere, when he seems to have turned away from it to invisible things.[58]

---

[55] Wolfgang Iser considers Pater as a precursor to Woolf. *Walter Pater. The Aesthetic Moment* (Cambridge: CUP, 1987 [1960]), 60. Meisel's study, with its emphasis on the notion of 'incandescence' or reflection in "The chemistry of the crystal", in a way reads Pater via Plato, or at least examines the Platonic notions of vision inherent in Pater's conception of art. Meisel, *The Absent Father*.
[56] Ibid., 12. On Woolf reading *Plato and Platonism* see: Meisel, 16–17; Brenda Silver, *Virginia Woolf's Reading Notebooks* (Princeton: Princeton UP, 1983).
[57] On Woolf's learning Greek with Clara Pater and Janet Case, and her reading of Plato see: Quentin Bell, *Virginia Woolf. A Biography*. 2 vols. (New York: Harcourt Brace Jovanovich, 1972), 71–72; 337. Meisel, *The Absent Father*, 21.
[58] Walter Pater, *Plato and Platonism. A Series of Lectures* (New York: Greenwood Press, 1969 [1925]), 126.

Pater advocates a renaissance of the Greek spirit in contemporary culture, and in *Plato and Platonism* argues in a similar vein as he had done in *The Renaissance*, where he sought to balance Greek philosophy and Christian religion.[59] Woolf, however, does not follow Pater in his attempt to incorporate Plato into the aesthetic avant-garde nor does she explicitly share his assumption that Plato "would have been an excellent writer of fiction".[60] Although Woolf does not argue in favour of a redemption of the senses in Plato, she was interested in the poetic and aesthetic implications of the constellation between experience and idea.

Other than for Plato, knowledge and understanding as well as aesthetic experience, for Woolf, are not exclusively achieved through the dispassionate and disinterested stance of the philosopher. While Platonic thought in its meta-aesthetic orientation is more concerned with eternal, immutable forms and invisible ideas, and their imperfect resemblances in the world of human perception, Woolf's aesthetics is neither disinterested nor unemotional, but it remains immanent in her works, and constantly reflects and includes the relation of vision to the material world of substance accessible to the senses. Even at singular moments of illuminated vision in her novels, knowledge is not separated from perspective, personality, emotions or images. The presentation of vision in Woolf's works is therefore founded on the idea of reciprocating significance between the particular and the universal. Aesthetic vision at the same time fixes meaning, and lets it emerge.

Classical Greek literature, and particularly Platonic thought, provides Woolf's works with a heuristic rather than epistemological model of aesthetic vision, which constantly requires the projection of hypotheses about the relations between parts and wholes, between the immediately visible and the unvisual which cannot be reached by the eye. Woolf describes aesthetic vision as a two-way-process: details have to be regarded in relation to the whole they compose,

---

59 Anne Varty, "Flux, rest, and number: Pater's Plato", *Platonism and the English Imagination*, ed. by Anna Baldwin and Sarah Hutton (Cambridge: CUP, 1994), 259: "Pater never emphasized the distance which the metaphysical imagination had to travel in order to meet Plato; he always wrote of the philosopher's proximity and in 1893 even claimed him as a contemporary, aligning him with the aesthetic movement by putting unattributed statements by its proponents into his mouth". In his essay on Pico della Mirandola, Pater states that: "But it was inevitable that from time to time minds should arise deeply enough impressed by its beauty and power to ask themselves whether the religion of Greece was indeed a rival to the religion of Christ. [...] The restored Greek literature had made it familiar, at least in Plato, with a style of expression concerning the earlier gods, which had about it something of the warmth and unction of a Christian hymn". *The Renaissance. Studies in Art and Poetry* (London: Macmillan, 1912), 32.
60 Pater, *Plato and Platonism*, 132.

and yet the entirety of a phenomenon can only be understood by working through its parts. Her presentation of vision thus acquaints the reader with the provisional nature of any hypothesis and makes him project expectations of what lies beyond the grasp of the visible. In this way Woolf's aesthetics of vision essentially follows a classical hermeneutic model which leads to a constant modification and refinement of the readers' projections.

Whereas Platonism professes a metaphysical over-determination of the signified and the ideal, Woolf's narratives reorient the readers' awareness to the ambiguity of vision, and transform the discursive philosophical concern with epistemology into the aesthetic reflexivity of the text. Although Woolf shares the Platonist notion that visual perception alone has become problematic as an epistemological tool, since it reaches only the surface but never the thing itself, her works do not categorically denounce the realm of the visible. Her reassessment of Platonism with regard to vision is substantiated by the paradigmatic polarity of the ideal and the phenomenal, which makes possible the interaction and mutual pervasiveness of ideas and experience, reality and possibility. Vision, conceived of as an aesthetic rather than epistemological category, can neither completely abstain from the visual, nor can it ever be entirely content with what can be seen.

1.3.2 The dynamics of the image in *To the Lighthouse*

In *To the Lighthouse* two aspects are central to Woolf's reception and transformation of Platonic elements: the dynamics of the image between immediate perception and idea and the notion of artistic creation which is developed as a figure of refinement, perfection and perfectibility in the structures of the text.

To the Lighthouse emphasises the relational quality of vision. The journey to the lighthouse is guided by the trajectory of promise which determines the process between approximation and arrival. The lighthouse creates an analogy to Lily Briscoe's work of art and initiates tension between promise and fulfilment, possibility and impossibility, projection and representation. In the first part of the novel, Mrs. Ramsay's unfulfilled promise to her son James corresponds to Lily's futile attempt to finish painting Mrs. Ramsay's portrait.

Even though the tripartite structure of the novel uses the *topos* of time as a journey, this journey is not merely chronological, but relies on processes of inversion between approximation and distancing and a shift of background and foreground, presence and absence. The plot not only follows the linearity implied by the anticipated journey to the lighthouse, but it also describes a cyclical movement of loss and renewal, which culminates in the idea of recreation and fulfilment. Hence the second part of the novel "Time Passes" depicts the decline and restoration of the summer house. Presented from the perspective of Mrs. McNab, the choric figure of the housekeeper, the reader learns that in the meantime ten years have passed, that both Mrs. Ramsay and her daughter have died and that one of her sons has been killed in the war. Whereas the first and the last part of the novel each comprise a single day, the middle part spans a period of ten years. Figuratively it comprises the duration of one night, as the first part ends with the family going to sleep and the last part begins with Lily Briscoe waking up in the morning. Within this paradox of expansion in contraction, the middle section of the novel inverts narrative time and time narrated, foreground and background, presence and absence as well as the impact and significance of events taking place.[61]

The last part of the novel narrates Mr. Ramsay's journey to the lighthouse with his two grown-up children Cam and James. The narration takes up the parallel between the dynamics of the journey to the lighthouse and the dynamics of the artistic process in which Lily eventually paints her picture. As Erich Auerbach has shown[62] and as Woolf herself had envisioned it, the narrative strategy, which underlies the tripartite structure of the novel is that of a parenthesis to invoke "the sense of reading the two things at the same time".[63] The lighthouse is finally reached, the picture is completed and the novel ends.

The image of the lighthouse operates within a symbolic configuration which focuses on the conception of self-contained beauty and on the light-emitting object which brings other objects into the view of the spectator. The image of the lighthouse is paradoxical in many ways. It not only denotes stability, but is in itself highly dynamic and relies on reciprocating projections. The lighthouse is not only a central object of desire which attracts numerous projections, but also an object which in its orbit of light projects light on other objects. The lighthouse

---

[61] Temporality was central to Woolf when she sketched out her ideas for *To the Lighthouse* in her diary. She creates a link between the "flight of time & the consequent break of unity in my design" (*D* III, 36), and conceives of temporality as a textual strategy to oppose unity.

[62] Erich Auerbach, "The Brown Stocking". *Mimesis. The Representation of Reality in Western Literature*, transl. by Willard R. Trask (Princeton: Princeton UP, 1953), 525–553.

[63] In an entry into her diary on September 5, 1926, Woolf expresses the wish for the arrival at the lighthouse and the completion of Lily's picture to coincide: "The problem is how to bring Lily & Mr R. together & make a combination of interest at the end. I am feathering about with various ideas. The last chapter which I begin tomorrow is In the Boat: I had meant to end with R. climbing on to the rock. If so, what becomes [of] Lily & her picture? Should there be a final page about her & Carmichael looking at the picture & summing up R.'s character? In that case I lose the intensity of the moment. If this intervenes, between R. & the lighthouse, there's too much chop & change, I think. Could I do it in a parenthesis? so that one had the sense of reading the two things at the same time?" (*D* III, 106).

creates a polarity of perspectives which is constitutive for the novel as a whole. The lighthouse which inspires the journey towards itself becomes a metaphor of its own symbolic function for the reader. It creates a landmark that guides the reader's navigations in the text, marks the beginning and the end of the journey and becomes a point of continuous return.

The structural dynamics within the image of the lighthouse describes a movement of thought which is inherent in Plotinus' metaphysics of light. Plotinus conceives of light as an element of being[64] that comprises both the unvisual intelligible light and the light accessible to the senses. In order to grasp the intelligible light, thought needs to gradually detach itself from sense perceptions and turn towards itself. This figure of 'thought which thinks itself', which Plotinus terms *epistrophé* as the return of the mind to its origin, characterises repetition as an inherent element of thought, and describes thought itself as both inherently differentiated and identical with itself. "Indem (das Denkende) denkt, macht es sich zu Zweien, oder vielmehr: weil es denkt, ist es Zwei, und weil es sich selbst denkt ist es Eines".[65] ("When thought thinks, it divides itself into two, or rather: because it thinks it is two, and because it thinks itself, it is one" Transl. C.O.) Werner Beierwaltes uses the image of the circle to illustrate this structure in which thought is at the same time static and dynamic. In *To the Lighthouse*, the figure of thought which creates itself as its own object is presented in the image of the lighthouse. The self-constitution of the image between identity and difference, which unfolds in the structures of the text is accomplished against the background of a central Neoplatonist configuration.

The image of the lighthouse is not only inherently differentiated as both moving and stable, but it gains a further dynamics when regarded in relation to Mrs. Ramsay. Like the lighthouse Mrs. Ramsay attracts projections, views and affections of other characters who in seeing her become aware of their own shortcomings. Whereas characters like the scientist Bankes idealise her appearance: "He saw her at the end of the line very clearly Greek, straight, blue eyed" (*TL*, 29), Mrs. Ramsay's reflection of herself is directed towards the lighthouse as her counterpart:

> She looked up over her knitting and met the third stroke and it seemed to her like her own eyes meeting her own eyes, searching as she alone could search into her mind and her heart, purifying out of existence that lie, any lie. She praised herself in praising the light, without vanity, for she was stern, she was searching, she was beautiful like that light (*TL*, 63).

---

64 Werner Beierwaltes, "Plotins Metaphysik des Lichtes", *Die Philosophie des Neuplatonismus*, hrsg. von C. Zintzen (Darmstadt: WB, 1977), 76.
65 Ibid., 84–85. Plotinus, *Enneade* V 6, 1, 22–23.

Her eyes meeting the stroke of the lighthouse grants her a moment of cathartic illumination, in which she becomes subject and object to herself at the same time. In analogy to the lighthouse Mrs. Ramsay is innately differentiated and unites different traits of her character. In the same way as the lighthouse alternately casts light or shadow on its surroundings, Mrs. Ramsay's visible beauty (the "torch of her beauty" (*TL*, 41)) illuminates the darkness of other characters, while her invisible inside remains a "wedge-shaped core of darkness" (*TL*, 62).[66] Mrs. Ramsay's innermost being not only presents itself as a 'Heart of Darkness', but can be read against Plotinus' interpretation of invisible beauty which participates in form.[67] The Neoplatonist notion of unity as self-differentiation and doubling of the self is rendered in the opposition of Mrs. Ramsay and the lighthouse, and in the circular image of light as a metaphor of the repetitive and alternating movement of the text.

The differential imagery of the novel and the relation between subject and object are further reflected in the process of artistic creation in which Mrs. Ramsay becomes an object of art. When Lily Briscoe attempts to paint Mrs. Ramsay's portrait, she experiences the difficulty to perceive 'two things at the same time':

> Such was the complexity of things. For what happened to her, especially staying with the Ramsays, was to be made to feel violently two opposite things at the same time; that's what you feel, was one; that's what I feel, was the other, and then they fought together in her mind as now (*TL*, 102).

Conflicting oppositions create a prerequisite for Lily's creative process in which she searches for a non-discursive form of vision to integrate the multiplicity of impressions into the unity of artistic expression. Her aesthetics relies on the notion of difference within unity and the necessity of synoptic vision in the work of art, and she discards alternatives which might break this unity of expression: "the danger was that by doing that the unity of the whole might be broken" (*TL*, 53). Unity which is built through self-differentiation constitutes the logic of Lily's picture in which light and shadow are simultaneously integrated: "A light here required a shadow there" (*TL*, 53). Lily strives for both formal unity within the aesthetic object and for emotional unity with her model, Mrs. Ramsay:

> 'Could loving, as people called it, make her and Mrs. Ramsay one?' for it was not knowledge but unity that she desired, not inscriptions on tablets, nothing that could be written in any language known to men, but intimacy itself, which is knowledge (*TL*, 51).

---

[66] The chiaroscuro opposition of light and shadow is also presented in the relation between Mr. and Mrs. Ramsay: "she could feel his mind like a raised hand shadowing her mind" (*TL*, 123).
[67] Plotinus, *Enneade* I 6, 2, 239.

"Loving" does not refer to sensual desire, but to a form of Platonic love, which is directed towards an abstract and invisible other that is never to be grasped in its entirety: "love that never attempted to clutch its object; but, like the love which mathematicians bear their symbols, or poets their phrases, was meant to spread over the world and become part of the human gain" (*TL*, 47).

The artist's gaze focuses on form that cannot be immediately derived from sense impressions. Lily hence conceives of her object, Mrs. Ramsay, as an "august shape" or the "shape of a dome", which materialises in the purple triangle in her painting (*TL*, 52). In choosing the purple triangle to present Mrs. Ramsay, Lily participates in Mrs. Ramsay's view of her inside as a "wedge-shaped core of darkness" – a form that remains concealed from other characters and emerges as an underlying structure of the novel's tripartite design. Mrs. Ramsay, Lily and the lighthouse are related in a similar triangular fashion in which Lily's painting, like Mrs. Ramsay, becomes a corresponding counterpart to the lighthouse.[68]

Not only is the lighthouse reached when also the painting and the novel are completed, but the threefold structure of *To the Lighthouse* is formally reflected in the two parts of the painting and its central line. From the beginning of the novel, Lily had been preoccupied with the question of "how to connect this mass on the right hand with that on the left" (*TL*, 53), and in the end, she decides to finish the painting by drawing a central line (*TL*, 209).[69] The formal centrality of "Time Passes" and its correspondence to Lily's central line is reflected in the symbolic centrality of the lighthouse. The verticality of the lighthouse creates the central

---

[68] Woolf clearly provided for the picture to end the novel, and, in doing so, to release the reader into a realm beyond it: "It strikes me that it might all end with a picture. These stories about people would fill half the book: and then the other thing would loom up and one should step into quite a different place and people? But what?". Virginia Woolf, "Notes for Writing". Holograph notebook, unsigned, dated March 1922-March 1925, 10. BERG

[69] Lily's line can be read with reference to Roger Fry's reflections on the central line in painting. According to Fry, the central line is necessary to create unity and order within a painting, which to him are the main aesthetic principles of a self-contained work of art: "In a picture this unity is due to a balancing of the attractions of the eye about the central line of the picture. The result of this balance of attractions is that the eye rests willingly within the bounds of the picture" (*VD*, 22). Fry generally conceives of lines as symbolic forms: "Certain relations of directions of line become for him full of meaning; he apprehends them no longer casually or merely curiously, but passionately, and these lines begin to be so stressed and stand out so clearly from the rest that he sees them far more distinctly than he did at first" (*VD*, 36). Lily's central line certainly emphasises the importance of formal relations, and adds symbolic significance to the two parts of the painting as well as those of the novel. Rather than conveying final unity, however, it implies the fragility of any conception of unity, and shows that unity, for instance between Lily and Mrs. Ramsay, that is between present and past, or subject and object, cannot be reached.

line of the novel into which its past, present, and future converge. The lighthouse motivates both the horizontal movement towards itself, and the vertical movement back in time. It sets up spatial and temporal distance, which releases the movement of approximation.

The effect of simultaneity and the mutual pervasiveness of perspectives is achieved when Lily makes her second attempt to paint her picture at exactly the same moment when Mr. Ramsay and the children embark on their journey to the lighthouse, and when their arrival at the lighthouse coincides with Lily's last brushstroke. Lily's distanced view of the lighthouse as an abstract object far away is paralleled by the travelers' immediate and detailed view, and this juxtaposition of perspectives describes a narrative strategy in which the image duplicates itself, becomes divided and is made visible from different angles.

The image of the lighthouse reflects back on itself and renders the dichotomy between the original and the replica obsolete. The lighthouse does not create any reference beyond itself, and in this sense becomes self-referential. The relation between perception and idea in the image of the lighthouse departs from the metaphysical conception of the sign in Platonism and brings sign and signifier into a reciprocal relation. As the novel's central icon, it at the same time grants insights into the mechanisms of this kind of iconicity in which sign and signifier are simultaneously present and mutually define each other without ever becoming entirely congruent.

In *To the Lighthouse*, the Platonic distinction between an abstract idea and phenomenal vision is transformed into the text's doubling of perspectives and the narrative rendering of the opposition between concrete observation and general idea. The "double vision"[70] of the lighthouse is paralleled to Lily Briscoe's vision as a painter, who feels "curiously divided" (*TL*, 156) when she starts painting. The novel destabilises the notion of vision as representation in dividing vision itself into a present and an absent view. Whereas Lily is unable to paint Mrs. Ramsay when she was alive, it is her absence which finally leads to the completion of the painting. The novel achieves the simultaneity of presence and absence by creating a dialectic necessity for the characters to make a literal and metaphorical transition to the other side. In the same way as James at the end gains a close view of the lighthouse, Lily completes her painting precisely because she creates the idea of her no longer present model. The course of the journey which aims at the unmediated view of the lighthouse is contrasted by the retreat of the immediately

---

[70] Norman Friedmann coined the term double vision. "The Waters of Annihilation: Double Vision in *To the Lighthouse*", *Journal of English Literary History*, 22 (1955), 61–79.

present object which Lily performs in her artistic process of creation: "so much depends, [...] she thought, upon distance" (*TL*, 191).

The dynamics of the image in *To the Lighthouse* is a result of the creation of vision in time, which does not follow a linear pattern, but is characterised by processes of inversion between approximation and distance. The anticipatory movement of the plot towards proximity and presence is balanced by a counter-movement of retreat into absence and the past. The presence of the lighthouse at the moment of the arrival corresponds to the absence of Mrs. Ramsay as Lily's model.

Although Mrs. Ramsay's promise is kept in the end, and James sails to the lighthouse, the journey in which the no longer children Cam and James now merely do their father a favour creates an anticlimactic element. The children eventually get what they once desired, but only when they no longer wish for it. The initial promise and the childhood illusion have lost their former meaning at the moment of their fulfilment.

The structure of the journey as a quest of promise, deferral, and fulfilment corresponds to the twofold vision of the lighthouse. When approaching the lighthouse, James Ramsay compares his present view with his former vision and asserts the reality and truth of his childhood vision of the lighthouse.

> The Lighthouse was then a silvery, misty-looking tower with a yellow eye, that opened suddenly, and softly in the evening. Now – James looked at the Lighthouse. He could see the white-washed rocks; the tower, stark and straight; he could see that it was barred with black and white; he could see windows in it; he could even see washing spread on the rocks to dry. So that was the Lighthouse, was it? No, the other was also the Lighthouse. For nothing was simply one thing. The other Lighthouse was true too (*TL*, 186).

James balances both views of the lighthouse and becomes aware of the distinct truth they bear for him.[71] The doubling of both views of the lighthouse when the travelers reach it corresponds to the self-division in the gaze of the artist: "She felt curiously divided as if one part of her were drawn out there – it was a still day, hazy; the Lighthouse looked this morning at an immense distance; the other fixed itself doggedly, solidly, here on the lawn" (*TL*, 156). Lily's vision finally does not disclose any transcendent reality, but emphasises the idea of a dynamic process

---

[71] For the notion of balance as the balance achieved by androgynous vision cf. Nancy Bazin, *Virginia Woolf and the Androgynous Vision* (New Brunswick, N.J.: Rutgers UP, 1973), 44–46, 124–138; Carolyn G. Heilbrun, *Toward a Recognition of Androgyny* (New York: Harper, 1973), 151–163. Mr. Ramsay repeats the opposition between the exact and the vague in his exasperation about Cam's failure to see, and connects the accurate gaze with masculinity and vagueness to the minds of women (*TL*, 167).

in the artist's vision, rather than the attachment to a particular model: "But what she wished to get hold of was that very jar on the nerves, the thing itself before it has been made anything. Get that and start afresh; get that and start afresh, she said desperately" (*TL*, 193). The insight into the impossibility of mimetic representation in art is linked to Lily's insight into the Neoplatonist analogy between the world of sense perceptions and the intelligible world: "One wanted, she thought, dipping her brush deliberately, to be on a level with ordinary experience, to feel simply that's a chair, that's a table, and yet at the same time, It's a miracle, it's an ecstasy" (*TL*, 202).

The text creates an analogy between two modes of existence of the image; one present and one absent, one immediate, solid and material and the other abstract and distant, and it does not attempt to give priority to one over the other, but presents them in simultaneous interaction. James Ramsay discovers this constitutive dynamics of the image of the lighthouse and his discovery marks a process of approximation which the novel succinctly and metonymically describes as '*To*' *the Lighthouse*.

1.3.3 Light, love and perfection: Platonic *eros* and the dynamics of narrative in *To the Lighthouse*

The metaphorical presence of light in the image of the lighthouse, its capacity to bring out form, and to make it possible to see the unseen is crucial to Woolf's transformation of Platonic thought. Light, however, like the Platonic *logos*, does not merely change conventional perception and mediate between opposites, but is in itself a creative energy, which overcomes dialectic constellations.

Light, love and the idea of perfection are connected in the dinner scene at the end of the first part of the novel. The dinner scene in *To the Lighthouse* can be read as an equivalent to Plato's *Symposion*, and it reflects the link between light, creation and love as form-giving principles of cohesion. Instead of openly declaring their praise for *eros* and discussing its many features, as do the seven speakers in the *Symposion*, the single guests at the Ramsays' house at first rather display their lack of love or emotion. When looking at her husband, Mrs. Ramsay "could not understand how she had ever felt any emotion or affection for him" (*TL*, 83). Her feeling of dearth is complemented by her glance at her surroundings: "The room (she looked round it) was very shabby. There was no beauty anywhere. She forbore to look at Mr. Tansley. Nothing seemed to have merged. They all sat separate. And the whole of the effort of merging and flowing and creating rested on her" (*TL*, 83). The profound sense of separation, isolation and unease between the guests is described by Mr. Ramsay in a phrase that becomes characteristic of the desolation of the audience in *Between the Acts*: "at this moment, sitting stuck there with an empty seat beside him, nothing had shaped itself at all. It was all in scraps and fragments" (*TL*, 90).

Whereas the scene at the beginning of the dinner is characterised by the isolation of the guests, their sense of unease is gradually suspended, when light directs their attention away from themselves and towards the detailed view of the dish of fruit:

> Now eight candles were stood down the table, and after the first stoop the flames stood upright and drew with them into visibility the long table entire, and in the middle a yellow and purple dish of fruit. What had she done with it, Mrs. Ramsay wondered, for Rose's arrangement of the grapes and pears, of the horny pink-lined shell, of the bananas, made her think of a trophy fetched from the bottom of the sea, of Neptune's banquet, of the bunch that hangs with vine leaves over the shoulder of Bacchus (in some picture), among the leopard skins and the torches lolloping red and gold.... Thus brought up suddenly into the light it seemed possessed of great size and depth, was like a world in which one could take one's staff and climb hills, she thought, and go down into valleys, and to her pleasure (for it brought them into sympathy momentarily) she saw that Augustus too feasted his eyes on the same plate of fruit, plunged in, broke off a bloom there, a tassel here, and returned, after feasting, to his hive. That was his way of looking, different from hers. But looking together united them (*TL*, 96).

Looking at the plate of fruit in candlelight changes Mrs. Ramsay's sense of time and space. In her imagination, she sees the arrangement of fruit as a *cornucopia*, the remnant of an extravagant mythical banquet, and the outlines of the fruit to her become the microcosm of a landscape on its own through which she lets her gaze wander. Her way of looking at real objects in her world transcends mere perceptual experience or functional reference, and produces unworldly and unreal features of the object.

The spreading light not only makes objects on the table visible, but it enfolds the scene inside the room against the darkness outside it. The eight candles symbolically stand for the eight children and prefigure the notion of unity in difference. It is only when all the lights are lit, that everybody at the table becomes aware of this sense of unity: "Some change at once went through them all, as if this had really happened, and they were all conscious of making a party together in a hollow, on an island; had their common cause against that fluidity out there" (*TL*, 97).

The climactic structure of the dinner scene is created by the different stages of transformation of the minds of the characters, the concurrent action of light, and the courses of the meal all leading towards a culmination of aesthetic experience expressed in the composition of the scene. The illumination of the scene changes when the main course is served, and characters virtually see each other in a different light. To Mrs. Ramsay her husband now: "[he] seemed a young man; a man very attractive to women" (*TL*, 99). The mutual pervasion of the elements of light, love and the main dish gives shape to the internal world of the individual mind and initiates a sense of taking part in an experience of communion. The narrative and symbolic density of the scene creates aesthetic experience as a momentary enriched presence, detaches it from ordinary reality and endows it with spiritual and sensual perfection. The dish, the "Bœuf en Daube", in itself materialises perfection and creates a link between the sensuous and the spiritual: "It was rich; it was tender. It was perfectly cooked. [...] She was a wonderful woman. All his love, all his reverence, had returned; and she knew it" (*TL*, 100).

The passage stages the inherently Platonic notion of perfection within an anti-Platonic dialectical paradigm. In the dinner scene the experiences of sensuality and perfection converge. The scene elevates the quotidian into the realm of the abstract and ideal, and, in doing so, provides what is abstract with reference to the concrete. It is the idea of perfection that is present in the main course "the perfect dish", the "perfect triumph" which enhances profane experience, and it is experience, which brings the idea to life and allocates significance to it within the text. In the dinner scene the notion of culminating unity is achieved within this process of convergence of the idea of perfection and the experience of it in the materiality of the dish. The dinner scene describes an aesthetics which neither abandons the link to sense perceptions, nor consists of them exclusively.

In focusing on the object of perfection the text integrates it into an immanent metaphysics. The hypostatisation of the main course corresponds to an even further-reaching elation of Mrs. Ramsay, and Lily Briscoe gains an almost metaphysical vision of her, who not only emanates magnetic attraction and lasting beauty: "There was something frightening about her. She was irresistible. [...] (for her face was all lit up – without looking young, she looked radiant)" (*TL*, 101), but love itself: "It came over her too now – the emotion, the vibration, of love" (*TL*, 101). The emotions evoked in the dinner scene create an irresistible draw on the participants which can be compared to the effect of the party concluding *Mrs. Dalloway*, or the farewell and reunion dinners in *The Waves*: "We are drawn into this communion by some deep, some common emotion. Shall we call it, conveniently, 'love'?" (*W*, 126).

In the character of Mrs. Ramsay who epitomises this kind of animating, life-giving love, Woolf creates a parallel to the notion of *eros*, as it appears in Plato's *Symposion*. As Socrates in the *Symposion* explains it in the enigmatic voice of the prophetess Diotima, *eros* is the love of the beautiful[72] and it develops out

---

72 *Symp.*, 203 D, 23.

of a feeling of deficiency. The missing good and beautiful (καλόν) that is perceived in the other causes the desire to possess it. It creates an ideal and makes the beholder fall in love with it in order to approach perfection. The continuous attraction by beauty without which one cannot reach perfection thus expresses both a fundamental dearth and a way to overcome it. In the same way as beauty is defined as the beauty of character, and only secondarily as bodily beauty,[73] *eros* is not just the god of sensual pleasure, but a driving force of creation. Love, in this sense, is always directed towards something, driven by the desire to be in possession of the good forever (*Symp.* 205 E, 24). The only way for the lover to capture the everlasting, and to participate in eternity is by creating new life, either bodily or spiritually (*Symp.* 208 C, 27), whereas the ultimate generation of immortality is reserved to spiritual creation alone (*Symp.* 209 B, 27).

Mrs. Ramsay combines light, beauty, and the generative force of love. She is not merely a medium in the service of some supernatural entity, but can be seen as a creative force herself, that activates what lies dormant and hidden in the world of her reality. Mrs. Ramsay does not only unfold her own beauty and goodness, but also brings to light a sense of community in which the aesthetic verges upon the ethical.[74]

Like the central perspective of Socrates/Diotima she mediates between the singular perspectives of the other characters. Her reflections on intimacy, perfection and the potential permanence of the moment, however, are ironically contrasted by their link to concrete materiality:

> Nothing need be said; nothing could be said. There it was, all round them. It partook, she felt, carefully helping Mr. Bankes to a specially tender piece, of eternity; [...] Of such moments, she thought, the thing is made that endures. 'Yes,' she assured William Bankes, 'there is plenty for everybody' (*TL*, 105).

---

[73] In his chapter on Plato's aesthetics, Walter Pater argues for a consideration of physical beauty in Plato: "We have seen again that not in theory only, by the large place he assigns to our experiences regarding visible beauty in the formation of his doctrine of ideas, but that in the practical sphere also, this great fact of experience, the reality of beauty, has its importance with him. The loveliness of virtue as a harmony, the winning aspect of those 'images' of the absolute and unseen Temperance, Bravery, Justice, shed around us in the visible world for eyes that can see, the claim of the virtues as a visible representation by human persons and their acts of the eternal qualities of 'the eternal', after all far out-weigh, as he thinks, the claim of their mere utility". *Plato and Platonism*, 268.
[74] In discussing Plato's aesthetics, Pater emphatically refers to the link between ethics and aesthetics: "And Platonic aesthetics, remember! as such, are ever in close connection with Plato's ethics". *Plato and Platonism*, 282.

The dish not only expresses eternity, but also continuity between generations: "'It is a French recipe of my grandmother's', said Mrs. Ramsay" (*TL*, 100).[75] Within the thematic frame of reference provided by the *Symposion*, the dinner scene exposes the comprehensive richness of aesthetic experience, and its fleeting nature, and rather than have the moment give way under the pressure of its own intensity, the scene ends with Mrs. Ramsay retreating from it.

The composition of the scene does not follow a teleological pattern leading to the celebration of immortality. It rather finds a meaningful basis in itself, and is not subservient to immutable eternity. Like Lily who steps back from her picture, Mrs. Ramsay retreats from what she has created, and her final reflection once again asserts the temporality of human existence, and marks aesthetic experience as the transformation of the fugitive moment into a kind of perfection inaccessible to ordinary reality. In her final contemplation she abandons any aspirations towards eternity, acknowledges the present, and captures the vanishing point of the present moment, which creates an almost imperceptible dividing line between present and past:

> With her foot on the threshold she waited a moment longer in a scene which was vanishing even as she looked, and then, as she moved and took Minta's arm and left the room, it changed, it shaped itself differently; it had become, she knew, giving one last look at it over her shoulder, already the past (*TL*, 111).

The temporary dissolution of the moment of unity and perfection, once again, all the more creates a return to the desire for fulfilment. When Lily resumes painting, she remains a Platonic lover: "To want and not to have, sent all up her body a hardness, a hollowness, a strain. And then to want and not to have – to want and want – […] Oh Mrs. Ramsay!" (*TL*, 178). For Lily art which gives presence to an absent ideal is the only way to temporarily participate in beauty and goodness. Lily is in love with her idea of Mrs. Ramsay, and her desire causes Mrs. Ramsay's return as an image, an abstract form of "perfect goodness" (*TL*, 202).

The mechanisms of procreation, preservation and renewal, however, are not abandoned at the end of the novel, but they are handed over to the reader as immanent structures of reflection which inaugurate processes of reading and re-reading. These are inspired and sustained by the narrative dynamics of desire that seeks to gain perfection and fulfils itself precisely in doing so.

---

75 The dish goes back to a favourite recipe of Roger Fry. Frances Spalding, *Roger Fry: Art and Life* (Berkeley: U of California Press, 1980), 128. It can also be found in Linda Wolfe, *Literary Gourmet: Menus for Masterpieces* (New York: Harmony Books, 1989), 234–235.

2 Modalities of the Gaze: Windows, Mirrors, and the Veil

2.1 The window and the novel as narrative space

> Moreover, a book is not made of sentences laid end to end, but of sentences built, if an image helps, into arcades or domes (*AROO*, 83).

In *A Room of One's Own* Woolf envisions the novel as an architectural form and describes the ways in which it takes shape in the reader's imagination: "it is a structure leaving a shape on the mind's eye, built now in squares, now pagoda shaped, now throwing out wings and arcades, now solidly compact and domed like the Cathedral of Saint Sofia at Constantinople" (*AROO*, 77). Architectural metaphors define the novel as an aesthetic space and give prominence to its formal construction.[1] Apart from Henry James' classical description of the house of fiction,[2] works such as *The Fall of the House of Usher*, *Bleak House*, or *The House of the Seven Gables* abound with the trope of windows and houses, they produce new types of observers, and experiment with modes of seeing and narrative.[3] Modernist works like *A Room of One's Own*, *A Room with a View*, and *Jacob's Room* indicate a shift both in focus and perspective, which is increasingly directed into the house, the room, and the mind of the individual.

Within this turn towards the interior through internal focalisation, free indirect discourse, and intradiegetic narrators, images of glass and fabric become a means through which the text focuses on the boundary between the character's mind and the world of the novel and renders perceptual experience as mediated. The window presents a complex metaphorical form which expands or con-

---

[1] See for instance: Joseph Kestner, *The Spatiality of the Novel* (Detroit: Wayne State UP, 1978); Gaston Bachelard, *The Poetics of Space. The Classic Look at How We Experience Intimate Places*, transl. by Maria Jolas, ed. by John R. Stilgoe (Boston: Beacon Press, 1994); *Spatial Change in English Literature*, hrsg. von Joachim Frenk (Trier: WVT, 2000).
[2] Henry James, *The Portrait of a Lady*, Preface (Oxford: Everyman, 1999), 8–9.
[3] A number of narratological concepts are subsumed under 'modes of seeing': narrative perspective, focalising instances, metaphorical vision, and the eye of the text. None of these refers to actual perception, but they induce a new, imaginative kind of seeing in the absence of the object to be seen. Generally, the question of vision and perspective in fiction can be approached from the established narratological views of Stanzel and Genette. What Franz Stanzel calls figural narration and Gerard Genette internal focalisation refers to the presentation of fictional events as filtered through the experience of a character, involving free indirect discourse as a preferred narrative technique.

tracts narrative focus, and in which the subject's introspection and its relation to an outside world converge. Ruth Miller stresses the synaesthetic function of windows in mediating between art and life:

> Windows may be seen as effecting certain syntheses Virginia Woolf wished to achieve in her writing: their medium is protective yet transparent; the perspective they afford is detached yet comprehensive. They also combine significant features of the other frames of life, sharing the mirror's sheet of glass, the room's creation of an inside and an outside, and the threshold's position as a passage between two spheres. Since rooms often serve as metaphors of the mind in Virginia Woolf's works, it is not surprising that windows are connected with the eyes, which usually represent metonymically the various ways in which the mind apprehends the external world. Although eyes themselves have a figurative function, windows add a further dimension by representing not the direct means of perception but the circumstances which both enable and restrict that perception.[4]

In the same way as the window allows for both participation in and separation from "life", it invokes the notion of an existence of two worlds or realities. Windows signify both solidity and transparency, and as Martha Nussbaum states: "Woolf's image of the window suggests that people are not completely sealed to one another. There is an opening, one can see through or see in, even if one cannot enter".[5] Interacting with a fragmentation of viewpoint, narrative time and language, windows and mirrors formally constitute textual frames.[6] They metaphorically facilitate the interaction between narrator and reader, and in her essay on Turgenev, Woolf uses the window as a metaphor to describe the effect of reading: "And when in some pause we look out of the window, the emotion is returned to us, deepened, because it is given through another medium" (*CE* I, 248).[7]

---

[4] Ruth Miller, *Virginia Woolf: The Frames of Art and Life* (New York: St. Martin's Press, 1989), 100–101.

[5] Martha Craven Nussbaum, "The Window: Knowledge of Other Minds in Virginia Woolf's *To the Lighthouse*", *NLH*, 26 (1995), 743. Dorrit Cohn, *Transparent Minds: Narrative Modes for Presenting Consciousness in Fiction* (Princeton: Princeton UP, 1978). Unlike previous theories of transparency as a mode of conveying consciousness, Cohn foregrounds the narrative use of the medium, which is expressive of the failure of words, and creates a visual barrier.

[6] Irving Goffman, *Frame Analysis* (Cambridge: Harvard UP, 1974), 3. Mary Ann Caws describes the effect of perceptual framing in Modernist texts and regards frames as "a static arrest within the normal flow of the text" and a "condensation of action and vision". *Reading Frames in Modern Fiction* (Princeton: Princeton UP, 1985), 3.

[7] James Naremore asserts that windows in Woolf's works are both symbolic of the reader's experience, and of the artist's relationship to the world. *The World Without a Self. Virginia Woolf and the Novel* (New Haven and London: Yale UP, 1973), 241.

Windows, mirrors and veils present what Woolf emphasises as "another medium". They not only create a boundary of perception or a threshold, but they foreground metaphorical materiality which disrupts any kind of direct and unmediated vision, and emphasises subjectivity, fragmentation, selectivity and aesthetic distance. The narrative use of windows, mirrors and the veil supports the notion of semi-transparency, semi-permeability, and mediated vision, which never directly attains its object.

In reading windows, mirrors and veils as formal, material, and metaphorical modalities of the gaze, this chapter intends to show that Woolf's aesthetics creates vision as a theme, strategy and function of the text. Three modalities of the gaze will be examined as this chapter proceeds from the transparency suggested by the window, to the semi-transparency of the veil, and finally to the opacity of the looking glass.

Windows, veils and looking glasses are considered as what Ernst Cassirer in his development of the Kantian critique of rationality, has defined as "Anschauungsformen" or symbolic forms. In his conception of the symbolic form, which he describes as a synthesis of subject and object, presence and absence, sense impression and intellectual meaning, Cassirer confronts representational realism. Symbolic forms facilitate insights which are not solely founded on experience, but they relate experience to intellectual and imaginative meaning. According to Cassirer symbolic forms are a constituent part in negotiating one's relation to the world. They are not an imitation of any given reality, but first of all create ways in which reality can be perceived: "alle echte Darstellung ist keineswegs ein bloßes Nachbilden der Welt; sondern ein neues Verhältnis, in das sich der Mensch zur Welt setzt" ("all real presentation is by no means a mimetic reconstruction of the world it creates but it establishes a new relation between human beings and the world". Transl. C.O.).[8] Cassirer's notion of symbolic form provides a connection between presentation and reception which creates an interpretive paradigm to describe aesthetic vision. The received critical view of the novel as an architectural shape materialises into a narrative practice in which the novel creates itself by means of symbolic forms and structural units such as the window and prefigures the ways in which it is to be read.[9]

---

[8] Ernst Cassirer, *Philosophie der Symbolischen Formen I: Die Sprache*, Text und Anm. bearb. v. Claus Rosenkranz. *Gesammelte Werke*, hrsg. von Birgit Recki. Bd. 11 (Darmstadt: WB, 1953), 9. Ernst Cassirer, "Mythischer, ästhetischer und theoretischer Raum", *Landschaft und Raum in der Erzählkunst*, hrsg. von Alexander Ritter (Darmstadt: WB, 1975), 29.

[9] Erwin Panofsky, applies Cassirer's concept of the 'symbolic form' to art history. Symbolic form, according to Panofsky permits the artist to combine an absent and abstract meaning with a concrete perceivable sign: Erwin Panofsky, "Die Perspektive als 'symbolische Form'", *Aufsätze zu*

In symbolic forms as they are metaphorically present as glass, fabric and frames, Woolf's aesthetics transforms the presentational conventions connected to the window, and she uses windows and the view out of a window within her critique of realist fiction.[10] In looking through the window, her characters never see reality as it is, but a reality which is discursively mediated, and in which the transparency of the material is contrasted by its impermeability. The window presents a textual strategy of selection, it negotiates between proximity and distance, and establishes the relation between what a character sees, and the presentation of that seeing to the reader. The notion of symbolic form becomes a prerequisite for aesthetic vision in *To the Lighthouse*, where the window figures as a main compositional principle.

In her early notes adumbrating the structure of the novel, Virginia Woolf famously speaks of it as "two blocks joined by a window",[11] and on the margin of the manuscript she adds a little sketch, which shows two squares linked by a rectangular bridge or channel to illustrate her concept.[12] She also provides outlines of single chapters: "One about perhaps looking out of the window and realising the Islands or [...] some other world [...] related to this one".[13] The first part of *To the Lighthouse*, "The Window",[14] likewise plays on the notion of the window as an imaginary trajectory into the fictional world of the novel, and invites the reader to follow the text's inquiry into "'[s]ubject and object and the nature of reality'" (*TL*, 23).

Windows, mirrors and the veil provide analogues to fictional form, and serve as models for aesthetic vision as a mode that reflects back on perception.[15] They become strategies in which the text imitates the materiality it presents, and trans-

---

Grundfragen der Kunstwissenschaft, hrsg. von Hariolf Oberer und Egon Verheyen (Berlin: Hessling, 1964), 108.
10 J. Oates Smith summarises the early reception of James and Woolf with regard to narrative reality and subjective vision: "For James and Woolf reality is a subjective phenomenon – more accurately, an endless series of subjective phenomena that may or may not be related. The secret lives of other people remain secret; one cannot penetrate into them [...]". J. Oates Smith, "Henry James and Virginia Woolf: The Art of Relationships", *Twentieth Century Literature*, 10 (1964), 119.
11 Virginia Woolf, Notes for Writing. Holograph notebook, unsigned, dated March 1922-March 1925, 11. BERG.
12 Ibid.
13 Ibid.
14 In her diary, Woolf outlines her early conception of the novel's structure: "I conceive the book in 3 parts: 1. at the drawing room window; 2. seven years passed; 3. the voyage" (*D* III, 36).
15 Marilyn Kurtz emphasises these formal and narrative functions of the window: "fictional form and subjective consciousness are revealed at the window – concerns of the modernists". *Virginia Woolf. Reflections and Reverberations* (New York et al.: Lang, 1990), 32.

form an inherently representational aesthetics into one that gives prominence to presentation and subjective creation.

2.1.1 The mediated gaze in *The Voyage Out*

In *The Voyage Out*, windows are metaphors of the subject's relation to the world of the novel, and indicate different stages in the development of its protagonist, Rachel Vinrace. The novel's immanent tensions in the presentation of perception range between projection and actuality, form and matter, and they recurrently appear in terms of windows and frames.

The curtained window creates an analogy to the stage and the theatre as Helen seeks company and expresses her longing for life outside the villa in her preference to keep the windows without curtains. The impressionistic nightly spectacle which surfaces in the dusk less tropics reveals a world that is unseen by day:

> The dinner table was set between two long windows which were left uncurtained by Helen's orders. Darkness fell as sharply as a knife in this climate, and the town then sprang out in circles and lines of bright dots beneath them. Buildings which never showed by day showed by night, and the sea flowed right over the land judging by the moving lights of the steamers. The sight fulfilled the same purpose as an orchestra in a London restaurant, and silence had its setting (*TVO*, 83).

The formal pattern of the emerging light appeals to the eye in the same way as the sound pattern of an orchestra does to the ear. Sight and sound merge into a synaesthetic union, which is further sustained by the dissolution of the visual boundary between land and sea that become indistinguishable in the darkness. The nightly spectacle is compared to a silent, almost visual form of background music, as it reconnects the Ambroses to London.

Curtains are ambivalent in that they mediate between the inside and the outside, and Helen's desire to open the nightly scene to the senses is not shared by characters who prefer the reassurance of a room without a view: "'What about those curtains?' asked Hirst. The crimson curtains were drawn across the long windows. 'It's a perfect night outside.' 'Yes, but curtains inspire confidence,' Miss Allan decided" (*TVO*, 138). In balancing familiarity and distance, the uncurtained windows also illustrate Helen's twofold task of exposing Rachel to life and protecting her from it:

> 'We're going to see life, You promised.' 'Seeing life' was the phrase they used for their habit of strolling through the town after dark. The social life of Santa Marina was carried on

almost entirely by lamp-light, which the warmth of the nights and the scents culled from flowers made pleasant enough. [...] At the open windows merchants could be seen making up the day's account, and older women lifting jars from shelf to shelf (*TVO*, 88–89).

"Seeing life" not only expresses her detachment from the object of her gaze through the windows, and offers scenes and fragments, but also involves the necessity for the observers to remain unseen in the guise of darkness. Rachel does not take part in the social life of the city and is mainly acquainted to it as a spectator, or rather through playing the role of the unseen observer. In the same way as "seeing life" becomes their evening entertainment, the open curtain characterises Helen and Rachel as theatregoers who are watching scenes of life from a distance.

A row of long windows opened almost to the ground. They were all of them uncurtained, and all brilliantly lighted, so that they could see everything inside. Each window revealed a different section of the life of the hotel. They drew into one of the broad columns of shadow which separated the windows and gazed in. [...] Creeping on, they found that the next window revealed two men in shirt-sleeves playing billiards with two young ladies. [...] 'Take care or we shall be seen', whispered Helen, plucking Rachel by the arm. Incautiously her head had risen to the middle of the window. [...] Turning the corner they came to the largest room in the hotel, which was supplied with four windows, and was called the Lounge, although it was really a hall. [...] Mr. Hewet turned his full face towards the window. They could see that he had large eyes obscured by glasses; his complexion was rosy; his lips clean-shaven; and, seen among ordinary people, it appeared to be an interesting face. He came straight towards them, but his eyes were fixed not upon the eavesdroppers but upon a spot where the curtain hung in folds. [...] Helen and Rachel started to think that some one had been sitting near to them unobserved all the time. [...] A scuffling was heard on the gravel. The women had fled. They did not stop running until they felt certain that no eye could penetrate the darkness and the hotel was only a square shadow in the distance, with red holes regularly cut in it (*TVO*, 90–92).

The uncurtained windows exhibit slices of life to the passing voyeurs. The serial procession of scenes in the windows is marked by the alteration of light and shadow, and the ever-present anxiety about being discovered intensifies the pleasure of watching. The spell of their disguise, however, is broken when the unseen observers are themselves confronted with the presence of an observer invisible to them. Seeking shelter in distance and darkness, Helen and Rachel only find themselves safe when they are no longer within the reach of anybody's view, and when the hotel has merely become an immaterial abstract shape. The window not only mediates the women's perception on what they see and reduces the world on the other side to an animated picture, something solely visual, but it also becomes a barrier to sound. At the end of the scene, sound returns when the "scuffling on the gravel" was heard, and it introduces the end of the watching and the retreat into darkness.

In contrast to the women who leave the scene, the narration substitutes their gaze, and returns to the hotel. The next chapter begins with the narrator's inspection of the interior of the 'square shadow'. This time, it is the reader who is turned into an unseen observer, and is guided through the walls of a succession of rooms, "the little box-like squares": "Very different was the room through the wall, though as like in shape as one egg-box is like another" (*TVO*, 93). He assumes the role of an invisible, ghostly presence, which looks into the rooms and out of the windows:

> A glance into the next room revealed little more than a nose, prominent above the sheets. Growing accustomed to the darkness, for the windows were open and showed grey squares with splinters of starlight, one could distinguish a lean form, terribly like the body of a dead person (*TVO*, 95).

Sustained by the uncanny atmosphere created in the dim light, the narrative focuses on the perception of form, the grey outline of the window and the broken starlight prefigure the death watch and the image of shattered glass at the end of the novel.

The narrator's ability to overcome the boundaries of walls and windows, and to move from one consciousness into another is rendered in formal and spatial terms. Although the hotel guests cannot see, but only speculate about what or who is behind the artificial walls, they are connected to one another as the visual boundary between them turns into audible materiality: "Miss Allan, the elderly lady who had been playing bridge, determined, giving the wall a smart rap with her knuckles. It was only matchboard, she decided, run up to make many little rooms of one large one" (*TVO*, 93).

In *The Voyage Out* the 'house of fiction' is successively transformed into houses and rooms that become metonymical of the characters' consciousness, and the readers' process of passing between them. In her essay "How should one read a book?" Virginia Woolf compares the process of reading biographies or memoirs to the inquisitive view into the lit windows of a house:

> Shall we read them in the first place to satisfy that curiosity which possesses us sometimes when in the evening we linger in front of a house where the lights are lit and the blinds not yet drawn, and each floor of the house shows us a different section of human life in being? (*CE* II, 3).[16]

---

[16] In an early entry into her diary, Woolf notes that looking into windows presents the beauty of life unseen, which affects her in a similar way as reading Shakespeare: "the squares with their regular houses & their leafless trees, & people very clearly outlined filled me with joy [...] when

In the same way as the lit window provides insight into an otherwise invisible interior, the reader of a biography gains an idea of a person's life, but is unable to reach beneath the surface: "This, then, is one of the ways in which we can read these lives and letters; we can make them light up the many windows of the past; we can watch the famous dead in their familiar habits and fancy sometimes that we are very close and can surprise their secrets" (*CE* II, 5).

In *The Voyage Out*, Rachel's and Terence's inability to relate to one another is illustrated in the juxtaposition of scenes in which they observe each other through the window. The distance between them is spatially encoded in the distance between the hotel and the villa, and it is through the windows of both buildings that their encounters are negotiated. They remain spectators of each other, and for Rachel the window provides a metaphorical entrance into Terence's room:

> When it was dark she was drawn to the window by the lights of the hotel. A light that went in and out was the light in Terence's window: there he sat, reading perhaps, or now he was walking up and down pulling out one book after another; and now he was seated in his chair again, and she tried to imagine what he was thinking about (*TVO*, 210).

The window mediates between the characters' consciousnesses and the social life inside the house, and both draws them to it and excludes them from it. Rachel and Terence remain outsiders,[17] who try to get beyond the boundaries imposed by perception, and thereby are more influenced by the inevitable divide between what they see and what is actually there. In the same way as they do not gain access to the world behind the window, the reader is not granted direct insights into their consciousness. The window rather becomes a metaphor for the characters' detachment from the world of the novel, and the reader's distance from the characters' inner life.

The sense of enclosure conveyed by rooms is symbolical of the colonial enclave in Santa Marina, and it also stands for the futile attempts of Terence and Rachel to overcome the boundaries of their consciousness. To Rachel, the

---

live people, seeming happy produce an effect of beauty, & you dont have it offered as a work of art [...] somehow it affected me as I am affected by reading Shakespeare. No: its life" (*D* II, 273).

17 Like Rachel and Helen, he epitomises the metaphor of the moth. Moths represent the twofold movement of being attracted to light, and needing distance from it. Moths appear in *The Voyage Out* in Mrs. Flushing's report about reading at night: "'tiger moths, yellow moths, and horrid cockchafers. Louisa, my sister, would have the window open. I wanted it shut. We fought every night of our lives over that window. Have you ever seen a moth dyin' in a night-light?' she enquired" (*TVO*, 184). In this passage the window asserts the need of distance in protecting both the character from the moths and the moths from their death. The dispute about opening and closing windows is also carried out in *To the Lighthouse* (*TL*, 27).

view through the window illustrates her sense of safety in isolation, and it both attaches her to what she sees and defamiliarises her from it:

> Rachel turned abruptly to the window. She did not know now what it was that had put her into such a passion; the sight of Terence in the hall had confused her thoughts, leaving her merely indignant. She looked straight at their own villa, half-way up the side of the mountain. The most familiar view seen framed through glass has a certain unfamiliar distinction, and she grew calm as she gazed (*TVO*, 220).

Although she searches for acquaintances, Rachel never builds up a lasting relation to any of the people she meets, and although she visits different rooms, she remains unattached to their inhabitants: "every room and passage and chair in the place had a character of its own in Rachel's eyes; but she could not bring herself to stay in one place any longer. She moved slowly towards the door" (*TVO*, 238). When she is successively invited into the private rooms of Evelyn and Miss Allan, Rachel does not feel comfortable with their attempts to 'read her character'. She resists their indiscretions and prefers to stay outside their reach. Instead, she opens the window and desires to escape both the stifling enclosure of their rooms, and the conversation about what to her are mere abstract ideas:

> Rachel at last put down the photographs, walked to the window and remarked, 'It's odd. People talk as much about love as they do about religion.' 'I wish you'd sit down and talk,' said Evelyn impatiently. Instead Rachel opened the window, which was made in two long panes, and looked down into the garden below (*TVO*, 238).

Rachel senses the gap between her way of seeing and that of others, and opening a window for her becomes an unconscious attempt of liberating herself from their confining gaze, and to connect to an outside world. Rachel's own room, however, does not confine or isolate her, but becomes a sheltered world of her girlish imagination and the freedom created in 'the room of one's own'.

> Among the promises which Mrs. Ambrose had made her niece should she stay was a room cut off from the rest of the house, large, private – a room in which she could play, read, think, defy the world, a fortress as well as a sanctuary. Rooms, she knew, became more like worlds than rooms at the age of twenty-four. Her judgment was correct, and when she shut the door Rachel entered an enchanted place, where the poets sang and things fell into their right proportions (*TVO*, 112).

In her own room, Rachel is inspired to approach the world surrounding her in a different way and to enter an imaginary realm of reading. Delving into Ibsen's *Nora*, Rachel's view of the world around her changes, and she gains a sense of actively playing a part in it, instead of being reduced to the role of the passive spectator:

> At last she shut the book sharply, lay back, and drew a deep breath, expressive of the wonder which always marks the transition from the imaginary world to the real world. 'What I want to know,' she said aloud, 'is this: What is the truth? What's the truth of it all?' She was speaking partly as herself, and partly as the heroine of the play she had just read. The landscape outside, because she had seen nothing but print for the space of two hours, now appeared amazingly solid and clear, but although there were men on the hill washing the trunks of trees with a white liquid, for the moment she herself was the most vivid thing in it – an heroic statue in the middle of the foreground, dominating the view. Ibsen's plays always left her in that condition. [...] she turned round, slid comfortably down into it, and gazed out over the furniture through the window opposite which opened on the garden (*TVO*, 112–113).

Rachel's renewed view of herself is rendered as a mediated experience. It is through reading the play and her transitory view out of the window that she momentarily gains resolution and clarity in seeing herself as an actress in a scene. In "How Should one Read a Book?", Woolf likewise regards the investigation into what she calls one's "own creative powers" as an effect of reading, and discusses the transition and mediation between art and life in terms of reading and the intermittent view out of the window:

> But also we can read such books with another aim, not to throw light on literature, not to become familiar with famous people, but to refresh and exercise our own creative powers. Is there not an open window on the right hand of the bookcase? How delightful to stop reading and look out! How stimulating the scene is, in its unconsciousness, its irrelevance, its perpetual movement (*CE* II, 5).

Reading, like the view out of a window marks a phase of transition. It introduces a dynamics between closeness and distance, between a focussed and a blurred view. The window marks Rachel's own undefined position between two worlds, and her sense of herself playing a role and not belonging to either one of them is further supported by her unsteady gaze: "She threw the book down, looked out of the window, turned away from the window, and relapsed into an arm-chair" (*TVO*, 114). At the end of the scene, the impetus gained by reading recedes, and Rachel discontinues her reflections and remains within the confines of the room, which is suspended between the outside world, and the inner world of her consciousness.

The novel stresses Rachel's need to see the world through the protective interface of the window, which illustrates her dilemma of wanting and yet not being able to get closer to her surroundings. She can neither bear the distance to the group of people, nor the direct sight of them, when she walks out of the house:

> Thinking was no escape. Physical movement was the only refuge, in and out of rooms, in and out of peoples' minds, seeking she knew not what. Therefore she rose, pushed back the table, and went downstairs. She went out of the hall door, and, turning the corner of the hotel, found herself among the people whom she had seen from the window. But owing to the broad sunshine after shaded passages, and to the substance of living people after dreams, the group appeared with startling intensity, as though the dusty surface had been peeled off everything, leaving only reality and the instant. It had the look of a vision printed on the dark at night (*TVO*, 245).

Rachel's distance to the world increases during her illness, and in her fever visions the world to her appears not only colourless, but also opaque, and the window no longer provides any access to the outside: "waking from a transparent kind of sleep, she saw the windows white in front of her" (*TVO*, 310). Rachel becomes increasingly aware of being separated from the familiar world, and her dislike of curtains expresses her sense of being trapped in the passive role of the spectator: "'What's so detestable in this country,' she exclaimed, 'is the blue – always blue sky and blue sea. It's like a curtain – all the things one wants are on the other side of that. I want to know what's going on behind it. I hate these divisions, don't you, Terence?'" (*TVO*, 285).[18]

Rachel's growing isolation is rendered in metaphors of glass. They are expressive of her fragile and secluded character, and Terence's premonition about losing her is compared to a painful experience of glass breaking: "his sense of dismay and catastrophe were almost physically painful; all round him he seemed to hear the shiver of broken glass" (*TVO*, 309). During her illness Rachel repeatedly tries to recall the lines from Milton's *Comus*, which Terence had read to her. Images of glass that is transparent yet impenetrable describe her state of consciousness, and as she becomes irretrievably remote from her surroundings, glass and water become indistinguishable in her imagination and indicate a transition from solidity into flux: "The glassy, cool, translucent wave was almost visible before her, curling up at the end of the bed, and as it was refreshingly cool she tried to keep her mind fixed upon it" (*TVO*, 311).

In one of the novel's final views out of the window, Terence expresses his hope for the individual mind to continue within a universal design in an appeasing, post-romantic vision of the sublime in nature.

---

18 The curtain signifying both division and ending is given further emphasis when Hirst and Hewet choose Thomas Hardy's poem to be read to the elderly hotel guests: "I speak as one who plumbs/Life's dim profound,/ One who at length can sound/ Clear views and certain./ But – after love what comes?/ A scene that lours,/ a few sad vacant hours,/ And then, the Curtain" (*TVO*, 100). The poem is also used to foreshadow Hewet's situation at the end of the novel.

> The light of his candle flickered over the boughs of a tree outside the window, and as the branch swayed in the darkness there came before his mind a picture of all the world that lay outside this window; he thought of the immense river and the immense forest, the vast stretches of dry earth and the plains of the sea that encircled the earth; from the sea the sky rose steep and enormous, and the air washed profoundly between the sky and the sea (*TVO*, 326).

The creational design in this passage – which is also taken up at the beginning of *The Waves* (*W*, 1) – focuses on the division between sky and sea and suggests the idea of repetition as a cyclical pattern of loss and renewal in nature. At the end of the novel, Terence reiterates Rachel's former concern with the possibility of life going on without her.[19] In his closing view out of the window, Terence continues to ask Rachel's questions. As he repeats her vision of life in which creation relies on the interchange of light and darkness, both characters appear no longer sealed from one another but have reached a kind of unity that goes beyond death: "And life, what was that? It was only a light passing over the surface and vanishing, as in time she would vanish, though the furniture in the room would remain" (*TVO*, 114).

2.1.2 The multiplicity of symbolic form in *Jacob's Room*

The significance of rooms and objects which potentially outlast the individual but fail to replace it is one of the central themes in *Jacob's Room*. In an entry into her Holograph notebook, dated April 15th, 1920, Virginia Woolf notes down her "Reflections upon beginning a work of fiction to be called, perhaps, Jacob's Room".[20] She voices her concern with form and the room, and with the interplay of life and lifelessness:

> I think the main point is that it should be free.
> Yet what about form?
> Let us suppose that the Room will hold it together.
> Intensity of life compared with immobility.

---

19 "'It's impossible to believe that it's all going on still!'" (*TVO*, 129). "Suddenly he saw it all. He saw the room and the garden and the trees moving in the air, they could go on without her; she could die" (*TVO*, 328).
20 *Virginia Woolf: The Critical Heritage*, ed. by Robin Majumdar and Allen McLaurin (London: Routledge and Kegan Paul, 1975), 101; 107. Early reviews of *Jacob's Room* emphasised the novel's seriality and compared it to "snapshot photography, with a highly sensitive, perfected camera", or, more mockingly, to a "crowded little album of pictures".

Experiences.
To change style at will.[21]

Although critics have stressed the kinetic qualities of *Jacob's Room*, they do not relate the window to the novel's sequence of formal units.[22] In *Jacob's Room*, however, the window both becomes a metaphor of perception limited by a material boundary, and describes a metonymical sequence of spatial entities of geometric form. The window encapsulates spatial and temporal components,[23] and becomes an element in the progression of scenes. In *Jacob's Room*, the window is used as a formal device to express the opposition between motion and standstill as well as the contrast between inside and outside, life and lifelessness. Windows in *Jacob's Room* symbolically express both, the desire of the many characters to get closer to life ("from the very windows, even in the dusk, you see a swelling run through the street, an aspiration, as with arms outstretched, eyes desiring, mouths agape" (JR, 165)), and the distance from it: "Strangely enough he'd never been in St Paul's these fifty years, though his office windows looked on the churchyard" (JR, 87).

Formally, windows describe the condition of seeing life in general, or the life of a character in the novel as partial, momentary and superficial. Windows create viewing situations, in which characters are never wholly revealed, in which only their outside is shown, and in which they are connected to the novel's central problem of how to represent the unrepresentable. As a symbolic form, the window asserts the multiplicity of perspectives, and relates it to the novel's dominating sense of the unfinished and ungraspable, which is created in the continuous need of characters and readers to readjust their angle of vision. The formal and metaphorical use of windows reflects the novel's repeated insistence that: "It is no use trying to sum people up" (JR, 37; 214) and the assertion that: "Nobody sees any one as he is" (JR, 36), with its avoidance of "character mongering" (JR, 214) as well as "the human eye" (JR, 109).

---

[21] Jacob's Room. Holograph unsigned dated April 15, 1920-March 12, 1922. BERG.
[22] Francesca Kazan investigates the question of the pictorial in *Jacob's Room* and examines ways in which Woolf's narrative technique approximates conventions of the visual arts. "Description and the Pictorial in *Jacob's Room*", *ELH*, 55 (1988), 703. Kazan conceives of the fragmented structure of "*Jacob's Room* as a series of frames", in which descriptive passages and pictorial moments interchange and mediate between motion and stasis.
[23] One of Jacob's views out of the window for instance conveys movement in a span of time: "The dinner would never end, Jacob thought, and he did not wish it to end, though the ship had sailed from one corner of the window-frame to the other" (JR, 75–76).

Like in *The Voyage Out*, the notion of vacancy that is intrinsically connected to the centre of the novel and its main character, is conveyed through the empty room, the empty chair (JR, 49; 247), and the distancing view provided by the window. The narrator mostly enters Jacob's room when he is not there (JR, 48, 246–247), or approaches him from the outside through the window: "the young man came to the window and stood there, looking out across the court? It was Jacob. He stood smoking his pipe while the last stroke of the clock purred softly round him" (JR, 57). Like the other characters ("Fanny Elmer passed beneath Jacob's window" (JR, 156)), the narrator remains outside the "window box" (JR, 54), taking a look inside (JR, 56), or, in an act of self-imposed modesty, wilfully refrains from further pursuing Jacob: "He has turned to go. As for following him back to his rooms, no – that we won't do" (JR, 128).

The processes of partially acquainting and understanding a character are recurrently compared to taking an imaginary walk beneath a window: "The march that the mind keeps beneath the windows of others is queer enough [...] – yet all the while having for centre, for magnet, a young man alone in his room" (JR, 129). The almost magnetic tension between Jacob as the centre of the novel, and the periphery around him is mediated by the gaze of the passing narrator, who is irresistibly drawn to the centre of attention, but prevented from getting too close. Jacob's inner life is screened even from the narrator, and the view of Jacob through the window therefore does not grant the spectator any transparent view of his character or insight into his mind: "Jacob came out from the dark place by the window where he had hovered. The light poured over him, illuminating every cranny of his skin; but not a muscle of his face moved as he sat looking out into the garden" (JR, 80). Jacob's passage from darkness into light creates a metaphorical analogy to a moth that is drawn to the lamplight, but needs distance to sustain itself. As Francesca Kazan notes, "[t]he literal frame of the window serves to accent the figural frame of the moment"[24], in which Jacob appears as a saintly, larger than life figure, who "occupies a border between subject and object, life and art".[25] Even though he becomes exposed to visibility, the inside of his mind and the essence of his character remain hidden to the observer, who merely looks at an illuminated, static object frozen into lifelessness.

As an essential modality of the gaze in *Jacob's Room* the window creates the boundary between the inside and the outside of its central character, and provides the novel's narrative perspectives with form. The search for form is also one of Jacob's declared aims. He acknowledges that "He was a young man of sub-

---

24 Francesca Kazan, "Description and the Pictorial in *Jacob's Room*", 713.
25 Ibid., 714.

stance" (*JR*, 44), for which he himself needs to create the appropriate form in the development of his character: "'I am what I am, and intend to be it,' for which there will be no form in the world unless Jacob makes one for himself" (*JR*, 44).

The text uses the window to relate multiple views of Jacob, and to present the impossibility to arrive at a single truthful view of him in metaphorically invoking forms and shapes similar to a cubist painting. The window creates a poetic image in a double process between contraction and expansion of focus. It frames a miniature view of broken particles and from there opens into a world of multiplicity in which forms and colours are composites of a kaleidoscopic reflection, and in which the object of the gaze corresponds to the presentation of the subject: "She looked out of the window. Little windows, and the lilac and green of the garden were reflected in her eyes" (*JR*, 34).

Glass is used as a metaphor to describe the flawed impetus to gain insight through visibility when the reader's view is compared to the futile movement of the moth, that strives towards the light of a lantern, but is prohibited by glass: "If you stand a lantern under a tree every insect in the forest creeps up to it – a curious assembly, since though they scramble and swing and knock their heads against the glass, they seem to have no purpose – something senseless inspires them" (*JR*, 39).[26] *Jacob's Room* uses vision to describe the process of approximation and retreat of the aesthetic object, and creates an analogy between the characters, the reader's and the narrator's position, which are all encapsulated in the metaphor of the moth: "But something is always impelling one to hum vibrating, like the hawk moth, at the mouth of the cavern of mystery, endowing Jacob Flanders with all sorts of qualities he had not at all [...] what remains is mostly a matter of guess work. Yet over him we hang vibrating" (*JR*, 97–98).[27]

The metaphor of the moth expresses the opposition between blindness and sight and the attraction of light, and it also describes a narrative strategy that illustrates both the impetus to represent, and the impossibility of representation. The window and metaphors of glass in general are not merely used as a critique of the reliance on visibility as a means to attain the truth about a character, but they describe a necessary condition of aesthetic vision. Glass does not prohibit the spectator from the object of his gaze, but rather protects him from a kind of vision which in itself would be blindness.

---

26 The same relation is expressed by the frequent image of "insects knocking against the window" (*JR*, 38), but unable to get inside the house.

27 Harvena Richter regards the moth as a symbol of the reader's creative imagination: "Hunting the Moth: Virginia Woolf and the Creative Imagination", *Virginia Woolf: Revaluation and Continuity*, ed. by Ralph Freedmann (Berkeley: U of California Press, 1980), 13–28.

Both the metaphorical use of windows as a precondition of perception, and their metonymical function substantiate the narrative strategies of selection, amalgamation and shifting significance between single structural units in *Jacob's Room*. The window creates distance, but also confines the objects, people or scenes to the space behind it. Apart from the room as a trope illustrating the impossibility of truly knowing Jacob, the novel deals with the dilemma of the confining view. Boxes and containers are metonymical for the structure of the novel. *Jacob's Room* juxtaposes numerous different types of boxes, such as train compartments, students' lodgings in Cambridge (*JR*, 49), compartments in the British Library (*JR*, 143 ff.), boxes at the opera (*JR*, 90), and also graves and tombstones (*JR*, 156). These containers provide formal frames within the procession of scenes in the novel, and, at the same time, expose the impossibility of gaining direct access to a character, or to understand him as a whole.

The dialectics of exposure and withdrawal revealed in the presentation of rooms and containers is again expressed in the use of glass: the "window box" (*JR*, 54), the glass box of the ticket seller (*JR*, 163), and the glass cases in which Jacob keeps his butterflies, or the jewellery box in which Jinny Carslake looks at her collection of pebbles to discover a holistic microcosm: "a little jeweller's box containing ordinary pebbles picked off the road. But if you look at them steadily, she says, multiplicity becomes unity, which is somehow the secret of life" (*JR*, 180).[28]

The imagery of boxes in *Jacob's Room* is employed within a process of *mise-en-abîme*, which culminates in the impenetrable black wooden box which contains Jacob's belongings: "This black wooden box, upon which his name was still legible in white paint, stood between the long windows of the sitting-room. The street ran beneath" (*JR*, 93). The spatial organisation of the scene relies on a concentration and a concomitant extension of the narrative focus from the wooden box through the window and to the background of the street. The house, the room and the box are arranged as a set of Chinese boxes around an empty centre. Jacob's box, however, is not entirely empty, but contains letters and a pair of trousers as remnants from his past. The black box with the white name on it symbolically brings the contrast between the visible and the invisible into play. It evokes the opposition between black and white, light and darkness, and presents the problem, that neither Jacob's name, nor the belongings stored in the coffin-like

---

28 Peter Walsh in *Mrs. Dalloway* is amused by a little girl he observes in Regent's Park: "little Elise Mitchell, who had been picking up pebbles to add to the pebble collection which she and her brother were making on the nursery mantelpiece, plumped her handful down on the nurse's knee and scudded off again full tilt into a lady's legs" (*MD*, 71).

box can be of any help in getting closer to him. His absence is rather conveyed through the written presence of his name.

The box which cannot be seen through the windows, but is placed between them, simultaneously implies that existence unrestricted by a name might be possible, and yet, that knowledge is based on naming, and that the self which is signified and condensed by a name remains partly anchored in the actual world of the visible: "our very perception of nature is already mediated by the necessity of naming – that naming and perception are virtually one and the same process, with the world itself as a text or matrix of texts".[29] *Jacob's Room* unfolds single layers which conceal the central character, and encourages a process of reading which involves looking for traces, amalgamating fragments, and adopting multiple perspectives, it also leads to the awareness that ultimately, the black box will remain closed, and the reader will have to remain an onlooker outside the room.

The idea of the reader as a passer-by on the street, and a spectator of partial views is prominent in *Jacob's Room*, where illuminated windows and scenes are compared to the pages and pictures of a book:

> rude illustrations, pictures in a book whose pages we turn over and over as if we should at last find what we look for. Every face, every shop, bedroom window, public-house, and dark square is a picture feverishly turned – in search of what? It is the same with books. What do we seek through millions of pages? Still hopefully turning the pages – oh, here is Jacob's room (JR, 132).

Moments of insight and understanding in *Jacob's Room* are not entirely impossible, but they remain partial and transitory. They emphasise the nature of aesthetic vision that captures the shadowy, fictional essence of character.

> In any case life is but a procession of shadows, and God knows why it is that we embrace them so eagerly, and see them depart with such anguish, being shadows. And why, if this and much more than this is true, why are we yet surprised in the window corner by a sudden vision that the young man in the chair is of all things in the world the most real, the most solid, the best known to us – why indeed? For the moment after we know nothing about him. Such is the manner of our seeing. Such the conditions of our love (JR, 96).

Similar to *The Voyage Out*, windows in *Jacob's Room* also mark the dividing line between Western, especially English, and other civilisations. Whereas in *The Voyage Out*, the florid tropics of South America provide a counterpart to London,

---

[29] Meisel, *The Absent Father*, 117. Meisel regards Woolf's treatment of names and naming within the context of Walter Pater's largely ironic approach to the language of science in which he denies the existence of nature as objective reality.

in *Jacob's Room*, Greece as the ancient cradle of civilisation, history, philosophy and knowledge, for Jacob represents an unattainable ideal. After he embarks on his journey to Italy and Greece, his attempt to liberate himself from the confines of civilisation is indicated in the comparative absence of windows (*JR*, 202). The unobstructed view he gains in Greece at the landscape and the sky had already occurred during Jacob's journey to the Scilly Isles, in the passage where he looks at the cloudless sky: "Jacob sang, lying on his back, looking up into the sky at mid-day, from which every shred of cloud had been withdrawn, so that it was like something permanently displayed with the cover off" (*JR*, 67).[30]

It is only at solitary instances that Jacob looks out of the window and in a moment of introspection feels united with the people outside through his loneliness: "Jacob went to the window and stood with his hands in his pockets. [...] some more profound conviction was the cause of his gloom – it was not that he himself happened to be lonely, but that all people are" (*JR*, 194). Both Jacob's and Rachel's juvenile viewpoints, their desire to connect to the world, and yet their distance from it are expressed in situations where they stand at the window.

Both protagonists die young, and at the end of both novels, windows acquire a more impersonal and hostile character. In *Jacob's Room*, the "fiery flushing windows" of Kensington Palace indicate the impending final disappearance of Jacob (*JR*, 242). Likewise, Mrs. Durrant and Clara look at "blazing windows" (*JR*, 244) in Covent Garden at the end of the novel. For Betty Flanders, the window becomes a premonition of Jacob's death, and an emblem of mourning, when it is "decorated with a fringe of dark leaves" (*JR*, 246). Bonamy in his final view out of the window senses confusion, and when he sees the leaves raising themselves (*JR*, 247), he repeats Archer's initial search for his brother and calls out for Jacob twice (*JR*, 4–5; 247). Like Archer, however, he does not receive an answer, and turns away from the window. At the end of the novel, the view through the window reiterates the characters' initial search for Jacob, and after its display of multiple views of him, returns to the distant perspective of the spectator. Windows are a means of multiplying reference and are linked to the novel's structure. Even though they present crucial stages in the central character's development, they distance him from others and prefigure a way of reading as viewing through a transparent, yet impermeable surface.

---

30 Cf. Rachel's experience: "She was conscious of an extraordinary intensity in everything, as though their presence stripped some cover off the surface of things" (*TVO*, 184).

2.1.3 The dialectics of perspective: windows in *Mrs. Dalloway*

The display of a kaleidoscopic, indeed almost cubist multiplicity of geometric form, presented in the symbolic form of the window in *Jacob's Room*, is further condensed in *Mrs. Dalloway*. The window denotes the novel's binary structure, which is reflected in Clarissa Dalloway's distance to herself, and in the juxtaposition of Clarissa and Septimus Smith. In her notes for writing *Mrs. Dalloway*, Woolf devises the early scenes of the novel as: "Mrs. Dalloway comes on alone (as in the first chapter). We then go on to a general statement, introducing Septimus. They are linked together by the aeroplane. We then return to Mrs. Dalloway alone in her drawing room + settle into her".[31]

The window prompts Clarissa Dalloway's introspection and remembrance. It not only opens up into the distant, youthful world of her past ("when, with a little squeak of the hinges, which she could hear now, she had burst open the French windows and plunged at Bourton into the open air" (*MD*, 3)), but also indicates her detachment from the world surrounding her in the present. Even though significant moments in Clarissa Dalloway's life are marked by her view out of the window, they always occur at a distance, and prevent her from directly relating to the world outside. When Clarissa looks into the window of the bookshop, the Shakespearean leitmotif "Fear no more"[32] is introduced and expresses the equanimity of her character that stands apart from life and its extremes. [33]

The dual quality of glass which is transparent and reflecting, but not permeable supports the idea of an ambiguous surface space only accessible to the eye, which protects the observer, but keeps him at distance from what he sees, and hence prevents unity between the subject and the reality perceived. Clarissa Dalloway's way of seeing largely consists of the surface world accessible to the senses: "There were flowers: delphiniums, sweet peas, bunches of lilac; and carnations, masses of carnations. There were roses; there were irises. Ah yes…" (*MD*, 13). According to Woolf, the presentation of life in the streets of London is a means to emphasise that it contains "happiness – or rather intense feeling or see-

---

31 Virginia Woolf, Holograph Notes. Nov, 9, 1922-Aug, 2, 1923. BERG.
32 Peter te Boekhorst, *Das literarische Leitmotiv und seine Funktionen in Romanen von Aldous Huxley, Virginia Woolf und James Joyce* (Frankfurt am Main: Lang, 1987).
33 In *The Waves*, Bernard even more censoriously describes the lack of self-awareness of the masses: "these starers and trippers; these errand-boys and furtive and fugitive girls who, ignoring their doom, look in at shop-windows?" (*W*, 74). Likewise, *Mrs. Dalloway* uses shop windows to render Rezia's stare: "And there were the shops – hat shops, dress shops, shops with leather bags in the window, where she would stand staring" (*MD*, 97).

ing".³⁴ Clarissa loves "life; London; this moment of June" (*MD*, 4), as well as "this right in front of her" (*MD*, 9), but remains herself barred from it and unknown to most of the people she sees. Upon returning to her house, her view out of the window expresses her disappointment and her sense of being excluded from life in general and from the social life represented by Lady Bruton's lunch party:

> she paused by the open staircase window which let in blinds flapping, dogs barking, let in, she thought, feeling herself suddenly shrivelled, aged, breastless, the grinding, blowing, flowering of the day, out of doors, out of the window, out of her body and brain which now failed, since Lady Bruton, whose lunch parties were said to be extraordinarily amusing, had not asked her (*MD*, 33).

The process of her walking up the stairs and withdrawing into her room is supported by the use of free indirect discourse to indicate the notion of retreat in subjective as well as spatial terms: "There was an emptiness about the heart of life; an attic room" (*MD*, 33). Clarissa's gaze is both directed into her self and into the room, and her growing sense of emptiness is paralleled by the gradual narrowing of her focus. She envisages the course of her own life drawing towards its end in the image of her bed becoming "narrower and narrower" (*MD*, 33), which gives way to her retreat into the past.

The window in *Mrs. Dalloway* is a formal device to indicate the parallel existence of Clarissa and Septimus. In forging a link in perspective and symbolism between both characters, it not only creates a paradoxical unity between them, but also provides a metaphor of the ways in which they approach reality. When Virginia Woolf sketches out her ideas for *Mrs. Dalloway* in an entry in her diary of October 14th 1922 she emphasises the ambivalence and two-sidedness of vision as a central concern of the novel: "Mrs. Dalloway has branched into a book; and I adumbrate here a study of insanity and suicide; the world seen by the sane and the insane side by side".³⁵ Inspired by her reading of Dostoevsky,³⁶ Woolf in her writing notes for *Mrs. Dalloway* envisages the dramatic structure of the novel which was to be sustained by two kinds of vision epitomised by the main characters: "*Mrs.* D. seeing the truth, S.S. seeing the insane truth. The work to have

---

34 Virginia Woolf, Holograph Notes. Nov, 9, 1922-Aug, 2, 1923. BERG.
35 Virginia Woolf, *A Writer's Diary: Being Extracts from the Diary of Virginia Woolf*, ed. by Leonard Woolf (New York: Harcourt, Brace, 1954), 52.
36 Willi Erzgräber, "The 'Moment of Vision' im Modernen Englischen Roman", *Augenblick und Zeitpunkt. Studien zur Zeitstruktur und Zeitmetaphorik in Kunst und Wissenschaften*, hrsg. von Christian W. Thomsen und Hans Holländer (Darmstadt: WB, 1984), 372.

the inventory of a play: only in narrative. Some revision therefore needed".[37] In her notes for writing *Mrs. Dalloway* Woolf further subdivides the central parallel structure of perspective of Clarissa and Septimus by introducing the point of view of numerous minor characters:

> Septimus must be seen by someone. His wife? She to be founded on L? Simple, instinctive, childless. They sit in Regents Park, for example. But the interview with the specialist must be in the middle. She is to be a real character. He only real insofar as she sees him. Otherwise to exist in his view of things: which is always to be contrasting with Mrs. Dalloway's. [...]

> Mrs. Dalloway must be seen by other people. As she sits in her drawing room. But there must be a general idea – one must not get lost in detail, her chapter must correspond with his. Question of closure that is to say of links between chapters: also could the scenes be divided like acts of a play into five, say in six?[38]

The structure of *Doppelgaenger* on the level of character is paralleled by the ambivalent nature of vision itself. Creating the borderline between different kinds of reality, vision can at the same time unite characters with a reality and separate them from it.

During Clarissa's visit to the flower shop, after the noise of the explosion in the street has drawn her towards the window, the window of a passing car becomes the focus of attention which unites the different perspectives of the passers-by, and creates a transition between them: "For thirty seconds all heads were inclined the same way – to the window" (*MD*, 19). In this scene, the window of the car ("a square of dove grey" (*MD*, 15)) not only becomes a focal point, attracting the characters' attention ("Septimus thought, and this gradual drawing together of everything to one centre before his eyes" (*MD*, 16)), but also connects Septimus' view from outside and Clarissa's from the inside of the house.[39] It becomes a metonymy for the novel's strategies of focalisation and its division between perspectives. The link between Clarissa and Septimus is established early in the novel, where the window conveys both the sense of duplicity and impending danger, and Clarissa's sombre foreboding presages Septimus' death: "feeling as she did, standing there at the open window, that something awful was about to happen" (*MD*, 3).

---

[37] Virginia Woolf "Thoughts when beginning a book to be called perhaps At Home: or The Party", Oct 16th, 1922 153r. BERG.
[38] "Mrs. Dalloway Holograph Notes", Nov, 9, 1922; Feb 26, 1923. BERG.
[39] Symbolic relations between both characters are established on numerous levels, for instance when the leitmotif 'fear no more' is repeated by Septimus (*MD*, 153).

For Clarissa Dalloway, the "mystery of life" consists of the question of how to relate to others: "here was one room; there another" (*MD*, 140), and to her mind neither love nor religion can solve it. Before she married Richard Dalloway, a different kind of harmony and unity was still possible between her and Peter Walsh, who remarks: "he and Clarissa. They went in and out of each other's minds without any effort" (*MD*, 69). In her present role, she is unable to directly relate to another person, and therefore is touched by the sight of the woman she regularly observes through the window (*MD*, 139), and whom she has taken to symbolise the 'privacy of the soul' (*MD*, 138). On the night of her party, however, Clarissa's protective invisibility is suspended similar to that of Rachel and Helen in *The Voyage Out*, when her alter ego looks at her, and the window does no longer offer any protection: "She walked to the window [...] She parted the curtains; she looked. Oh, but how surprising! – in the room opposite the old lady stared straight at her!" (*MD*, 203)

Whereas Clarissa is able to maintain a life on the surface, symbolised by the interface of the window, and when retiring to her room also delights in the feeling of distance and anonymity, Septimus senses imprisonment when the seemingly transparent inhibits him from getting close to the things themselves. His feeling of being irrevocably cut off from life, truth and beauty is expressed in his vision of an impenetrable screen, which confines him to the world of his traumatic memories: "but beauty was behind a pane of glass, a voice spoke from behind the screen" (*MD*, 102; 96; 159; 73).[40] Septimus remains isolated, and his only escape from his phobic visions is not the deictic return to sensuous seeing, which would assert the reality of the visible and which was both prescribed by Holmes and readily followed by Lucrezia, but the retreat from it: "But he would not go mad. He would shut his eyes; he would see no more" (*MD*, 24).[41]

---

[40] Woolf dwells on the notion of ambivalence between biased detachment and empathy inherent in 'the screen making habit' of the mind when she reflects on the sight of two young girls. "My instinct at once throws up a screen, which condemns them [...] But all this is a great mistake: These screens shut me out. Have no screens, for screens are made out of our own integument; & get at the thing itself, which has nothing whatever in common with a screen. The screen making habit, though, is so universal, that probably it preserves our sanity. If we had not this device for shutting people off from our sympathies, we might, perhaps, dissolve utterly. Separateness would be impossible. But the screens are in the excess; not the sympathy" (*D* III, 104).
[41] Lucrezia Smith urges her husband to look at details, and to become aware of the world around him rather than succumbing to his traumatic visions: "'Look', she implored him, for Dr. Holmes had told her to make him notice real things [...] 'Oh look', she implored him. But what was there to look at? A few sheep. That was all" (*MD*, 27–28).

The idiosyncratic vacuum in which Septimus finds himself cannot be pierced through by Lukrezia's words, and he merely stares at his surroundings without acknowledging their everyday reality (*MD*, 24). Septimus, whose mental illness particularly affects his visual sense, is ostracised from society and lives in a hermetic world haunted by his mental visions.[42] Looking at actual life becomes particularly dangerous for him, because what he sees is never a reassuring, objective reality, but a vision of reality, which is always on the verge of transforming into hauntingly unreal images.

Septimus' loss of reality and feeling further amounts to his loss of imaginary vision ("Where he had once seen mountains, where he had seen faces, where

---

42 In both *Mrs. Dalloway* and its critical reception, Dr. Holmes has gained and maintained his reputation as a sinister practitioner of psychiatry, who is partly responsible for Septimus suicide. Mark Hussey in his entry on Dr. Holmes in *Virginia Woolf A-Z* mentions that "Woolf drew on her experience of doctors in portraying Holmes, but he also exhibits characteristics of the way the medical establishment viewed shell shock in the years following World War I" (Mark Hussey, *Virginia Woolf A-Z* (New York: Facts on File, 1995), 118). Woolf's portrait of Dr. Holmes is not only founded on the obvious reference to the prototypical detective and investigator into the devious mind, Sherlock Holmes, but can also be related to a leading medical authority on disturbances of sight in post-traumatic nervous disorders. This historical Dr. Gordon Holmes was a physician at the "Royal London Ophthalmic Hospital", and also worked as a physician to out-patients at the "National Hospital for the Paralysed and Epileptic" in London. After the end of World War I, he diagnosed patterns of trauma regarding the dichotomy of visual and spatial perception, and particularly identified the loss of recognition, disturbances of spatial orientation, and the lack of visual localisation of objects as results of cerebral lesions. (Gordon Holmes, "Disturbances of Visual Space Perception", *The British Medical Journal*, 2 (1919), 230–233). In one of the "Montgomery Lectures in Ophthalmology" which was delivered at Trinity College Dublin in June 1919 and printed in *The British Medical Journal*, he bases his empiricist analyses on George Berkeley's "Essay towards a new theory of vision", and lists different kinds of perceptive disorders in post-war patients (230). Among Holmes diagnoses are mainly symptoms of disturbance in visual attention and irregularities in perception affecting ocular movements. Holmes describes the situation of a patient which is reminiscent of Septimus plight: "the patient first stared blankly in front of him [...] it was only after some time and searching that he could bring his eyes directly to an object on one side of his visual axes at which he was asked to look." (232) *Mrs. Dalloway*, however, leaves it open whether Septimus traumatic visions are caused by physical injuries, and only portrays his intuitous rejection of Holmes "the coward" (*MD*, 164). Although Alex Zwerdling, in *Virginia Woolf and the Real World*, notes Woolf's sensitivity towards post-war mental disorders, it remains questionable whether Woolf was familiar with contemporary neurophysiological research, which would substantiate the reference to Gordon Holmes. Furthermore, it is to be doubted that, if she were indeed referring to the historical Holmes, whether she would have used the same name. The question whether the present speculations are drifting too extensively towards the empirical, and whether or not Woolf has engaged the reader in what Joyce in *Ulysses* calls 'Sherlockholmesing' has to be left unresolved (*U*, 16, 831).

he had seen beauty, there was a screen" (*MD*, 159)), and ultimately the loss of his self: "There remained only the window, the large Bloomsbury lodging house window; the tiresome, the troublesome, and rather melodramatic business of opening the window and throwing himself out" (*MD*, 163). Septimus' death, and the flight from the imminent confinement to 'proportion' prescribed by Dr. Holmes, is treated as a desperate attempt to relate to the outer world: "Death was an attempt to communicate, people feeling the impossibility of reaching the centre which, mystically, evaded them; closeness drew apart; rapture faded; one was alone. There was an embrace in death" (*MD*, 202).[43]

In further condensing the parallels laid out between both characters, the novel juxtaposes the last window encounters of Clarissa and Septimus. In the final description of Clarissa's view out of the window, looking at the old woman in the house opposite, the window, for Clarissa, becomes a mirror, when the old woman 'stares' at her. Similarly, before he is about to commit suicide, Septimus notices an old man from across the street likewise 'staring' at him (*MD*, 164). Eventually, both Septimus and Clarissa act as mirrors and as windows to each other, coexisting with and reflecting each other, when they, like Terence and Rachel, only achieve unity after death. In *Mrs. Dalloway*, similar to *The Voyage Out*, the broken window signifies death. For both Clarissa and Septimus, windows mark the borderline between life and death. In contrast to Clarissa, who exists on the surface of life, on "the ebb and flow" of things, and epitomises Freud's definition of the "ego as a surface", Septimus, in breaking the window, refutes surfaces, transcends the surface of the window, delves into the unconscious, and, in doing so, acknowledges a dimension to his life beyond surfaces, which he tragically only seeks in death. Although Clarissa does not take the same radical consequences and returns to the community of her friends, after his death, she senses a kind of union with Septimus: "She felt somehow very like him" (*MD*, 204). Whereas Clarissa feels estranged by the other characters at the party, where even her old relations Sally Seton and Peter have become unfamiliar to her, it is finally Septimus, who remains anonymous to her, but with whom she experiences familiarity.

The window is a structural element of passage and eventually becomes a symbol of aesthetic vision, which is described as a process of convergence, but of ultimate incompatibility of the inside and the outside view. As such it both evokes and refutes closeness. It creates a passage between characters and, at the same

---

43 Whereas Septimus' suicide expresses his wish to liberate himself, after his death, his wife Rezia also senses a kind of liberation symbolised by the window she envisions in her medicine-induced daydream: "It seemed to her as she drank the sweet stuff that she was opening long windows, stepping out into some garden" (*MD*, 164).

time, constructs a barrier between them. It suggests transparency, but refuses to become a vehicle for the equation between transparency and mimesis.

2.2 "The veil of words" and the poetics of the diaphanous

2.2.1 The diaphanous in Modernist aesthetics

The veil, like the window, establishes the notion of a boundary between seeing and being, public space and privacy, immediacy and distance. Whereas the window plays on the notions of framing and perceptual distance, the veil dwells on the interplay of a visible foreground and an invisible background. Other than the transparency conveyed by the window, the veil foregrounds its materiality as semi-transparent or diaphanous.

The diaphanous traditionally conveys the notion of phenomenal in-between-ness. It can be conceived within the notion of iconic difference, which exists between the object and the medium.[44] Creating a liminal space between the object itself and the way in which it appears to the viewer, the diaphanous suggests that there is no immediate or unmediated relation between the eye and the object of perception. Rather than focusing on the 'whatness' of the object, the diaphanous undermines the clear-cut distinction between appearance and essence in directing the viewer's attention to the way in which the object appears. The notion of the diaphanous inherent in the image of the veil presents a perceptual situation, in which vision depends on a medium.

The discursive foundation for the discussion of the diaphanous had been laid by Aristotle in *De anima* and *De sensu et sensibili*, where he regards the diaphanous or translucent as a part of the natural constitution of bodies to partake in colour. Aristotle does not logically prove or legitimise the existence of the diaphanous, but succinctly remarks "εστί δή διαφανής" (there is the diaphanous).[45] In the course of the history of the term, the Aristotelian idea of translucency increasingly converged with that of transparency, until it almost became synonymous with it. Medieval interpretations of Aristotle, for instance in the scholasticism of St. Thomas Aquinas, treated the diaphanous within the broader notion of *perspicuitas*,[46] and

---

[44] Gottfried Boehm describes the notion of iconic difference inherent in a work of art. Art presents visible materiality and at the same time creates significance beyond materiality. "Die Wiederkehr der Bilder", *Was ist ein Bild?*, 30–31.
[45] Aristotle, *De anima*, ed. by William D. Ross (Oxford: Clarendon, 1998), 418b3.
[46] Quint. Inst. VIII, 3, 61; "perspicuitas" VIII, 2, 1–24.

from its earliest appearance in the English language onwards, the term *diaphane* or *diaphanous* has been entwined with the notion of transparency.[47] The equation of the diaphanous with the transparent is likewise reflected in examples from technical history, where a diaphanometer in 1789 is described as an instrument for measuring the transparency of the atmosphere, and a diaphanoscope in 1886 as "a contrivance for viewing transparent positive photographs".[48]

In Modernist fiction, and particularly in the works of Virginia Woolf, the diaphanous expresses a modality of aesthetic vision that playfully refutes immediacy. As a central paradigm of perception, the figure of the diaphanous rather constitutes a narrative strategy of visualisation, which emphasises the mediated nature of aesthetic experience that is mediated by the text itself. In both Woolf's novels and her critical works the diaphanous materialises in modes of perception which are metaphorically related to the veil, and lay emphasis on vagueness, hazy and blurred vision as well as on seeing through tears. In analysing the narrative and aesthetic functions of the metaphor of the veil and the concomitant perceptual modes of vagueness, this chapter will focus on the use of the symbolic materiality of words, and the overall presentation of narrative situations governed by twilight and the diaphanous haze.

The veil traditionally marks a material boundary of perception.[49] It dwells on the interplay of a visible foreground and an invisible background, and it presents a "symbolic form" in Ernst Cassirer's definition.[50] In giving the onlooker an idea of something which is visible and yet kept from direct visibility, the veil mediates between presence and absence, and, as Patricia Oster explains it, becomes an image for the aesthetic creation of the imaginary.[51] The attraction of the absent inherent in the veil is emphasised by Jean Starobinski, who reads the veil as a

---

47 Cf: *OED* "diaphanity", Norton Ord. Alch. Iii, in Ashm (1652) 42: "A goodly stone glittering with perspecuitie, Being of wonderfull and excellent Diaphanity." The diaphanous is often linked to materiality of glass or fabric, as in Caulfeild & Saward's Dictionary of needlework: "a woven silk stuff, having transparent coloured figures" (1882).
48 *OED*, "diaphanometer, "diaphanoscope".
49 This dominant notion concerning the metaphor of the veil manifests itself in the work of Aleida and Jan Assmann, *Schleier und Schwelle* I-III (München: Fink, 1997–1999).
50 Ernst Cassirer, *Philosophie der symbolischen Formen I: Die Sprache*.
51 Patrizia Oster, "Der Schleier zwischen religiöser und ästhetischer Erfahrung", *Schleier und Schwelle II. Geheimnis und Offenbarung*, hrsg. von Aleida und Jan Assmann (München: Fink, 1998), 237. For the use of the veil in Early Modern art history see: Klaus Krüger. *Das Bild als Schleier des Unsichtbaren ästhetischer Illusion in der Kunst der frühen Neuzeit in Italien* (München: Fink, 2001). Ralf Konersmann, *Der Schleier des Timanthes. Perspektiven der historischen Semantik* (Frankfurt am Main: Fischer, 1994).

characteristic modality of aesthetic vision.⁵² As a mode of expressing the inexpressible in iconography and fine art, the veil marks the transition between factual, immanent reality and a world beyond it, and becomes an emblem of both religious and aesthetic experience. Moshe Barasch stresses this twofold function of the veil in naming it a "visible metaphor of the secret".⁵³

Founded on a rhetoric of concealment and revelation, the veil not only presents religious, erotic and aesthetic experience as a mode of perception, but at the same time provides an image for the experience of the imaginary, which guides and structures perception.⁵⁴ Veiled, an object or a person is only present within this ambiguity, and directs the view at, and possibly through the veil. Among the many ambiguities which govern the image of the veil, the main perceptive difficulty it introduces lies in its presentation of visible materiality, which coexists with what is shown, and also points to what invisibly exists beyond it. The veil makes possible a specific form of perception, which emphasises the notion of in-between-ness and ambiguity, and leaves the viewer in a position of being able to see, and yet unable to see clearly.

Because of its textile structure, the interface formed by the veil is intertwined with the textual web of words, which does not so much emphasise the impenetrability of a densely-woven tapestry, but rather its delicate and see-through qualities. As an image of the text, however, the veil is ambiguous. On the one hand, it directs the reader's attention to itself and invalidates referential meaning outside the text, and, on the other hand, it generates the notion of something beyond itself. It both refers to the material presence of the text, and to the experience of reading, which is cast into a perceptual constellation and becomes a form of aesthetic vision.⁵⁵

In the critical works of Virginia Woolf, the notion of the diaphanous and the image of the veil become vital to her aesthetics. In an entry into her diary, she describes the intermediate position of the diaphanous between the revelatory stasis of a moment and the delicate elusive richness of life's flow:

---

52 Starobinski, "Le voile de Poppée", *L'Œil vivant* I (Paris: Gallimard, 1961), 27.
53 Moshe Barasch provides many examples of the veil from early iconography which illustrate the close connection between religious ritual and aesthetic presentation. "Der Schleier. Das Geheimnis in den Bildvorstellungen der Spätantike", *Schleier und Schwelle* II, 179–201.
54 Patrizia Oster, *Der Schleier im Text. Funktionsgeschichte eines Bildes für die neuzeitliche Erfahrung des Imaginären* (München: Fink, 2002), 10.
55 Starobinski describes the ambiguity of the text between proximity and distance: "Ainsi, malgré notre désir de nous abîmer dans la profondeur vivante de l'œuvre, nous sommes contraints de nous distancer d'elle pour pouvoir en parler. [...] Il ne faut refuser ni le vertige de la distance, ni celui de la proximité: il faut désirer ce double excès où le regard est chaque fois près de perdre tout pouvoir." Jean Starobinski, "Le voile de Poppée", *L'Œil vivant* I, 26–27.

> Now is life very solid or very shifting? I am haunted by the two contradictions. This has gone on for ever; will last for ever; goes down to the bottom of the world – this moment I stand on. Also it is transitory, flying, diaphanous. I shall pass like a cloud on the waves. Perhaps it may be that though we change, one flying after another, so quick, so quick, yet we are somehow successive and continuous we human beings, and show the light through. But what is the light? (*AWD*, 137)

The centrality of the diaphanous, the semi-transparent and the translucent in Woolf's literary aesthetics is expressed in her programmatic essay "Modern Fiction". In "Modern Fiction", Woolf analyses contemporary writing and distinguishes it from the materialism inherent in Edwardian realism, which is represented in the works of Wells, Bennett and Galsworthy. The hermetic vacuum of Bennett's novels – "He can make a book so well constructed and solid in craftsmanship that it is difficult for the most exacting of critics to see through what chink or crevice decay can creep in" (*CE* II, 104) – to Woolf is equally disappointing as Galsworthy's "delight in the solidity of his fabric" (*CE* II, 104).

Woolf diagnoses the futility of historical realism to "prove solidity", and "to catch life" in creating a mimetic likeness to it. Since what she calls life is irreconcilable with any finite expression of it, to maintain that any single vision can exclusively capture the essence of life would be invidious. "Life escapes", she writes, "and perhaps without life nothing else is worth while. It is a confession of vagueness to have to make use of such a figure as this, but we scarcely better the matter by speaking, as critics are prone to do, of reality" (*CE* II, 105).

Woolf replaces the sense of solidity provided by an unambiguous reference between medium and meaning by the notion of the uncreated, the possible and the incomplete, and in her definition of life seeks to liberate writing from generic conventions imposed upon it by a realist aesthetics: "Life is not a series of gig-lamps symmetrically arranged; life is a luminous halo, a semi-transparent envelope surrounding us from the beginning of consciousness to the end" (*CE* II, 106).[56]

Similar to Woolf, Joyce uses the anglicised Aristotelian term *diaphane* in *Ulysses* to describe Stephen Dedalus's view of the relation between language and reality in the "Proteus"-episode of the novel. The "ineluctable modality of the

---

[56] The notion of life as a semi-transparent membrane is not to be confused with what Woolf, in *Moments of Being*, calls "the cotton wool of daily life". Whereas the "cotton wool" refers to the explicit quotidian immediacy of the visible, the semi-transparent suggests that there is more to life than meets the eye, and opens up a realm of aesthetic possibility in which "nothing is simply one thing".

visible" expressed by Joyce's protagonist on his walk along Sandymount beach relates to his visual and tactile perception, and unfolds the protean nature of language that Stephen inhabits. Stephen reflects on Aristotle's definition of the *diaphane* in bodies[57]:

> Snotgreen, bluesilver, rust: coloured signs. Limits of the diaphane. But he adds: in bodies. Then he was aware of them bodies before of them coloured. How? By knocking his sconce against them, sure. [...] Diaphane, adiaphane. If you can put your five fingers through it it is a gate, if not a door. Shut your eyes and see (*U*, 3, 7–9).

Throughout *Ulysses*, the *diaphane* describes Stephen's way of seeing "the signatures of all things" which is opposed to the practical materialism of his counterpart Leopold Bloom.[58] As many readers of this section have noted, Stephen's shutting his eyes is a turn to a reliance upon hearing to make his way across the beach ("Exactly: and this is the ineluctable modality of the audible" (*U*, 3, 13)). I take this and the experience of having his eyes closed ("I am getting along nicely in the dark" (*U*, 3, 15)) as an experiment that ends with a very different conclusion from the empiricist *esse est percipi*: "Open your eyes now. I will. One moment. Has all vanished since? If I open and am forever in the black adiaphane. *Basta*! I will see if I can see. See now. There all the time without you: and ever shall be, world without end" (*U*, 3, 27–28). Joyce's take on the visual is different from the empiricists because Joyce approaches experience itself in a different way. The novel not only brings into question how Stephen experiences his day but also how we as readers experience the text. Joyce, like Woolf, embraces the empiricist reliance on experience, but he dispenses with their totalising systems of knowledge and their search for unified approaches to experience. The reason "Proteus" begins this way – and the reason it ends the "Telemachiad" and sets the tone for the rest of the novel – is that it signals the break with the traditional unquestioned reliance on clear vision to provide for knowledge and truth.[59]

---

[57] For Stephen, Plato and Aristotle create the Skylla and Charybdis of Western Thought: "John Eglinton, frowning, said, waxing wroth: "'Upon my word it makes my blood boil to hear anyone compare Aristotle with Plato'. 'Which of the two', Stephen asked, 'would have banished me from his commonwealth?'" (*U*, 9, 79–83).

[58] Sheldon Brivic, "The Veil of Signs: Perception as Language in Joyce's *Ulysses*", *ELH*, 57 (1990), 743–745.

[59] Prior to both Joyce and Woolf, Walter Pater in his early essay "Diaphaneitè" (1864) uses the term in a context emerging from Platonism, where he is concerned with the ethical dimensions of the artistic mind. Pater speaks of "a mind of taste lighted up by some spiritual ray within". Walter Pater, "Diaphaneitè", *Miscellaneous Studies. A Series of Essays* (London: Macmillan, 1924), 250. Pater describes the relation between the artist and life: "The artist and he who has treated life in

In Woolf's critical essays, the veil presents an aesthetic category. The "veil of fiction", she refers to in "The Captain's Death Bed",⁶⁰ describes aesthetic experience as permitting a distant, subjective and necessarily differing view. Whereas in her novels "the veil of words" (*W*, 76) signifies poetic language, in her literary criticism Woolf regards the veil as a productive image for aesthetic creation, and uses it as a metaphorical analogue to the narrative interplay of veiling and unveiling, concealing and revealing for which she provides examples from literary history.

In "The Pastons and Chaucer", Woolf praises Chaucer's sentences as a procession of veiled beauties: "a stately and memorable beauty in the undraped sentences which follow each other like women so slightly veiled that you see the lines of their bodies as they go" (*CR* I, 19). In her essay on Ruskin, she focuses on the relation between word and meaning in Ruskin's style and compares the experience of reading to a perceptual situation: "Compared with much of his writing, it is extremely simple in style; but the simplicity is the flower of perfect skill. The words lie like a transparent veil upon his meaning" (*CDB*, 52). In the essay "The Novels of E.M. Forster" she compares Forster to Ibsen and uses the veil to describe the intermediary position of his fiction between the empirical world and an imaginary world beyond it: "A room is to him a room, a writing table a writing table, and a waste-paper basked a waste-paper basket. At the same time, the paraphernalia of reality have at certain moments to become the veil through which we see infinity" (*CE* I, 346).

The diaphanous in Modernist aesthetics is both a subject of fiction, and a narrative strategy, which confirms neither to empiricist nor idealist claims. Rather than pointing to a transcendental reality, Woolf concentrates on language to transform the potential into the actual. When Jacob, in *Jacob's Room*, for instance, looks at the girls sitting opposite him, they appear to him in hazy shades: "Opposite him were hazy, semi-transparent shapes of yellow and blue.

---

the spirit of art desires only to be shown to the world as he really is; as he comes nearer and nearer to perfection, the veil of an outer life not simply expressive of the inward becomes thinner and thinner" (249). He regards translucency as a property of original genius and identifies it with the moral perfection of a character. (247–254). Meisel, *The Absent Father*, 92. Cf. *Politeia* V, 478d, 5–9.
60 The veil provides an altered state of fictional reality: "In short, after a fine burst of pleasure there comes a time when the spell that Captain Marryat lays upon us wears thin, and we see through the veil of fiction facts – facts, it is true, that are interesting in themselves, [...] but their interest is another kind of interest, and as much out of harmony with imagination as a bedroom cupboard is with the dream of someone waking from sleep. Often in a shallow book, when we wake, we wake to nothing at all; but here when we wake, we wake to the presence of a personage" (*CDB*, 45).

[...] 'Clara, Clara', Jacob named the shape in yellow gauze Timothy's sister, Clara" (*JR*, 75). For Jacob, Clara does not stand for the Thomistic *claritas*, but appears as a coloured shape, expressive of translucent vagueness: "She looked semi-transparent, pale, wonderfully beautiful up there among the vine leaves and the yellow and purple bunches, the lights swimming over her in coloured islands" (*JR*, 82). To Jacob, Clara has become an epitome of the diaphanous, a tissue of a poetic image which enables the viewer to perceive colours.

"The veil of words" does not only create the aesthetic object through language, but, at the same time, marks its intangibility. What characters and readers see is language, and the world of Woolf's novels is made visible by making language a medium which generates aesthetic vision.

2.2.2 Twilight and fog: vague and fading vision

Woolf's presentation of modes of perception explores the liminal space between transparency and opacity, and it is concerned with visions of the vague, the hazy, the fading, and the almost invisible. The creation of perceptive situations which emphasise obscurity, indeterminacy, and vagueness expresses the reluctance of Woolf's aesthetics to conform to pre-defined standards, and to rather expose their contingency. The fusion of light and darkness into a diffuse, diaphanous haze challenges any direct link between the subjectivity of perception and objective perceptibility. Its structural ambiguity opens up a realm of possibility which questions what is given, entails an abstraction from it, and creates an open horizon of possible meaning. Woolf analyses the experimental narrative potential inherent in the fusion of contrasts and blurred boundaries, and compares the reading of Tchekov's stories to looking at a scene in twilight, which departs from conventional definitions of genre:

> and then, as the eyes accustom themselves to twilight and discern the shapes of things in a room we see how complete the story is, how profound, and how truly in obedience to his vision Tchekov has chosen this, that and the other, and placed them together to compose something new. But it is impossible to say 'this is comic', or 'that is tragic', nor are we certain, since short stories, we have been taught, should be brief and conclusive, whether this, which is vague and inconclusive, should be called a short story at all (*CE* II, 108–109).[61]

---

[61] Metaphorically, she describes the effect reading certain novels has on eyesight in similar terms: "After reading the romances of Scott and Stevenson and Mrs. Radcliffe, our eyes seem stretched, their sight a little blurred, as if they had been gazing into the distance" (*GR*, 110).

Half-visibility and twilight not only encourage a way of looking more closely at what one sees to grasp it in its profundity, but create distinct viewing situations in narrative. The veil becomes a compositional principle of Woolf's texts, when they play on the borderline between visibility and invisibility, and are set in the indistinct atmosphere of twilight.

Expressing a fundamental perceptive indeterminacy, many of Woolf's novels begin either at dawn or at dusk. Like *The Waves*, and *The Voyage Out*, *The Years*, after its initial account of the uncertain April weather in London, embarks on a description of the spreading light against the darkness of the setting dusk. The "Present-Day" – section of the novel begins with the setting on an Arcadian landscape and conveys an illuminated, half-transparent world seen through a veil:

> It was a summer evening; the sun was setting; the sky was blue still, but tinged with gold, as if a thin veil of gauze hung over it, and here and there in the gold-blue amplitude an island of cloud lay suspended. In the fields the trees stood majestically caparisoned, with their innumerable leaves gilt. Sheep and cows, pearl-white and parti-coloured, lay recumbent or munched their way through the half-transparent grass. An edge of light surrounded everything (*TY*, 224).

The veil rendered in the suggestive mode of an "as if" multiplies the ways in which something can be seen, and makes possible an aesthetic vision of colour and form, which exceeds impressionistic immediacy.

At the beginning of *The Voyage Out*, the uncertainty looming over the farewell scene with the still nameless couple who find themselves in-between their home and their destination is expressed by a view of the world which is rendered only partly visible by fog: "From a world [...] half-obliterated too in a fine yellow fog, they got neither help or attention" (*TVO*, 6). The fog obliges them to sharpen their way of looking at the world, and enables them to see a world of form rather than of substance: "Very dimly in the falling dusk they could see the lines of the rigging, the masts and the dark flag which the breeze blew out squarely behind" (*TVO*, 7). Whereas fog figures as a poetic image in T.S. Eliot's "The love song of J. Alfred Prufrock", the Ambroses' hazy view of London at the point of leaving it expresses their distance to it, and similar to the beginning of *Night and Day*, fog and mist indicate an alienated view of familiar surroundings: "A fine white mist, the etherealized essence of the fog, hung visibly in the wide and rather empty space of the drawing room, all silver where the candles were grouped on the tea-table, and ruddy again in the firelight" (*ND*, 4).

The loss of determinacy expressed in vague and blurred vision not only affects the subject's ways of seeing and being, but narrative reality at large. The uncertainty of perception denotes a transitional reality which can no longer be encompassed by a single conceptual view, but one which leads to a dispersal of perspectives and meaning, releases chains of associations, and enables the reader to establish connections between them.

Like the journey into the heart of the jungle narrated in *The Voyage Out*, Joseph Conrad's *Heart of Darkness*, from its very beginning, sets a mood of ambiguity and uses the notion of the diaphanous to introduce the novel's central idea of the inscrutable, which questions clear vision: "The water shone pacifically; the sky, without a speck, was a benign immensity of unstained light; the very mist on the Essex marshes was like a gauzy and radiant fabric, hung from the wooded rises inland, and draping the low shores in diaphanous folds" (*HoD*, 6).

Mist and fog create perceptual situations in which clear-cut distinctions between the self and others can no longer be maintained. The insubstantiality of fog and mist inhibits clear vision and emphasises the indistinctness of what is seen. Although the optical properties of fog, unlike the veil, are not created by a textile structure, but by tiny water droplets, similar to the veil, fog both hides and reveals an object of perception, encases the individual, and both protects and encumbers it. Mist and fog allow for an extension of perceptive capacities, and are also used to illustrate the extension and merging of characters. In *Mrs. Dalloway*, Clarissa conceives of herself as a mist to describe the way in which she connects people to each other, and extends the boundaries of her self: "being laid out like a mist between the people she knew best, who lifted her on their branches as she had seen the trees lift the mist, but it spread even so far, her life, herself" (*MD*, 10).

In *The Waves* the six characters are linked in a similar way, when mist is compared to the language which temporarily suspends the boundaries between them. The thoughts and words of the six protagonists have become permeable, and Bernard, the poet, describes their childhood relation: "'But when we sit together, close', said Bernard, 'we melt into each other with phrases. We are edged with mist. We make an unsubstantial territory'" (*W*, 7). Later in the novel, Neville describes Bernard's way of seeing: "He sees everyone with blurred edges" (*W*, 31). In Bernard's view, people are not confined to a definite outline, but capable of redefining themselves in merging with others: "The veils drop between us. I am admitted to the warmth and privacy of another soul" (*W*, 67). In the relations between characters, vague and blurred vision assumes an intersubjective dimension which aims at the momentary dissolution of the boundaries of the individual mind.

2.2.3 Seeing through tears

Corresponding to "the confession of vagueness" and the notion of life as "a semi-transparent envelope" in "Modern Fiction", vague and blurred vision is linked to emotion when it is rendered as seeing through tears. Woolf's presentation of perception is once again neither anonymous nor neutral, but in rendering emotional states of seeing, her novels present individualised kinds of perception which are made accessible to the reader in the mode of 'how' something is seen, and which in turn affect 'what' is seen.

The externalisation of inward feeling creates a correspondence between the perceiving subject and the object perceived, and leads to a transformation of the visible. Feeling releases perception in the same way as perception releases feeling. Seeing through tears thus introduces a sense of detachment that leads to the reshaping of impressions in the mind of the beholder, and turns the reality perceived into a poetic image.

In the farewell-scene at the beginning of *The Voyage Out* the narrative gradually moves from a view of the anonymous outside of Helen Ambrose to her inner way of seeing. Helen gains a growing sense of solitude and detachment, and as the narrator focuses on her, the reader is acquainted with her mood in the description of her way of looking at the river:

> But this lady looked neither up nor down; the only thing she had seen, since she stood there, was a circular iridescent patch slowly floating past with a straw in the middle of it. The straw and the patch swam again and again behind the tremulous medium of a great welling tear, and the tear rose and fell and dropped into the river (*TVO*, 4).

Tears cause a prismatic multiplication of the object perceived, and a merging of the individual with the outside world. The patch and the straw floating on the river, which capture Helen's gaze, also metonymically prefigure the ship's journey across the ocean. The image links together Helen's present grief with life's flow, and anticipates the journey on the river which awaits her at the end of the novel.

Seeing through tears is seeing objects in motion, and not being able to fix them into a referential frame. The motion of tears combines the inner vision of the subject, and the way in which it appears from the outside, when the recursive, wave-like movement of the rising and falling tears is paralleled to the rising and falling of Helen's shoulders: "Yes, she knew she must go back to all that, but at present she must weep. Screening her face she sobbed more steadily than she had yet done, her shoulders rising and falling with great regularity. It was this figure that her husband saw [...]" (*TVO*, 4).[62] The narrator's external focus is further complemented by Mr. Ambrose's view of his wife, who, unlike the reader, only 'sees' her from the outside:

---

[62] Similarly, in *Mrs. Dalloway*, the wave-like movement of rising and falling marks Lucrezia's existential insecurity: "Slightly waved by tears the broad path, the nurse, the man in grey, the perambulator, rose and fell before her eyes" (*MD*, 71–72).

> As he did not leave her, however, she had to wipe her eyes, and to raise them to the level of the factory chimneys on the other bank. She saw also the arches of Waterloo Bridge and the carts moving across them, like the line of animals in a shooting gallery. They were seen blankly, but to see anything was of course to end her weeping and begin to walk (*TVO*, 5).

Seeing through tears takes place on the margin where sight verges on blindness, and causes a solitary and unique way of seeing. The presentation of vision through tears grants insights into the characters' emotional states of desperation, grief and anger, which they do not communicate to any of the other characters. Like Helen, Rachel increasingly feels the difference which separates her from the things she sees. Her anger at finding herself trapped inside a world which to her has become oppressive and its elements interchangeable is reflected in her vision of the outside world, which lacks significance:

> She walked quickly and blindly in the opposite direction, and found herself at the end of a *cul de sac*. There was a window, and a table and a chair in the window, and upon the table stood a rusty inkstand, an ash-tray, an old copy of a French newspaper, and a pen with a broken nib. Rachel sat down, as if to study the French newspaper, but a tear fell on the blurred French print, raising a soft blot. She lifted her head sharply, exclaiming aloud, 'It's intolerable!' Looking out of the window with eyes that would have seen nothing even had they not been dazed by tears, she indulged herself at last in violent abuse of the entire day. [...] Vaguely seeing that there were people down in the garden beneath she represented them as aimless masses of matter, floating hither and thither, without aim except to impede her. What were they doing, those other people in the world? 'Nobody knows,' she said. The force of her rage was beginning to spend itself, and the vision of the world which had been so vivid became dim (*TVO*, 244).

Helen's view of the floating patch is paralleled by Rachel's more distanced and objectified view of the people outside. Unlike Helen, however, Rachel interprets what she sees and thereby creates distance between her and the reader. Helen's seeing through tears brings forth a different vision of the world, one in which the emotional state of the subject merges with the appearance of the object, and communicates it to the reader in a poetic image.[63]

Like *The Voyage Out*, *Jacob's Room* also starts with a view through tears. It is revealing that one of the main conceptual changes Woolf undertook in *Jacob's Room* was to change the beginning of the novel. Instead of starting with Jacob looking at the light coming from across the waves, as she did in the Holograph

---

[63] Tears not only dissolve the boundary between subject and object, but also bring about the merging of two subjects. In *The Waves*, Bernard relates to other characters: "My eyes fill with Susan's tears. I see far away, quivering like a gold thread, the pillar Rhoda saw, and feel the rush of the wind of her flight when she leapt" (*W*, 194).

draft,⁶⁴ in the final version, she chose to begin with Jacob's mother's view at the sea:

> 'So of course,' wrote Betty Flanders, pressing her heals rather deeper in the sand, 'there was nothing for it but to leave.' Slowly welling from the point of her gold nib, pale blue ink dissolved the full stop; for there her pen stuck; her eyes fixed, and tears slowly filled them. The entire bay quivered; the lighthouse wobbled; and she had the illusion that the mast of Mr. Connor's little yacht was bending like a wax candle in the sun. She winked quickly. Accidents were awful things. She winked again, the mast was straight; the waves were regular; the lighthouse was upright; but the blot had spread (*JR*, 3).

Mrs. Flanders' blurred vision through her rising tears is paralleled by the spilling of the ink on a page.⁶⁵ Even though Mrs. Flanders readjusts her vision to normalcy, the spread ink mark fixes the moment of grief, and instead of any explanatory intervention by the narrator, the perceived image alone is employed to convey her mood and state of mind to the reader. The passage is not merely a mimetic rendition of what the world looks like when seen through tears. Instead, Mrs. Flanders' vision simulates both the ephemeral diffusion of fluid watercolour and its fixity, expressing a temporary view of reality. Similar to a watercolour painting, her view blurred by tears dwells on the surface of things, and presents a momentary state of emotional distress rendered as visual diffusion.

The aesthetic rather than mimetic quality of her vision is even further elaborated by the fact that Betty Flanders in this passage unwittingly figures as the object in a watercolour painted by the artist Mr. Steele. Mrs. Flanders' inability to clearly perceive her surroundings is itself reflected in the exasperation of Charles Steele, who is unable to paint Mrs. Flanders in clear-cut outlines: "It was too pale – greys flowing into lavenders, and one star or a white gull suspended just so – too pale as usual" (*JR*, 5).

The momentary dissolution of referentiality in Mrs. Flanders' view of life is paralleled by the failure of the artist to condense life into a definite picture. Seeing through tears describes a world in constant flow, which is paling into colourlessness and does not offer the eye anything to attach itself to. Presenting a vague vision of life, blurred by tears, suggests a critique of perception, which

---

64 *Virginia Woolf's Jacob's Room: The Holograph Draft*. Based on the holograph manuscript in the Henry W. and Albert A. Berg Collection of English and American Literature at the New York Public Library. Transcr. and ed. by Edward L. Bishop (New York: Pace, 1998), 2.
65 Elfi Bettinger offers a narratological reading of the passage. "Jacob Out of Focus. Virginia Woolfs experimentelles Erzählen zwischen Lyrik und Prosa", *Erzählen und Erzähltheorie im 20. Jahrhundert. Festschrift für Wilhelm Füger*, hrsg. von Jörg Helbig (Heidelberg: Winter, 2001), 325–326.

questions any claims of a true nature of the view. Tears not merely challenge the stability of signifiers, but expand and rearrange them in creating an externalised image of the character's inner state. Mrs. Flanders' sight is rendered as blurred by tears and anticipates her grief at the end of the novel: "Tears made all the dahlias in her garden undulate in red waves and flashed the glass house in her eyes, and spangled the kitchen with bright knives" (*JR*, 4). *Jacob's Room* expresses the discursive inscrutability of the character's feelings, which are only present in the poetic image. In presenting a character's vision through tears, the novel dissolves outlines – "The equator swam behind tears" (*JR*, 239) – , and creates a distinct kind of aesthetic vision which resides in the dynamics of the poetic image.

In the Holograph version of *Jacob's Room*, which preceded the final draft, seeing through tears, as I would like to suggest, was at one stage meant to create a structural parenthesis of the novel as a whole. Woolf not only envisaged different beginnings for the novel, but also numerous different endings, and this is the ending of the novel as we know it in the final version:

> 'Jacob! Jacob!' cried Bonamy, standing by the window. The leaves sank down again.
> 'Such confusion everywhere!' exclaimed Betty Flanders, bursting open the bedroom door.
> Bonamy turned away from the window.
> 'What am I to do with these, Mr Bonamy?'
> She held out a pair of Jacob's old shoes. (*JR*, 247)

In the ending of the Holograph draft, however, Woolf once again uses Mrs. Flanders' view through tears to furnish the last line of the novel:

> Jacob, Jacob said Bonamy, standing by the window.
> 'Such confusion everywhere!' said Betty Flanders, opening the bedroom door
> 'What is one to do with these Mr. Bonamy?'
> She held out a pair of Jacob's old shoes.
> ~~They both laughed.~~
> The room waved behind her tears.[66]

In having Betty Flanders' vision through tears begin rather than end the novel, Woolf in her final version gives less prominence to Mrs. Flanders' emotional state. Instead, Jacob's shoes are presented as an object which appears within a poetic texture of language through which the absence of the subject becomes visible.

Unclear, vague and fading vision, and the metaphor of the veil reframe the question of form in Modernist texts. The insistence on semi-transparency of the view gives prominence to the state of in-between-ness, breaks the illusion of direct

---

[66] *Virginia Woolf's Jacob's Room: The Holograph Draft*, 275.

perception, and gives prominence to a distant, but not entirely obstructed view. The aesthetic transformation of impressions never produces something immediately accessible to the eye, but remains ambiguous. Within the constellations between subject and object in Woolf's aesthetics, the notion of the diaphanous becomes a means of conceptualising the relation between seeing and aesthetics. It is both a critique of conventionalised vision, and an image for the imaginary which generates aesthetic vision.

2.3 The looking glass and the reflection of difference

In contrast to the window, which focuses on the borderline between the inside and the outside and juxtaposes different views of the self and the world, the looking glass stresses the iconic difference within the subject, and presents a seemingly objectified image of it. Similar to the window, the mirror's frame confines the field of vision to a segmented part of the world. Unlike the window, however, the mirror lacks transparency, and does not open up the view into an outside world. Instead, it depends on the reflection of light, in order to present the subject as an object.[67] While the window grants the spectator the possibility of seeing without being seen, the look into the mirror always involves the idea of being seen by somebody, if only by oneself. The mirror presents a different view of the self, one in which it is the 'glass' that sees. The reflecting properties of the mirror and its symbolic materiality introduce a break in perception and dwell on the interplay between the notions of surface and depth. Mirrors express epistemological uncertainty and emphasise the fragility of any construction of the self. [68] The ambivalence of the mirror image lies in its presentation of a material borderline that reflects the reproduction as well as the loss of the self.

---

[67] The image of the mirror prominently figures in psychoanalytic and biographic approaches to the subject in Woolf's works. Cf. for example Floris Delattre, *Le roman psychologique de Virginia Woolf* (Paris: J. Vrin, 1932); Makiko Minow-Pinkney, *Virginia Woolf and the Problem of the Subject* (Brighton: Harvester, 1987); Elizabeth Abel, *Virginia Woolf and the Fictions of Psychoanalysis* (Chicago: U of Chicago P, 1989). Katherine Dalsimer offers an interpretation of Woolf's novels from her point of view as a clinical psychologist, and regards writing as an activity to compensate for her illness. *Virginia Woolf: Becoming a Writer* (New Haven, London: Yale UP, 2001), xvii.
[68] Ralf Konersmann, *Spiegel und Bild. Zur Metaphorik neuzeitlicher Subjektivität* (Würzburg: Königshausen und Neumann, 1988), 28–30. As Konersmann and others have shown, Lacan in his analysis of 'the mirror stage' was not unprecedented in establishing the central equivalence of looking and being looked at. *Spiegel und Bild*, 35–42. Susan Squier explores the mirror en-

Whereas a painting relies on the physical absence or non-existence of what it presents, the mirror demands the immediate presence of its object of representation, and creates an almost causal link between existence and representation. The mirror creates the illusion of objective exactitude, and it remains the reflection of a surface. Mieke Bal explains the emptiness inherent in the opacity of the mirror itself, which, unlike the window or the veil, presents a boundary of perception that relies on reflecting substance and makes it impossible for the gaze to venture beyond it.[69] The mirror rather reflects its own emptiness: "the mirror mirrors its own status as a mirror."[70]

2.3.1 Beyond the looking glass: the surface and "the other side of life"

Woolf employs the metaphor of the mirror to reflect upon the nature of reflection. It is used to reveal surface views and the limits of positivist representation. As a critique of realist modes of narration, it challenges the ideal of empirical accuracy connected to the mirror, and sets itself against treating the mirror as a mimetic analogue to poetry and fiction.[71] In *Orlando*, for instance, the imaginary, magic, and almost fairy tale-like qualities of the looking glass prevail, and only assert themselves when Orlando transcends the surface of the looking glass to discover a more-dimensional world behind it. *Orlando* plays on the alleged truthfulness of reflection, and similar to *Alice in Wonderland* or *Through the Looking Glass*, in *Orlando* the mirror's material impenetrability is undermined by magic and serves to assert fictional truth. After Orlando has become a woman, she, for instance, looks at herself in the mirror to confirm the truthfulness of the change (*O*, 106), and when Queen Elizabeth destroys the mirror which reflects Orlando kissing a girl, she likewise acknowledges the reality of the reflection.[72] The novel weakens the notion of the mirror as an instrument aspiring to create an illusion of reality, and it illustrates the difference between the reflection and the original.

---

counter in Woolf's works in Lacanian terms. "Mirroring and Mothering: Reflections on the Mirror Encounter in Virginia Woolf's Works", *TCL*, 27 (1981), 272–289.
69 Mieke Bal, *Reading "Rembrandt". Beyond the Word-Image Opposition* (Cambridge: CUP, 1991), esp. 247–269.
70 Ibid., 266.
71 The use of the mirror in art criticism and aesthetic theory until Romanticism is elaborated on by M.H. Abrams: *The Mirror and the Lamp. Romantic Theory and the Critical Tradition* (London, Oxford, New York: OUP, 1971), 32–47.
72 (*O*, 21). Richter, *The Inward Voyage*, 99–113. Richter investigates into "mirror modes" as psychological reflections of the self.

As an instrument of perception, the mirror reveals both the viewer's expectations about the reflected image, and also the nature of its representation.[73] In *Mrs. Dalloway* the mirror facilitates negotiations between inner and outer reality and serves to constitute Clarissa's social and personal identity.[74] Clarissa has projected her social roles and duties on her image of her self, and hence, according to Peter Walsh, also adjusted her viewing habits to those of her husband: "With twice his wits, she had to see things through his eyes" (*MD*, 84). The process of her dissolving, and, at the same time, recapturing a vision of her self is illustrated in the passage in which Clarissa retreats to her room and looks into the mirror. The two-dimensional space encompassed by the mirror-frame functions as a filter of perception, and serves to integrate multiple impressions.

The image Clarissa Dalloway sees of herself mediates between fixity and flux, fragmentation and coherence, and the mirror serves as a unifying frame of self-projection: "seeing the glass, the dressing-table, and all the bottles afresh, collecting the whole of her at one point (as she looked into the glass), seeing the delicate pink face of the woman who was that very night to give a party; of Clarissa Dalloway; of herself" (*MD*, 40). Clarissa senses a moment of "contraction" (*MD*, 40), and by looking into the mirror, she "plunged into the very heart of the moment, transfixed it" (*MD*, 40), and "collect[s] the whole of her at one point" (*MD*, 40):

> That was her self when some effort, some call on her to be her self, drew the parts together, she alone knew how different, how incompatible and composed so for the world only into one centre, one diamond, one woman who sat in her drawing-room and made a meeting-point, a radiancy no doubt in some dull lives (*MD*, 40).

Clarissa both re-establishes her superficial public image by looking into the mirror, and escapes from the merely two-dimensional image of herself by means of a metonymical deference in which she takes up the mirror's qualities of glass and reflection, and becomes herself a centre of prismatic radiance. The condensed reflection Clarissa encounters in the mirror at the same time contracts and expands the image of herself, and points to the multiple reflections emanating from her which are illustrated in the image of the diamond. The diamond creates a counter-image to Clarissa's otherwise 'tinselly' character, but it remains ambivalent and presents a multiplication of surfaces.

---

[73] Jens Kulenkampff, "Spieglein, Spieglein an der Wand …", *Bild und Reflexion. Paradigmen und Perspektiven gegenwärtiger Ästhetik*, hrsg. von Birgit Recki und Lambert Wiesing (München: Fink, 1997), 271.

[74] Makiko Minow-Pinkney, "The Problem of the Subject in *Mrs. Dalloway*", *Clarissa Dalloway*, ed. by Harold Bloom (New York: Chelsea House, 1990), 184.

The potential emptiness of the opaque mirror is treated when the mirror appears as an uncanny presence in *To the Lighthouse* and reveals "the other side of life" in *The Waves*.[75] The inability of the looking glass to capture life or to render a truthful reflection of it is presented in the "Time Passes"-section of *To the Lighthouse*, where the blank looking glass appears as a material remnant of the world of the past, a non-presence which conveys absence and loss: "how once the looking-glass had held a face; had held a world hollowed out in which a figure turned, a hand flashed, the door opened, in came children rushing and tumbling; and went out again" (*TL*, 129). The empty mirror does not provide a look back in time, and it only reflects the disintegration of the house (*TL*, 130–131). In *To the Lighthouse*, the qualities of the mirror stand for superficiality and illusion, and although for some characters it momentarily holds out the promise of insight, the mirror cannot provide access to a truth beyond itself.

> That dream then, of sharing, completing, of finding in solitude on the beach an answer, was but a reflection in a mirror, and the mirror itself was but the surface glassiness which forms in quiescence when the nobler powers sleep beneath? [...] to pace the beach was impossible; contemplation was unendurable; the mirror was broken (*TL*, 134).

The ambiguous role of the mirror in *To the Lighthouse*, where it does not convey any insights, and presents life as void and meaningless, is further explored in *The Waves*. The looking glass appears in the third *Interlude* of the novel, where it creates a contrast to the generative energy of sunlight and suggests emptiness. While the sun brings out colour and form, the looking glass inside the room is present as a colourless blank: "Now, too, the rising sun came in at the window, touching the red-edged curtain, and began to bring out circles and lines. [...] The looking-glass whitened its pool upon the wall" (*W*, 47). The looking glass reappears in the last two *Interludes,* where it becomes an ominous witness to the disappearance of life from the novel. Other than the sunlight from outside the room, which renders a world in motion, the eye of the looking glass converts the scene it beholds into a still life: "Rimmed in a gold circle the looking-glass held the scene immobile as if everlasting in its eye" (*W*, 139). In the ninth *Interlude*, the looking glass eventually opens into the darkness: "The looking glass was pale as the mouth of a cave shadowed by hanging creepers" (*W*, 158).

The looking glass presents a counterpart to creation in the *Interludes*, and the six characters in *The Waves* are distinguished by their attitude and reaction

---

[75] "There were also reflections, looking glasses have an extraordinary fascination. They show one the other side of life". Virginia Woolf, *The Waves. The two Holograph Drafts*. Transcribed and edited by J.W. Graham (Toronto: U of Toronto Press, 1976), 363.

towards the looking glass, which reflect their adherence to surfaces or 'the other side of life'. Bernard needs the eyes of others to reflect his being ("I need eyes on me to draw out these frills and furbelows. To be myself (I note) I need the illumination of other people's eyes, and therefore cannot be entirely sure what is my self" (*W*, 75)). Jinny prefers mirrors which show her entire person, and despises the small looking glass because it separates the head from the body, and produces a distorted image of the face:

> 'I hate the small looking-glass on the stairs,' said Jinny. 'It shows our heads only; it cuts off our heads. And my lips are too wide, and my eyes are too close together; I show my gums too much when I laugh. [...] So I skip up the stairs past them, to the next landing, where the long glass hangs, and I see myself entire. I see my body and head in one now' (*W*, 24f).

While Jinny acknowledges the exactitude of the mirror's representation, Rhoda, by contrast, loathes the confrontation with her real face in the looking –glass: "I hate looking-glasses which show me my real face" (*W*, 26). In her visions, Rhoda seeks both to free herself from the material world, and to be anchored in it, and temporarily reassured of her existence. Her ability to leave the ordinary world in her imagination fills her both with fascination and terror: "Out of me now my mind can pour. I can think of my Armadas sailing on the high waves. I am relieved of hard contacts and collisions. I sail on alone under white cliffs. Oh but I sink, I fall! That is the corner of the cupboard; that is the nursery looking glass" (*W*, 15). The surface reality of the looking glass ends her imaginative journey and refers her back to the reality of her life. In the world of her mind, however, Rhoda desires a state of non-being, and prefers not to be seen, and to be unattached to solidity, certainty, or even her own face.

> 'That is my face'; said Rhoda, 'in the looking-glass behind Susan's shoulder – that face is my face. But I will duck behind her to hide it, for I am not here. I have no face. Other people have faces; Susan and Jinny have faces; they are here. Their world is the real world. The things they lift are heavy. They say Yes, they say No; whereas I shift and change and am seen through in a second' (*W*, 25).

In the scene when the six friends meet for Percival's farewell-dinner, each character passes the mirror, but only Louis looks into it, and reveals his self-consciousness through the attentive view of Neville as a "strange mixture of assurance and timidity. He looks at himself in the looking-glass as he comes in: he touches his hair; he is dissatisfied with his appearance" (*W*, 77). Whereas Bernard and Percival unconsciously avoid the glass, Louis needs his image in the mirror to assimilate to the group of friends, to which he still feels he does not belong: "I smoothed my hair when I came in, hoping to look like the rest of you. But I cannot, for I am not single and entire as you are" (*W*. 83). For Louis the glass reveals a standard of objectivity and acceptance which he strives to achieve, but which could never do justice to his real being. The looking glass in *The Waves* presents a two-directional view, it creates tension between the image and the viewer, but also reminds the viewer that what he looks at is always one-sided, fragile and superficial. The duality of the gaze inherent in the looking glass establishes the notion of two worlds, and contrasts life outside the looking glass with the lifelessness inside it. Lifelessness, stasis and the notion of objectivity are entwined with the mode of representation provided by the looking glass.

In Woolf's short story "The Lady in the Looking-Glass: A Reflection" the dynamics between the realms inside and outside the looking glass becomes a structural device to reflect on the nature of reflection. The story uses the figure of an uncanny narrator to display the anxiety about the objectifying disclosure invoked by the looking glass: "People should not leave looking-glasses hanging in their rooms any more than they should leave open cheque books or letters confessing some hideous crime" (*CSFVW*, 221). Although the narrator issues this ironical warning at the beginning of the story, he enters the seemingly empty domestic space and becomes both an investigator, and a ghost-like presence which itself is not reflected in the glass. The looking glass rather tempts him to inspect the surroundings, and as he yields to the compulsion to look into the glass – "One could not help looking, that summer afternoon, in the long glass that hung outside in the hall" (*CSFVW*, 221) – it permits him to see a part of the house. Instead of feeling like an intruder, he cautiously assumes the position of a camouflaged natural scientist observing rare species:[76]

> The house was empty, and one felt, since one was the only person in the drawing-room, like one of those naturalists who, covered with grass and leaves, lie watching the shyest animals – badgers, otters, kingfishers – moving about freely, themselves unseen. The room that afternoon was full of such shy creatures, lights and shadows, curtains blowing, petals falling – things that never happen, so it seems, if someone is looking (*CSFVW*, 222).

The perspective of the unseen observer watching the uninhibited course of timid creatures is contrasted by the perspective of the looking glass, which portrays objective reality like a photographic still-life:

> But, outside, the looking-glass reflected the hall table, the sun-flowers, the garden path so accurately and so fixedly that they seemed held there in their reality unescapably. It was a strange contrast – all changing here, all stillness there. One could not help looking from one to the other (*CSFVW*, 221).

---

[76] Alt, *Woolf and the Study of Nature*, 191.

The narrative shifts between the dynamics of life inside the room, and the stationary arrest of the image kept inside the looking glass. The looking glass does not provide access to an imaginary world, but conserves life at the cost of its liveliness: "in the looking-glass things had ceased to breathe and lay still in the trance of immortality" (*CSFVW*, 222). [77]

"The Lady in the Looking-Glass" contrasts two modes of narration, and uses the mirror as an image to illustrate methods of narrative realism: "Throughout her writing life, Woolf rejected what we might call the prosaics of the looking-glass, the flat two-dimensionality of conventional mimesis".[78] The gaze of the narrator moreover presents a version of what Woolf in *A Room of One's Own* had criticised as the "naturalist novelist" (*AROO*, 93)[79] who is content to merely describe and categorise his subject in accordance with a fixed system of classification.

From the beginning of the story, mimesis is treated within both a scientific, and a criminological discourse. Conforming to the notion of witnessing and giving proof of a "hideous crime", the mirror is used as a penitentiary instrument which points to the possibility that a sinister observer might exist behind it. The narrator in "The Lady in the Looking-Glass" resembles an objectifying observer who seeks to get as close to its object as possible, until he virtually becomes one with what he sees: "one must put oneself in her shoes" (*CSFVW*, 224).

The narrator undergoes different phases of investigative zeal which alternate between desire and delusion. When Isabella, the main character in the story and his main target of observation escapes from the reach of the looking glass, the narrator not only describes himself as a botanist when he compares Isabella to "a wreath or a tendril", but also as a voyeur. When his search for the truth of her character does not lead to the desired outcome, he, in a more aggressive vein,

---

77 Tracy Seeley and others have noted the story's binary structure ranging between "stasis of mimetic representation in the mirror, and the vibrant world's hum coming through the windows". Seeley analyses Woolf's construction of domestic space in the story in analogy to the Victorian interiors epitomising the cultural values of Victorian society which Woolf was both familiar with and critical of. "Virginia Woolf's Poetics of Space: 'The Lady in the Looking-Glass: A Reflection'", *Woolf Studies Annual*, 2 (1996), 106.
78 Ibid., 103. Hsiu-Chuang Deppman likewise distinguishes between the "mode of seeing, vs. the mode of imagining [...] Isabella in the garden and Isabella in the glass". "Rereading the Mirror Image: Looking-glasses, Gender and Mimeticism in Virginia Woolf's Writing", *Journal of Narrative Theory*, 31 (2001), 52.
79 In *A Room of One's Own*, Woolf is concerned that her character Mary Carmichael might become a "natural novelist": "Mary Carmichael, I thought, still hovering at a little distance above the page, will have her work cut out for her merely as an observer. I am afraid indeed that she will be tempted to become, what I think the less interesting branch of the species – the naturalist-novelist, and not the contemplative" (*AROO*, 93).

resorts to the naturalist's stance, and describes Isabella as an oyster or a butterfly, which he seeks to catch and "prize [her] open with the first tool that came to hand – the imagination. One must fix one's mind upon her that very moment. One must fasten her down there" (*CSFVW*, 223).

The narrator's self-imposed imperative ("must"), his detailed description of her belongings, and his assumptions about the possibility of a true representation, are for a second time frustrated. The narrator then recasts himself into the role of a detective, and turns to bodies of evidence other than Isabella herself: "In each of these cabinets were many little drawers, and each almost certainly held letters" (*CSFVW*, 222). The narrator's efforts are once again marred, when "at the critical moment a veil of cloud covered the sun, making the expression of her eyes doubtful" (*CSFVW*, 224).

Asserting the insufficiency of mimesis, and the essential elusiveness of character and narrative reality ("Her mind was like her room, in which lights advanced and retreated" (*CSFVW*, 225)), the text reaches its culminating point when Isabella advances into the reach of the looking glass. The narrator, who had hoped to find out the truth about her and to "penetrate" her mind, instead is confronted with a lifeless image of her:

> She stopped dead. [...] At once the looking-glass began to pour over her a light that seemed to fix her; that seemed like some acid to bite off the unessential and superficial and to leave only the truth. It was an enthralling spectacle. [...] Here was the hard wall beneath. Here was the woman herself. She stood naked in that pitiless light. And there was nothing. Isabella was perfectly empty (*CSFVW*, 225).

The transformation described is that of the image turning into a picture and of becoming merely the visibility of a surface: "the mirror has deprived the images of all their imaginative qualities".[80] The kind of visibility conveyed through the looking glass is a factual, objectifying disclosure of Isabella's outward appearance: "the world inside the looking-glass captures the realistic image of her appearance and stops all of her physical actions".[81]

Likewise, the letters the narrator had found, conform to the statuesque still-life in the looking glass "they were drawn in and arranged and composed and made part of the picture and granted that stillness and immortality which the looking-glass conferred [...] it would have needed a chisel to dislodge them from the table" (*CSFVW*, 223). The letters undergo a metamorphosis which eventually turns them into "marble looking envelopes" (*CSFVW*, 223) and in which they are

---

[80] Deppman, "Rereading the Mirror Image", 56.
[81] Ibid., 53.

reduced to their outward appearance: "the world inside captures the realistic image of her appearance and stops all of her physical actions. [...] the imagination frees and the looking-glass freezes".[82]

The mirror displays representational modes in terms of the scientific and scrutinising gaze of the observer who takes the life out of the object in the looking glass. It presents a kind of visible proof of seeming objectivity and truth in exposing facts about a character, and, at the same time, it reveals the emptiness of any view of a person which is based on objective fact. The look into the mirror confronts the viewer with the possibility that there may be no life, and that the look into the glass may reveal only emptiness. What one sees in the mirror is possibly "the world without a self".

2.3.2 Water and glass in *Between the Acts*

The image of glass breaking marks the ending of several of Woolf's novels. At the end of *The Voyage Out*, Terence seems "to hear the shiver of broken glass" (*TVO*, 309), in *To the Lighthouse*, James sees "the waves breaking in white splinters like smashed glass upon the rocks" (*TL*, 203), and *The Waves* finishes in a similar vein with 'the waves breaking on the shore'. The breaking of glass in connection with water is most prominently dealt with at the end of *Between the Acts* when the broken mirrors reflect the audience of the pageant in the incipient rain. *Between the Acts* explores the symbolic materiality of depths and surfaces, and reflects upon the nature of reflection within a binary constellation. Images of water and glass are used to mutually reveal their respective material and metaphorical properties, and they create formal analogues to the novel's structure as *Between the Acts* imitates the shift between fixity and flux. Water and glass describe the immanent movement of the narrative, which metaphorically juxtaposes the transparent solidity of glass to the opacity and fluidity of water to contrast imaginative vision and the reflection of emptiness in glass. In its episodic structure, and its alternation between scenes, intervals, and historical *tableaux vivants*, Woolf's last and unfinished novel *Between the Acts* takes up earlier experimentations with fragmented forms, circling around a central absence, as in *Jacob's Room* and *The Waves*.

In one of the earliest reviews of *Between the Acts*, F. R. Leavis notes the "extraordinary vacancy and pointlessness" as well as "the apparent absence of

---

82 Ibid.

concern for any appearance of grasp of point" in the novel.[83] He uses these observations in order to construct a critical fiction of decline and fall within Woolf's entire *œuvre* in which *To the Lighthouse* allegedly holds an uncontested superior position.[84] What Leavis and others have criticised is Woolf's purported failure to properly render morality, emotions and experience: "it seems to shut off all the ranges of experience accompanying those kinds of preoccupation, volitional and moral, with an external world which are not felt primarily with one's consciousness of it".[85] *Between the Acts* has indeed put critics under stress. The novel's conscious avoidance of reporting direct experience, its portrayal of the characters' inability to express emotions and to find any significance in life, and, above all, the fact that there are "no acts",[86] are likely to leave the reader with a sense of unease and dissatisfaction.

The sense of vacancy, of the action lingering in between is central to the structure and theme in *Between the Acts*,[87] and it is not the novel's failure, but indeed one of its particular aesthetic strengths. The gaps between the scenes of the pageant and the distance between the characters as well as between the actors and the audience are symbolically present in the novel's treatment of pools of water such as the lily pond and its more prosaic counterpart, the "cesspool". In *Between the Acts* the pond mediates between a changing surface and an unfathomable depth, and conveys the presence of uncanny remainders, of secrets, or of waste. The quality of the water itself, which can be either fluid or stagnant, is both an image of life and of the imagination.

Woolf's short story "The Fascination of the Pool" (1926) provides a parallel to her treatment of pools in *Between the Acts*. In "The Fascination of the Pool", the way of taking a close look at a pool of water provides access to the onlooker's mind, in which memories of former events and acquaintances come to the surface and generate images. To the viewer, the mirror-like opacity of the water gradually clears and the pool becomes a window into another world, which is both a world of the past, and a shared world of underlying currents of thought:

> the red and black letters and the white paper seemed to lie very thinly on the surface, while beneath went on some profound under-water life like the brooding, the ruminating of a mind. Many, many people must have come there alone, from time to time, from age to age,

---

[83] F. R. Leavis, "After 'To the Lighthouse'. *Between the Acts* reviewed", *Scrutiny*, 10 (1942), 295.
[84] Ibid., 297.
[85] Ibid.
[86] Naremore, *The World Without a Self*, 237.
[87] Geoffrey Hartmann states that the novel consists of unfilled spaces: "Virginia's Web", *Chicago Review*, 14 (1961), 28.

dropping their thoughts into the water, asking it some question, as one did oneself this summer evening (*CSFVW*, 226).

The symbolic structure of the pool itself encourages the lonely visitors to drop their thoughts like coins into a wishing-well, in order to make sense of their lives. The gaze into the pool creates communion with other minds, and inspires a play with identities, it stirs the imagination and induces an element of magic.

Between the Acts likewise begins on a summer's evening, but it refers to the factual conversation about the "cesspool" (*BA*, 1), and relates that Pointz Hall is waiting for the delivery of water. Water and glass are juxtaposed as the novel's opening metaphors, and like the window which opens into the night, the pool remains resiliently opaque. Similar to the pool in the short story, the lily pond is a source for the creation of legends,[88] and provides a vanishing point for the longings and desires of various characters. It marks a place into which their imagination, and the perception of reality converge, and where theatrical illusion is both built up and destroyed.

The pervasive notion of distance, vacancy, and emptiness in *Between the Acts* is rendered in modes of seeing as well as in the metaphorical and metonymical use of glass through which inside and outside are negotiated, but no meaningful relations are established. Characters become mere observers of themselves, and, like Isabella, are unable to create or re-create moments of being.

> She lifted it and stood in front of the three-folded mirror, so that she could see three separate versions of her rather heavy, yet handsome, face; and also, outside the glass, a slip of terrace, lawn and tree tops. Inside the glass, in her eyes, she saw what she had felt overnight for the ravaged, the silent, the romantic gentleman farmer. 'In love,' was in her eyes. But outside, on the washstand, on the dressing-table, among the silver boxes and toothbrushes, was the other love; love for her husband, the stockbroker – 'The father of my children,' she added, slipping into the cliché conveniently provided by fiction. Inner love was in the eyes; outer love on the dressing-table. But what feeling was it that stirred in her now when above the looking-glass, out of doors, she saw coming across the lawn the perambulator; two nurses; and her little boy George, lagging behind? (*BA*, 7)

Sensing the irreconcilable divisions within her self, Isabella turns to the window, longing for unity with her child, but like the mirror, the window makes it impossible for her to communicate with the outside world. The window and the looking

---

88 The story mentions a drowned girl, and the "giant carp" (*CSFVW*, 227). In *Between the Acts*, characters never visit the pool in company, and the significance of the pool is revealed in their respective ways of relating to it. The maid, when cooling her cheeks remembers the tale of the drowned lady: "It was in that deep centre, in that black heart, that the lady had drowned herself" (*BA*, 26).

glass epitomise her distance towards her own feelings and become barriers that do not permit any interaction between herself and others.

> She tapped on the window with her embossed hairbrush. They were too far off to hear. The drone of the trees was in their ears; the chirp of birds; other incidents of garden life, inaudible, invisible to her in the bedroom, absorbed them. Isolated on a green island, hedged about with snowdrops, laid with a counterpane of puckered silk, the innocent island floated under her window. Only George lagged behind (*BA*, 7).

Isabella is excluded from the world in motion by the glass of the window. Likewise, the looking glass to which she returns her gaze is devoid of any fairy tale-quality, and does not provide any answers or solutions. Her contemplation about her life and her search for words to express her plight do not lead her anywhere. The view of herself in the mirror rather makes her more dissatisfied with her looks and conveys a sense of futility and failure. Although her "glass green eyes" (*BA*, 65) suggest life and hope, they also allude to the possible emptiness of her being.

Analogous to the emptiness expressed in Isabella's view of herself, the novel's descriptions of space are dominated by the recurring notion of emptiness which lies at the core of life.[89] In contrast to the "black heart" of the pool of water, the "heart" of Pointz Hall, symbolised by the empty room and the alabaster vase, is devoid of meaning.

> The room was empty. Empty, empty, empty; silent, silent, silent. The room was a shell, singing of what was before time was; a vase stood in the heart of the house, alabaster, smooth, cold, holding the still, distilled essence of emptiness, silence (*BA*, 21–22).

The silence of the anonymous lady in the picture recalls the silence of the drowned lady, and is reflected in the emptiness of the dining room, which is further condensed into the image of the empty alabaster vase.[90] Reminiscent of both the "quintessence of dust" Hamlet muses about, and the "unravished bride of quietness!" in Keats' "Ode on a Grecian Urn", the "essence of emptiness, silence" in *Between the Acts* is presented in the metonymic image of the vase, which denotes

---

[89] See e.g. the pronounced and repeated mentioning of the empty barn, the empty stage, the empty cage, the empty closet (*BA*, 91). The notion of emptiness preoccupied Woolf. While she was working on *Between the Acts*, she notes in an entry into her diary on 6 September 1939, "Yes, it's an empty meaningless world now" (*D* IV, 234).

[90] The vase had already become a motif signifying aristocratic convention in *Mrs. Dalloway*: "At Bourton they always had stiff little vases all the way down the table" (*MD*, 36).

the emptiness of the house, and of Isabella's life, and refers back to the general lack of water.

The emptiness and confinement of life inside Pointz Hall is contrasted by the fluidity and opacity pertaining to the pool. The characters stranded inside the lifeless house are contrasted to the fish in the pool. Whereas the fish in the pond suggest the ungraspable fluidity of existence, and the verticality of the soul as opposed to a mere surface, the characters in the novel rather resemble the "filleted soles, the semi-transparent boneless fish" (*BA*, 19), which Isabella prepares for lunch.[91] Isabella's reminiscences about herself and her husband in connection to fishing similarly reveal the distance between the couple: "They had met first in Scotland, fishing – she from one rock, he from another" (*BA*, 29). Apart from the opposition of the two characters and life symbolised by water passing by 'in between them', the equation of fishing and her marriage for Isabella also means being taken out of a life-element, and to be exposed to an environment inimical to life and motion. Like a fish out of the water, Isabella faintly expresses her desire to regain liveliness: "'That's what I wished,' Isa added, 'when I dropped my pin. Water. Water...'" (*BA*, 64). The impossibility to reach her aim, however, is indicated by "the walls of shining glass" separating her from life: "'A beaker of cold water, a beaker of cold water,' she repeated, and saw water surrounded by walls of shining glass" (*BA*, 41). Instead of reviving water, however, boiled tea water is served during the interval: "'What delicious tea!' each exclaimed, disgusting though it was, like rust boiled in water" (*BA*, 64).

Like Isabella, Miss LaTrobe requires water to regain her creative vision when she realises that her attempt to communicate her vision in the pageant has failed: "What she wanted, like that carp (something moved in the water) was darkness in the mud; a whisky and soda at the pub; and coarse words descending like maggots through the waters" (*BA*, 126). Characters like Miss LaTrobe, Lucy Swithin, and Mrs. Manresa are distinguished from others in the way in which they relate to the pool. The workings of the minds of both Miss LaTrobe and Mrs. Manresa are paralleled to the verticality and liveliness of the pool. The metaphor

---

[91] The image of the fish is applied to the audience of the pageant, when the eyes of the spectators are compared to fish coming to the surface when an actress enters the stage of the pageant: "Eyes fed on her as fish rise to a crumb of bread on the water. Who was she? What did she represent?" (*BA*, 76–77). Likewise, the unbridgeable gap between the audience and the actors is emphasised, when the villagers on stage communicate fish-like with the wind taking the sound away: "the audience sat staring at the villagers, whose mouths opened, but no sound came" (*BA*, 87).

of the spring distinguishes Mrs. Manresa's way of thinking from the others – "A spring of feeling bubbled up through her mud. They had laid theirs with blocks of marble" (*BA*, 27) – , and Miss LaTrobe's way of developing her idea for a new play is described in the process of her drinking and the rising of words from the "fertile mud" of her imagination: "She raised her glass to her lips. And drank. And listened. Words of one syllable sank down into the mud. She drowsed; she nodded. The mud became fertile. Words rose above the intolerably laden dumb oxen plodding through the mud" (*BA*, 131).

The alternation between fixity and flux during the intervals is presented in the metaphorical opposition of glass and water. Images of water describe the motion of the audience during the intervals, when it is assembling, and "streaming along the paths and spreading across the lawn" (*BA*, 46), when Mrs. Manresa is "afloat on the stream of the melody" (*BA*, 49), or when "a small boy battled his way through the crowd, striking against skirts and trousers as if he were swimming blindly" (*BA*, 65).

The counter-notion of emptiness and vacuity between the single 'acts' is metonymically supported by the action 'in between' taking place in the glass-enclosed greenhouse. Like the boxes, rooms, and containers in *Jacob's Room* the greenhouse in *Between the Acts* is a paradoxical image of space denoting both nature and artifice. Similar to the vase, it becomes a container of emptiness, and the characters inside it transform into immobile statues: "At first they resented – serving as statues in a greenhouse. Then they liked it" (*BA*, 70). At the same time, the greenhouse suggests conservation, creation and natural growth. During the first intermission it provides a meeting place for Isabella and William, and it conveys both their attempt at relating to one another, and the emptiness of their unfulfilled lives: "They knew at once they had nothing to fear, nothing to hope" (*BA*, 70). The impossibility of communicating with each other is expressed in their dismal outlook into the future where no revelation is to be expected, and they cannot conceive of themselves as part of a larger design: "The future shadowed their present, like the sun coming through the many-veined transparent vine leaf; a criss-cross of lines making no pattern" (*BA*, 71).

In the next interval, a connection between the enclosed space of the greenhouse and the glassy depths of the pool is established when Giles feels that Mrs. Manresa "stirred the stagnant pool of his old heart even – where bones lay buried" (*BA*, 74). Farcically prompted by the play's allusion to Gretna Green, he invites her to visit the greenhouse: "'Like to see the greenhouse?', he said abruptly, turning to Mrs. Manresa" (*BA*, 92). The greenhouse not only marks a borderline between nature and artifice, and presents an ambivalent space in which nature is artificially cultivated, but it also symbolises the vacuum between characters who fail to establish any relation between each other.

Water and glass convey the alternation of motion and standstill in the climactic scene of *Between the Acts* at the end of the pageant.[92] The sudden confrontation of the audience with the broken mirrors intended as a cathartic element by LaTrobe[93] is preceded by a "sudden and universal" rainfall (*BA*, 111). The rain deflects the audience's attention away from the apparent failure of theatrical illusion, it creates communion among them, and re-establishes the bond with nature to bring about a new beginning. After the rain, "a fresh earthy smell" rises from the grass, and the characters tentatively interpret the rain as an equivalent to poetry which transcends their individual minds: "While we're waiting, tell me, did you feel when the shower fell, someone wept for us all? There's a poem, *Tears tears tears*, it begins. And goes on *O then the unloosened ocean* . . . but I can't remember the rest" (*BA*, 124).

With the rest remaining silent, the pageant which ends the novel as an anti-mimetic play within the novel is used as a device of *mise-en-abîme*.[94] The hope invested into the mirrors does not bring about self-recognition but rather reveals self-reflection as an empty gesture. In spite of the homiletic overtones of the request to "*calmly consider ourselves*" (*BA*, 115), this scene does not attempt to create finite meaning, contrition or catharsis, which could make up for the emptiness suggested by its metaphors of glass.

When the audience sees themselves reflected in the mirrors "not whole by any means, but at any rate sitting still" (*BA*, 115), the action comes to a standstill, in which, as Harvena Richter describes it, "reflector and reflected merge".[95] The arrested image, however, does not hold a moment of being, but rather presents a

---

92 As Allen McLaurin has noted, Woolf was reading Coleridge at the time when she was writing *Between the Acts*. In her essay on Coleridge written in September 1940, she remarks about the difficulty of editors to come to grips with his character: "Yet it is the only way of getting at the truth – to have it broken into many splinters by many mirrors and so select" (*CE* III, 220). In this respect, the novel only approximates a cathartic moment when the readers, or the audience in the play, are referred to the truth about themselves, which is the truth of being broken, dispersed, and no longer a community, revealed in the catalogue of fragmented impressions, "scraps, orts and fragments" (*BA*, 116, 117). Allen McLaurin, *The Echoes Enslaved* (Cambridge: CUP, 1973), 54.
93 The sense of doom and delusion is supported by the play's allusion to the dramatic irony Shakespeare uses in *Macbeth* upon the arrival of King Duncan: "The temple-haunting martins who come, have always come. ... Yes, perched on the wall, they seemed to foretell what after all the *Times* was saying yesterday" (*BA*, 113). King Duncan, upon his arrival at Cawdor, notices "This guest of summer,/ The temple-haunting martlet, does approve/By his lov'd mansionry that the heaven's breath/Smells wooingly here" (*MAC*, 1, 6, 3–6).
94 André Gide employs the *topos* of the mirror in terms of an infinite mirroring in a *mise en abîme*. Woolf read Gide's diaries in 1939 (*D* V, 227).
95 Harvena Richter, *The Inward Voyage*, 100.

photographic still created out of fragments, and reflects the remains of a surface. The fragmented and frozen view of the audience held by the looking glasses expresses not only the ending of a generation's view of themselves, but also the insufficiency of representation as reflection.

The broken mirrors express the futility of returning to an objective historical past, as well as the cultural pessimism of the older generation:

> O the irreverence of the generation which is only momentarily – thanks be – 'the young.' The young, who can't make, but only break; shiver into splinters the old vision; smash to atoms what was whole. [...] My dear, that's the cheval glass from the Rectory! And the mirror – that I lent her. My mother's. Cracked. What's the notion? Anything that's bright enough to reflect, presumably, ourselves? (*BA*, 113). [96]

The exclamation: "Ourselves! Ourselves" (*BA*, 114) does not convey any sense of community, but stresses the absence of any kind of community, and the shattering of the mirror refers to the disintegration of the audience into "scraps, orts and fragments" (*BA*, 116, 117).

The fragments reveal the potential emptiness of Mrs. Manresa, who stands between the younger and the older generation, and who constantly views herself in the mirror: "Mrs. Manresa had out her mirror and attended to her face" (*BA*, 110), and uses it to maintain the surface of her public self: "Mrs. Manresa had out her mirror and lipstick and attended to her lips and nose" (*BA*, 83). In contrast to all the other characters, who feel a certain unease at being exposed to the mirrors at the end of the pageant, Mrs. Manresa flouts their portent symbolism, and puts them to their everyday use: "All evaded or shaded themselves – save Mrs. Manresa, who, facing herself in the glass, used it as a glass; had out her mirror; powdered her nose; and moved one curl, disturbed by the breeze, to its place" (*BA*, 115). Rather than noting the sense of emptiness imposed on the audience by the broken mirrors, Mrs. Manresa notices the fragility of her outward appearance, and her own more profound breaking apart from inside: "Mrs. Manresa in the very centre smiled; but she felt as if her skin cracked when she smiled. There was a vast vacancy between her, the singing villagers and the piping child" (*BA*, 48).

Whereas the other characters do not arrive at any cathartic reflection by looking into the mirrors, after the pageant is over, Lucy Swithin gains faith and

---

[96] In her review of *The Green Mirror* by Hugh Walpole, Woolf uses the image of the breaking mirrors in a similar way to describe the clash between generations. "Very different in detail they all share a common belief that there is only one view of the world, and one family; and invariably *at* the end the mirrors break, and the new generation bursts in". Virginia Woolf, "The Green Mirror", *Contemporary Writers* (London: The Hogarth Press, 1965), 71.

consolation when she gazes into the pool. She repeats the words of the pageant ("ourselves") when looking at the coloured fish, feels connected to them, and attains a reconciliatory vision of multiplicity and beauty, which is set apart from the fragmentation displayed by the broken mirrors:

> Then something moved in the water; her favourite fantail. The golden orfe followed. Then she had a glimpse of silver – the great carp himself, who came to the surface so very seldom. They slid on, in and out between the stalks, silver, pink; gold; splashed; streaked; pied. 'Ourselves,' she murmured. And retrieving some glint of faith from the grey waters, hopefully, without much help from reason, she followed the fish; the speckled, streaked, and blotched; seeing in that vision beauty, power, and glory in ourselves (*BA*, 127).

Lucy Swithin is related to the life-giving elements of air and water, and inhabits a liminal vantage point from which to observe the present situation. Her view of the leaves floating on the pond symbolically presents a vision of the continents as islands on the surface of a world in transition:

> her eyes went water searching, looking for fish. The lilies were shutting; the red lily, the white lily, each on its plate of leaf. Above, the air rushed; beneath was water. She stood between two fluidities, caressing her cross. [...] Often the delight of the roaming eye seduced her – a sunbeam, a shadow. Now the jagged leaf at the corner suggested, by its contours, Europe. There were other leaves. She fluttered her eye over the surface, naming leaves India, Africa, America. Islands of security, glossy and thick (*BA*, 127).

The final scene of the pageant leaves behind a vision of a world of flotsam and jetsam from which theatrical illusion has parted: "As waves withdrawing uncover; as mist uplifting reveals; so, raising their eyes (Mrs. Manresa's were wet; for an instant tears ravaged her powder) they saw, as waters withdrawing leave visible a tramp's old boot, a man in a clergyman's collar surreptitiously mounting a soap box" (*BA*, 117). The breaking of mirrors, however, precedes a dynamic reassembly of fragments. The motion of the audience's gathering is described in terms of physical and chemical reactions within the fluid dynamics of dispersal and unification: "Like quicksilver sliding, filings magnetised, the distracted united" (*BA*, 117). Similar to the notion of the character of Jacob as the absent, but nevertheless magnetic centre in *Jacob's Room*, the audience in *Between the Acts* seeks to find a centre to which to relate: "What we need is a centre. Something to bring us all together..." (*BA*, 123). The novel does not grant the audience their wish in any straightforward way, but creates an analogy between the image of the pool and view out of the open window as points of convergence for individualised perspectives.

The novel begins and ends with a view through the open window. Like the view into the pond, the final view out of the window in *Between the Acts* does not convey transparency or clarity, but opens up into an inscrutable darkness: "The great square of the open window showed only sky now. It was drained of light, severe, stone cold. Shadows fell. Shadows crept over Bartholomew's high forehead" (*BA*, 135). The endings of both *The Voyage Out* and *Between the Acts* offer visions of a world in darkness: "The sky was once more a deep and solemn blue, and the shape of the earth was visible at the bottom of the air, enormous, dark, and solid" (*TVO*, 353). Darkness, however, does not merely denote hopelessness, but like the darkness at the bottom of the pool, becomes a means for the characters to regain themselves, and a condition for creation.

At the end of *Between the Acts*, the transparent boundary created by the window dissolves, and the 'house of fiction' provided by Pointz Hall not only loses its role as a shelter, but also its sense of confinement.

> The window was all sky without colour. The house had lost its shelter. It was night before roads were made, or houses. It was the night that dwellers in caves had watched from some high place among rocks. Then the curtain rose. They spoke (*BA*, 136).

The view out of the open window provides both a backwards and a forward pointing vision. The cave denotes a primeval cave as well as Platonic cave, which mankind inhabits without any opportunity of ever attaining a vision of reality. Characters who, like Bartholomew Oliver, struggle to bring the light of reason into the cave are contrasted to those like Lucy Swithin, who face the world outside the open window with ease: "He would carry the torch of reason till it went out in the darkness of the cave. For herself, every morning, kneeling, she protected her vision. Every night she opened the window and looked at leaves against the sky. Then slept" (*BA*, 127).

At the end of *Between the Acts*, the symbolic properties of the pool and the open window converge, and provide images for the imaginary. Similar to the pond, the open window provides a closing view into the vanishing point of a transient world in motion.

3 The Temporality of Aesthetic Vision

3.1 Modernist temporalities of the view

> Yet what composed the present moment? If you are young, the future lies upon the present, like a piece of glass, making it tremble and quiver. If you are old, the past lies upon the present, like a thick glass, making it waver, distorting it. All the same, everybody believes that the present is something, seeks out the different elements in this situation in order to compose the truth of it, the whole of it. To begin with: it is largely composed of visual and of sense impressions (*CE* II, 293).

The passage from "The Moment: Summer's Night" investigates into the quality of the moment and focuses on sense impressions as its distinctive components. The present it describes does not merely refer to an objective reality of things simply being there at a certain point of time, but it appears within a wider scope of individual interpretations that defer closure. The experience of time is conveyed through visual perceptions depending on different points in individual lives. The juxtaposition of two perspectives on the present moment introduces the principles of anachronism and anticipation, which determine the subjective perception of temporality, and the narrative structure of time. They render a notion of the present that resists representation and, at the same time, describe a way in which the text creates its own temporality through sense perceptions. "The Moment: Summer's Night" is an experiment of the imagination in creating a momentary vision of a moment in time, which is almost infinitely expandable by being infinitely divisible.

Modernist texts combine the experience of temporality with visual perception. The category of temporality is not only central to Modernity, but it also presents Modernity's central paradox: Modernist texts stand within a temporal continuum, and yet bring forth distinct kinds of temporality. This chapter analyses the temporality of aesthetic vision in Woolf's works with regard to its inherent dialectical dynamics between the revelatory stasis of a moment of being and the procedural condition of becoming inscribed into the temporal flow of the narration. The productive tension that governs the narrative lies in its twofold movement between contraction and expansion in which aesthetic vision emerges as a textual strategy to bring forth a distinct kind of temporality, one which both explores the singularity of the moment and provides a synthetic view of more than one level of time.

The notion of the present moment has preoccupied both the sciences and aesthetic theory of the early twentieth century, and formed part of a general interest in time.¹ Woolf's contemporaries such as John McTaggart, or Bertrand Russell treated temporality from an idealist or an empiricist perspective respectively. In his essay "On the experience of time" Russell, similar to Woolf's narrator in "The Moment: Summer's Night", is trying to define what is meant by "one (momentary) total experience".² He bases his investigation on the hypothesis that "4. An entity is said to be now if it is simultaneous with what is present to me, i.e. with this, where 'this' is the proper name of an object of sensation of which I am aware. 5. The present time may be defined as a class of all entities that are now".³

Although Woolf shares Russell's idea about the subjectivity of temporal experience, and his impetus to find out what a "momentary total experience" might consist of, her conception of temporality created in narrative does not find its referent in the solely empirical perception of the present, but rather in the creation of a present which is absent, which constitutes an imaginary object without objectivity. Woolf's texts regard the present not as a given category that determines sense perception, but as a discursive creation of aesthetic vision that emerges in the narrative structures of the text.

Philosophical theories of time have brought forth models of temporality which can be integrated into an overall aesthetic concern. From the late 19th century onwards, two main tendencies can be identified: One tendency emerging in philosophical theories on time is concerned with procedural models of time, which rely on ontological and phenomenological conceptions. Whereas Martin Heidegger regards time in terms of a hermeneutical analysis of existence, and as an event of being,⁴ Edmund Husserl treats time in terms of a continuity of consciousness.⁵ Henri Bergson emphasises temporality as memory of the body,⁶ and Hans Blumenberg focuses on the distinction between individual life-time and what he calls "time of the world" (Weltzeit).⁷ The second model of temporality, which gained particular importance, lays emphasis on the moment as a singular

---

1 Stephen Kern, *The Culture of Time and Space 1880–1918* (Cambridge, Mass.: Harvard UP, 1983). Ann Banfield, "Time Passes. Virginia Woolf, Postimpressionism and Cambridge Time", *Poetics Today*, 24 (2003), 471–516.
2 Bertrand Russell, "On the Experience of Time", *The Monist*, 25 (1915), 215.
3 Ibid., 213.
4 Martin Heidegger, *Sein und Zeit* (Tübingen: Niemeyer, 17. Aufl. 1993); ---, "Zeit und Sein". *Zur Sache des Denkens* (Tübingen: Mohr, 3. Aufl., 1988), 1–25.
5 Edmund Husserl, *Zur Phänomenologie des inneren Zeitbewußtseins* (1893–1917), hrsg. von R. Boehm, Husserliana X (Hamburg: Meiner, 1985).
6 Henri Bergson, *Matière et mémoire* (Paris: Presses du Compagnonage, 1962).
7 Hans Blumenberg, *Lebenszeit und Weltzeit* (Frankfurt am Main: Suhrkamp, 3. Aufl., 1986).

event stepping out of temporal continuity.⁸ The focus on the discontinuity of the experience of the singular moment therefore subverts the validity of those historical models of time, which are exclusively based on a teleological and linear construction.⁹ Hans-Robert Jauss considers the breaking of a linear time structure as characteristic of Modernist fiction, paradigmatically represented in Joyce's *Ulysses*, Thomas Mann's *Der Zauberberg*, and Marcel Proust's *À la Recherche du Temps Perdu*.¹⁰ Herbert Grabes describes the paradoxical impetus of writing within time, and yet against time as a characteristic feature of Modernist texts and as a means of undermining the chronological and irreversible succession of linear time dominant in 19th century literature.¹¹

In looking at the elusive nature of the moment, Modernist approaches intertwine the notion of time with aesthetic vision. In his influential definition of the "image" as a complex which takes place within time, and yet exceeds time, Ezra Pound provides a nexus between temporality and the image:

> An 'image' is that which presents an intellectual and emotional complex in an instant of time. I use the term 'complex' rather in the technical sense employed by the newer psychologists, such as Hart, though we might not agree absolutely in our application. It is the presentation of such a 'complex' instantaneously which gives that sense of sudden liberation; that sense of freedom from time limits and space limits; that sense of sudden growth, which we experience in the presence of the greatest works of art.¹²

In Pound's definition, the image is not to be separated from understanding or emotion, and reflects back on experience, enlarges and intensifies it. It creates

---

8 Theodor W. Adorno, *Ästhetische Theorie*. Gesamtausgabe Bd. 7, hrsg. von G. Adorno und R. Tiedemann, (Frankfurt am Main: Suhrkamp, 1970); Gilles Deleuze, *Cinéma 2. L'image-temps* (Paris: Minuit, 1985); ---. *Différence et Répétition*, (Paris: PUF, 11ème ed. 2003); Georges Didi-Huberman, *Devant le Temps. Histoire de l'art et anachronisme des images* (Paris: Minuit, 2000).
9 The conflict between historical time and the moment is a recurrent concern in Benjamin's and Kierkegaard's philosophy of history. Walter Benjamin, *Über den Begriff der Geschichte. Gesammelte Werke* Bd. 1.2, hrsg. von Rolf Tiedemann und Hermann Schweppenhäuser (Frankfurt am Main: Suhrkamp, 1974), 691–704; Sören Kierkegaard, *Der Augenblick. Aufsätze und Schriften des letzten Streits*, übers. von Hayo Gerdes. *Gesammelte Werke* Abt. 34, hrsg. von Emanuel Hirsch (Guetersloh: Mohn, 1994).
10 Hans Robert Jauss, *Zeit und Erinnerung in Marcel Prousts À la Recherche du Temps Perdu. Ein Beitrag zur Theorie des Romans* (Frankfurt am Main: Suhrkamp, 1986), 9.
11 Herbert Grabes, "Schreiben in der Zeit gegen die Zeit", *Zeit und Roman. Zeiterfahrung im historischen Wandel und ästhetischer Paradigmenwechsel vom sechzehnten Jahrhundert bis zur Postmoderne*, hrsg. von Martin Middeke (Würzburg: Königshausen & Neumann, 2002), 313–332; 314f.
12 Ezra Pound, "A Few Don'ts by an Imagiste", *Poetry* I (March 1912), *Literary Essays of Ezra Pound*, ed. by T. S. Eliot (London: Faber and Faber, 1968), 4.

aesthetic experience in an instant of time and reveals the potential of art to overcome time and space. The transformational, liberating and even redemptive potential of the image emerging in its unique and paradoxical temporality is described in similar terms by Walter Benjamin. The idea of condensation implied in Pound's "complex" is paralleled by Benjamin's term "constellation" in his definition of the dialectical image:

> It's not that what is past casts its light on what is present, or what is present its light on what is past; rather, image is that wherein what has been comes together in a flash with the now to form a constellation. In other words, image is dialectics at a standstill. ...Only dialectical images are genuine images.[13]

In forging an arbitrary relation between what has been and what is now, dialectical images defamiliarise the observer from what is factual, and transport him into a new critical awareness. The dialectical image also reveals itself as a visible means for the present to redeem the past from being obscured and forgotten, and, for Benjamin, it is the only form to provide, rather than replicate, genuine historical experience.[14] In aesthetic theories focusing on the moment, in the aftermath of Benjamin, the notion of the present hinges on the underlying assumption of a redemptive presence, which creates a time out of time and promises release from what was conceived as bourgeois historical reality.

The sense of liberation from linear and historical time in moments of an aesthetic temporality created by the work of art is an essential concern of Proust's *À la Recherche du Temps Perdu*. Woolf was familiar with the *Recherche*[15] and Proust's general popularity in Bloomsbury culminated in the publication of Clive Bell's monograph in 1928.[16] Proust's influential notion of involuntary memory describes a sudden emergence of a memory that momentarily brings about the a-temporal recognition of a link between past and present:

---

[13] Walter Benjamin, *The Arcades Project*, transl. by Howard Eiland and Kevin McLaughlin (Cambridge, Mass.: Belknap, 1999), 463 [N3,1].
[14] Susan Buck-Morss, *The Dialectics of Seeing: Walter Benjamin and the Arcades Project* (Cambridge, Mass: MIT Press, 1991); Richard Wolin, *Walter Benjamin: An Aesthetic of Redemption* (New York: Columbia UP, 1982).
[15] Cheryl Mares, "Woolf's Reading Proust", *Reading Proust Now*, ed. by Mary Ann Caws and Eugène Nicole (Frankfurt am Main, New York, et al.: Lang, 1990), 185–186.
[16] Brenda Silver, *Virginia Woolf's Reading Notebooks*, Guermantes, 87; Swann's Way, 82, 89. Bell focuses on the centrality of time and calls the *Recherche* "a shape in time" (*Proust*, 48): "Time is the stuff of which *A la recherche du temps perdu* is composed: the characters exist in time, and were the sense of time abstracted would cease to exist. In time they develop their relations, colour and extension all are temporal" (*Proust*, 45).

Involuntary memory provides an unexpected (shocking) link or association between a concrete experience in the present and its cognate in the past; as a sudden shock, the *mémoire involontaire* provides Proust with not a mere convolution, but a positive deliverance from temporality. [...] involuntary memory is, as Proust himself describes it, precisely the apprehension of "a fragment of time in the pure state" for "a moment brief as a flash of lightning" (*Remembrance* 3: 905).[17]

The element of suddenness pertaining to the moment in which a memory gains presence in the "flash of lightning" is related to the pervasive notion of shock in Modernist accounts of aesthetic method and production. Clive Bell describes and explains Proust's use of memory and his technique of relating present and past in the *Recherche*:

> *A la recherche du temps perdu* is a series of carefully planned explosions by means of which the submerged past is brought into the present, the deep-sea monster of memory to the surface.[18]
>
> Could we but recapture a past experience, dragging it up from the depths of the sub-conscious, a past experience with all its glamour, its intensity, its reality clinging about it, but with its sting drawn, should we not stand a chance of seeing the monster whole and seeing him steadily. The monster we know can be brought to the surface by an appropriate shock. Proust's first gift, the gift that conditioned his method, was his capacity for giving himself shocks.[19]

In her autobiographical reflection *A Sketch of the Past*, Woolf likewise observes the element of unpredictability, suddenness and even shock which pervade her reflections on writing: "Then, for no reason that I know about, there was a sudden violent shock; something happened so violently that I have remembered it all my life. [...] These are three instances of exceptional moments. I often tell them over, or rather they come to the surface unexpectedly" (*MB*, 71).[20] Like Proust and

---

17 Max Pensky, "Tactics of Remembrance: Proust, Surrealism, and the Origin of the Passagenwerk", *Walter Benjamin and the Demands of History*, ed. by Michael P. Steinberg (Ithaca, London: Cornell UP, 1996), 173–174. Concerning analogies in the time-structure of Woolf's novels and Proust's *Recherche* see Willi Erzgräber, "'The Moment of Vision' im Modernen Englischen Roman", *Augenblick und Zeitpunkt. Studien zur Zeitstruktur und Zeitmetaphorik in Kunst und Wissenschaften*, hrsg. von Christian W. Thomsen und Hans Holländer (Darmstadt: WB, 1984), 373.
18 Clive Bell, *Proust* (London: The Hogarth Press, 1928), 41.
19 Ibid., 44.
20 Benjamin reads Proust in a similar way, but invests the *Recherche* with the hope of redemption: "Proust emerges as a model for the tactics of an awakening, insightful remembrance of the truth of life – or of a historical epoch – through the collection and manipulation of concrete remembered objects and impressions". Pensky, "Tactics of Remembrance", 168.

Benjamin, Woolf acknowledges the productive potential brought about by the insightful shock, when she assumes "that the shock-receiving capacity is what makes [her] a writer" (*MB*, 72).

The creative shock does not only provide insights into a different quality of reality constituted by the bringing to light of significant patterns, but also marks the starting point of artistic production. Likewise, some of today's central theories of aesthetic experience propose a model of presence and treat it in an a-temporal sense.[21] Vision plays a critical role in the unfolding theories of presence, and Karl Heinz Bohrer links the notion of presence to the moment of insight in order to define the concentration on the present as a prerequisite for aesthetic perception. Bohrer regards the experience of an absolute present as characteristic of Modern literature[22] and bases his argument on the hypothesis that perception is fundamentally subjective.[23] Bohrer uses the term 'suddenness' to refer to this specifically Modernist experience of time,[24] and his theory of aesthetic experience centres on the autonomy of the aesthetic, which stands in opposition to history.[25] This approach towards an unmediated kind of presence is not entirely unproblematic because it implies an aesthetics which seems to be able to do without the dialectical distance between the work of art and the reader.

---

21 Hans Ulrich Gumbrecht, *The Production of Presence. What Meaning Cannot Convey* (Stanford: Stanford UP, 2004); Martin Seel, *Ästhetik des Erscheinens* (Frankfurt am Main: Suhrkamp, 2003); ---, "Ästhetik und Aisthetik. Über einige Besonderheiten ästhetischer Wahrnehmung. Mit einem Anhang über den Zeitraum der Landschaft", *Ethisch-Ästhetische Studien* (Frankfurt am Main: Suhrkamp, 1996), 36–69.
22 Karl Heinz Bohrer, *Das absolute Präsens. Die Semantik ästhetischer Zeit* (Frankfurt am Main: Suhrkamp, 1994); ---, *Ekstasen der Zeit. Augenblick, Gegenwart, Erinnerung* (München, Wien: Hanser, 2003). ---. "Utopie des 'Augenblicks' und Fiktionalität. Die Subjektivierung der Zeit in der modernen Literatur". *Zeit und Roman. Zeiterfahrung im historischen Wandel und ästhetischer Paradigmenwechsel vom sechzehnten Jahrhundert bis zur Postmoderne* (Würzburg: Königshausen & Neumann, 2002), 215–252.
23 The notion of time as becoming an increasingly subjective category in Modernism is likewise maintained by the sociological outline of Norbert Elias and the critical investigation into Modernism by Jürgen Habermas. Elias adumbrates the historical development of the notion of time as the product of an act of subjective synthesis. Norbert Elias, *Über die Zeit* (Frankfurt am Main: Suhrkamp, 1990), 1; XVII-XVIII. Jürgen Habermas, "Das Zeitbewußtsein der Moderne und ihr Bedürfnis nach Selbstvergewisserung", *Der Philosophische Diskurs der Moderne. Zwölf Vorlesungen* (Frankfurt am Main: Suhrkamp, 1989), 18.
24 Karl Heinz Bohrer, *Plötzlichkeit: Zum Augenblick des ästhetischen Scheins* (Frankfurt am Main: Suhrkamp, 1981).
25 Jürgen Habermas attests to Modernity a similar longing for 'real, immaculate presence'. Jürgen Habermas, "Die Moderne – ein unvollendetes Projekt", *Die Moderne ein unvollendetes Projekt. Philosophisch-Politische Aufsätze* (Leipzig: Reclam, 3. Aufl., 1994), 35.

Containing an element of absence in the process of reception, temporality rather allows for the interplay between difference and identity which exists between the past of the text and the present of the experience of reading.[26]

This chapter regards the temporality of aesthetic vision both as a quality of the text, and as a generative principle created in the act of reading.[27] The first part will analyse the rhetoric of beginnings in which Woolf's texts stage their own anteriority as in *A Sketch of the Past* where the sketch and the scene present minimalist forms in which vision is linked to temporality.

The second part is concerned with the notion of spatio-temporal constructions of aesthetic vision in anachronistic narrative movements of remembrance, recollection and retrieval within the central interplay of presence and absence. Whereas the trajectory of the narrative creates continuity, the element of stasis is presented in spatial and scenic constellations, which allow for a vision of time in space. In looking at the correlation of inner and outer spaces, rooms and containers of memory, this chapter investigates aesthetic vision between the localisation and the diffusion of a spatio-temporal order.

The third part focuses on *Between the Acts*, and its creation of paradox temporality in dialectical configurations between historical time and lifetime, between different generations, and between notions of immanent time and timelessness. It returns to the elements of the sketch, the scene, and the interlude as formal

---

26 Wolfgang Iser, "Von der Gegenwärtigkeit des Ästhetischen", *Dimensionen ästhetischer Erfahrung*, 176–202. Hans Robert Jauß, *Ästhetische Erfahrung und Literarische Hermeneutik* (Frankfurt am Main: Suhrkamp, 1982). *Zeit und Text. Philosophische, kulturanthropologische, literarhistorische und linguistische Beiträge*, hrsg. von Andreas Kablitz, Wulf Oesterreicher and Rainer Warning (München: Fink, 2003).
27 The significance of time in Woolf's novels has been pointed out in numerous works, and although scholarship has habitually recognised the influence of philosophical models of time on her works, there are no systematic analyses of the conception of time in Woolf's *œuvre* to date. Whereas early Woolf-scholarship from the 1930s until the 1950s was interested in time as a theme and motif (Church, 1955; Hartley, 1939; Kohler, 1948; Wilson, 1942; Graham, 1948), studies of the 1950s and 1960s mainly focused on the analyses of the momentariness of time (Baldanza, 1956; Beja, 1964; Francis, 1960). This tendency was also prolonged in German Woolf-scholarship until the 1980s (Erzgräber, 1984), in which aesthetic questions remained largely neglected. Instead, the readily invoked assumption of Bergson's influence had not only become a commonplace but was also boldly undermined by any non-Bergsonian approaches (Kumar, 1962). From the 1970s until the 1990s Woolf-scholarship concentrated on a number of diverging approaches, which focused on feminism, fine art and postcolonialism, in which temporality was conspicuously referred to the background. More recently, Vera Nünning and Theresa Prudente have drawn critical attention to the innovatory potential inherent in Woolf's novels when it comes to presenting a-linear models of time that modify conceptions of time established in 19th century fiction (V. Nünning, 2002, 307; Prudente, 2009).

prerequisites for aesthetic vision, and treats them as signatures of a distinct temporality.

3.2 Beginnings: the sketch and the scene

In an entry into her diary on May 28th, 1929, Virginia Woolf reflects on the difficulty of starting to write the novel then still called *The Moths*:

> How am I to begin it? And what is it to be? I feel no great impulse; no fever; only a great pressure of difficulty. Why write it then? Why write at all? Every morning I write a little sketch, to amuse myself. [...] I am not saying [...] that these sketches have any relevance. I am not trying to tell a story. Yet perhaps it might be done in that way. A mind thinking. They might be islands of light – islands in the stream that I am trying to convey: life itself going on (*D* III, 229).

What she called the sketch, a possible "island of light" in the stream of life, becomes an integral part of her aesthetics. The metaphors of the island and the stream illustrate the temporal dynamics of the narrative between continuous motion and temporary stasis. The inherently incomplete and seemingly random sketches referred to in this passage resemble the short-lived intensity of the "moments of being" described in Woolf's own memoir *A Sketch of the Past*.

In *A Sketch of the Past*, Woolf's aesthetic reflections upon temporality are treated within the twofold perspective of present and past, of presence and absence, and of the visible versus the invisible. While she was writing *A Sketch of the Past*, Woolf was deeply and at times distressfully immersed in working on the biography of Roger Fry: "As it happens that I am sick of writing Roger's life, perhaps I will spend two or three mornings making a sketch" (*MB*, 64). "Making a sketch" temporarily relieves her from the discursive pressures of encyclopedic completeness and descriptive fidelity to fact exerted by the genre of biography.[28] In its contingency, its playful randomness and resistance to linearity, the *Sketch*, an epithet referring both to its concept and form, reveals many dimensions relevant to Woolf's aesthetics of vision. It is above all the very sense of ostentatious incompleteness inherent in the notion of the sketch which becomes a particular

---

[28] Woolf expresses her exasperation with Fry's biography: "I have no energy at the moment to spend upon the horrid labour that it needs to make an orderly and expressed work of art; where one thing follows another and all are swept into a whole" (*MB*, 75). Elizabeth Hirsh, "Writing as Spatial Historiography", *Mapping the Self: Space, Identity, Discourse in British Auto/Biography*, ed. by Frédéric Regard (Saint-Etienne: Publications de l'Université de Saint-Etienne, 2003), 211.

strength of Virginia Woolf's fiction. Her works are fraught with the sense of openness and the unfinished. In *Jacob's Room*, which critics at first have dismissed as a "crowded little album of pictures",[29] the artist Charles Steele is exasperated by the seemingly impossible task of painting Mrs. Flanders and gives up painting her picture altogether (*JR*, 6). In *The Voyage Out*, Terence Hewet does not write the novel about silence that he intends to write, and the biography of the grandfather in *Night and Day* remains a fragment. In *To the Lighthouse*, Mr. Ramsay never completes the "Alphabet of Truth", and not until the very end of the novel does Lily Briscoe finish her painting.

The sketch anticipates the finished work yet acquires an aesthetic presence on its own that is founded on perceptual difference and temporal deferral. Woolf's fiction privileges moments of openness and invention. It focuses on the minimalist, the seemingly banal and quotidian, and implies that what is conventionally beneath notice is often in fact most noticeable. Instead of looking for the grand design, Lily Briscoe and the children in *To the Lighthouse* are able to perceive the whole in single, fragmented recognitions and fleeting memories: "The great revelation had never come. The great revelation perhaps never did come. Instead there were little daily miracles, illuminations, matches struck unexpectedly in the dark; here was one. This, that and the other" (*TL*, 161). The sketch carries this notion of illumination, enlightenment and even revelation, and becomes an analogue to images like "islands of light", "matches struck in the dark", or "the match burning in a crocus" (*MD*, 35) that Woolf uses to characterise her idea of the moment.[30]

Woolf includes the notion of the sketch in her poetic reflections and expresses the desire to develop a new way of writing which both preserves the unfinished nature of the sketch, and also displays the precision of the complete work:

> I wish I cd invent a new critical method – something swifter & lighter & more colloquial & yet intense: more to the point & less composed; more fluid & following the flight, than my C.R. essays. The old problem: how to keep the flight of the mind, yet be exact. All the difference between the sketch & the finished work (*D* V, 298 [sic]).

A Sketch of the Past can be regarded as an experiment in which fiction records its own processes of rendering the past and analyses them at the same time.[31]

---

29 *Virginia Woolf. The Critical Heritage*, 107.
30 Morris Beja, "Matches Struck in the Dark: Virginia Woolf's Moments of Vision", *The Critical Quarterly*, 6 (1964), 137.
31 Alex Zwerdling, "'Mastering the Memoir'. Woolf and the Family Legacy", *Modernism/Modernity*, 10 (2003), 168. Hermione Lee, *Virginia Woolf* (New York: Vintage, 1999), 19.

Departing from set conventions, Woolf's biographical fiction and her criticism of the traditional conception of biography rather investigate the peripheries of real and imagined lives, and her skepticism about established criteria of biographical writing gives way to new and experimental forms of creating character in biography and memoir.[32] *A Sketch of the Past* invokes the analogy to the painter's sketch, and hence extends the generic boundaries of biography. She conceives of the biographer as artist and of the artist as biographer when, in her essay on Walter Sickert, she speaks of him as "a great biographer, [...] when he paints a portrait I read a life".[33] In works like *A Sketch of the Past* Woolf develops a notion of temporality that relies on minimal formal units such as the sketch, the scene, and the interlude. Time and vision interact, when, for instance, in *A Sketch of the Past*, Woolf compares vision to memory, and reflects on how something that is seen in the past can gain presence and momentarily dissolve the link between presence and reality:

> The strength of these pictures – but sight was always then so much mixed with sound that picture is not the right word – the strength anyhow of these impressions makes me again digress. Those moments – in the nursery, on the road to the beach – can still be more real than the present moment [...]. But I was seeing them through the sight I saw here – the nursery and the road to the beach. At times I can go back to St Ives more completely than I can this morning. I can reach a state where I seem to be watching things happen as if I were there. That is, I suppose, that my memory supplies what I had forgotten, so that it seems as if it were happening independently, though I am really making it happen. In certain favourable moods, memories – what one has forgotten – come to the top. Now if this is so, is it not possible – I often wonder – that things we have felt with great intensity have an existence independent of our minds; are in fact still in existence? And if so, will it not be possible, in time, that some device will be invented by which we can tap them? I see it – the past – as an avenue lying behind; a long ribbon of scenes, emotions (*MB*, 67).

In *A Sketch of the Past*, Woolf expresses her desire to tap the reservoir of the unseen and forgotten in its continuity outside the reach of the subject's consciousness, to rescue the moment of aesthetically self-conscious being from non-being and oblivion, and to momentarily preserve it in narrative images that appear in the mode of an "as if".

In tracing her own method of rendering the past in which she asserts the productive and independent activity of the mind to create, Woolf identifies the scene

---

[32] Woolf herself was an avid reader of memoirs, and one of her earliest ventures into the genre of biography, "Reminiscences" (1907), was intended as a biography of her sister Vanessa and addressed to her children.
[33] Virginia Woolf, *Walter Sickert: A Conversation*, 10.

as the core from which her rendition of the past, and perhaps also her narrative evolve, and relates it to "the origin of her writing impulse":

> These scenes, by the way, are not altogether a literary device – a means of summing up and making innumerable details visible in one concrete picture. Details there were; still, if I stopped to think, I could collect a number. But, whatever the reason may be, I find that scene making is my natural way of marking the past. Always a scene has arranged itself: representative; enduring. This confirms me in my instinctive notion: (it will not bear arguing about; it is irrational) the sensation that we are sealed vessels afloat on what it is convenient to call reality; and at some moments, the sealing matter cracks; in floods reality; that is, these scenes – for why do they survive undamaged year after year unless they are made of something comparatively permanent? Is this liability to scenes the origin of my writing impulse? Are other people also scene makers? These are questions to which I have no answer. Perhaps sometime I will consider it more carefully. Obviously I have developed the faculty, because, in all the writing I have done, I have almost always had to make a scene, either when I am writing about a person; I must find a representative scene in their lives; or when I am writing about a book, I must find their poem, novel...But this may not be the same faculty (*MB*, 122).[34]

Woolf's synecdochal conception of the scene and her reflection upon the acts of scene-receiving and scene-making describe them as pre-discursive fusions between the reality of a scene and the invisible and "sealed" part of one's identity. In her essay "The Russian Point of View", Woolf calls the invisible content of the sealed vessels "the soul": "Whoever you are, you are the vessel of this perplexed liquid, this cloudy, yeasty, precious stuff, the soul. The soul is not restrained by barriers. It overflows, it floods, it mingles with the souls of others" (*CR*, 180).

The underlying idea of the vanishing point of an imaginative synthesis between souls is further explored in Woolf's reading of Dostoevsky, where she finds a model for expressing the emergence of a new amalgamation of elements of the soul. In a trajectory obliterating conventional temporality, the soul in Dostoevsky becomes indistinguishable from the souls of others and creates a new paradigm for the presentation of the human mind, which exceeds the singularity of scenes:

> The pace at which we are living is so tremendous that sparks must rush off our wheels as we fly. Moreover, when the speed is thus increased and the elements of the soul are seen, not separately in scenes of humour or scenes of passion as our slower English minds conceive them, but streaked, involved, inextricably confused, a new panorama of the human mind is revealed. The old divisions melt into each other (*CR*, 179).

---

34 The typescript of this passage reads threads instead of details, and less skeptically closes: "Or is this not quite the same faculty?" Virginia Woolf, *A Sketch of the Past*, Typescript I, BL ADD. MS. 61973, 120–121.

In *A Sketch of the Past*, Woolf renders the dialectic constellation between surface and depth in the metaphors of the river and the film to describe the interdependence, and mutual pervasiveness of present and past vision:

> The past only comes back when the present runs so smoothly that it is like the sliding surface of a deep river. Then one sees through the surface to the depths. In those moments I find one of my greatest satisfactions, not that I am thinking of the past; but that it is then that I am living most fully in the present. For the present when backed by the past is a thousand times deeper than the present when it presses so close that you can feel nothing else, when the film on the camera reaches only the eye (*MB*, 98).

Images, emotions and impressions of the past evoked by memory assert a reality of their own and question any exclusive ontological claim of the present towards representing an absolute given reality. Linked to the past, the present gains temporal significance and semantic depth, and allows for the experience of difference.[35] The view of the present sustained by the past brings forth a momentarily synthetic vision of past and present, which exceeds the sensation of the merely visible surface of experience, and shifts between the present actualisation of an impression and its temporal distancing into the past. In an entry into her diary, Woolf acknowledges this capacity of voluntary memory to shape the past:

> At the moment (I have 7 ½ before dinner) I can only note that the past is beautiful because one never realizes an emotion at the time. It expands later, & thus we don't have complete emotions about the present, only about the past. This struck me on Reading platform, watching Nessa & Quentin kiss, he coming up shyly, yet with some emotion. This I shall remember; & make more of, when separated from all the business of crossing the platform, finding our bus &c. That is why we dwell on the past, I think (*D* III, 5).

This passage from her diary, in itself a transitory record of a moment of vision, reveals the inherently dialectical tension between different configurations of temporality that are visually encoded. The text creates a dynamic union between past and present, and implies the paradox that any view on the present is inherently influenced by the past in the same way as any view on the past is mediated by the present. The idea of the present as a platform from which journeys into time depart and to which they return, implies a recursive model of time, and a dual vision of the present as present, and of the present as past. The metaphor of the platform as a narrative foothold of the present also gains significance in *A Sketch of the Past*:

---

35 "Woolf's novels [...] testify to a potential in human experience for perceiving a time out of time, for overcoming the limits of actual life through apprehension of a different mode of being altogether". Mark Hussey, *The Singing of the Real World*, 117.

2nd May ... I write the date, because I think that I have discovered a possible form for these notes. That is, to make them include the present – at least enough of the present to serve as platform to stand upon. It would be interesting to make the two people, I now, I then, come out in contrast. And further, this past is much affected by the present moment (*MB*, 75).

The date of the entry serves as a marker of the present and introduces the dialectic tension between similarity and difference, which constitutes the temporality of aesthetic vision. Within this temporal configuration the *Sketch* acquires an aesthetic presence of its own in a doubly encoded present. It both creates the present as a platform from which the narrative can cast itself into the role of a preliminary stage pointing towards a future fulfilment, and, in looking back and recording memories, it seeks to reconnect the work and the subject to its origins in an anachronistic, and a-temporal way. The text invokes both the idea of the linear progression of a journey in time, and, at the same time, it creates a cyclical hermeneutic dynamics of thought. The notion of temporality developed in *A Sketch of the Past* resists replacing a narrative of progress with one of eternal return and juxtaposes the two. When reflecting on her memoirs, Woolf refers to the metaphor of the platform to express this duality of vision that depends on one's temporal perspective: "My mother, I was thinking had 2 characters. I was thinking of my memoirs. The platform of time. How I see father from the 2 angles. As a child condemning; as a woman of 58 understanding – I shd say tolerating. Both views true?" (*D* V, 281 [sic]).

Corresponding to this doubling of her view on time, the way in which the subject recollects remnants of the past requires a kind of self-doubling in the narrative re-enactment of memory, and the creation of a simultaneous vision of past and present. It is this twofold structure of temporality that provides for a fictional play with identity.[36] In creating and maintaining the tension between the remembering and remembered self, memories, particularly when they are tied to images, can provide a narrative or pictorial sense of the self. Within a memory, the subject is able to conceive of itself both as an object and as the creator of the scene who is involved in the process of memorising. Woolf stresses the binary nature of reminiscence in *A Sketch of the Past*, and describes her two first childhood memories: "I begin: the first memory. This was of red and purple flowers on a black ground – my mother's dress; and she was sitting either in a train or in an omnibus, and I was on her lap" (*MB*, 64).

---

36 Ibid., 26: "Memory thus plays a double role, both disturbing and restoring the individual's sense of identity".

The text traces the way in which memories emerge from consciousness. It focuses on the image remembered, and successively supplies it with details of its initial context, expanding the perspective until the images resolve themselves into a scene. Woolf's ekphrastic use of parataxis balances telling and showing, and imitates children's language. The structure of the text thus purports to follow the perception of the eye, and, step by step, develops images into narration. This sense of becoming that is inscribed into the unfolding narrative exemplifies what classical rhetoric knew as *enargeia*,[37] the capacity of language to create images, which turn the reader or listener into a viewer.

Woolf's second memory relies even more strongly on repetition and alternates between stillness and motion, becoming and being in a way that is reminiscent of the recursive motion of the waves. Similar to the metaphor of the platform the images of the "base" and the "bowl" relate the memory to the present. The scene remembered, however, serves as a focal point to create an immanent temporality of the text, which is capable to expand or contract time according to the emotional breadth of the moment.

> If life has a base that it stands upon, if it is a bowl that one fills and fills and fills – then my bowl without a doubt stands upon this memory. It is of lying half asleep, half awake, in bed in the nursery at St Ives. It is of hearing the waves breaking, one, two, one, two, and sending a splash of water over the beach; and then breaking, one, two, one, two, behind a yellow blind. It is of hearing the blind draw its little acorn across the floor as the wind blew the blind out. It is of lying and hearing this splash and seeing this light, and feeling, it is almost impossible that I should be here; of feeling the purest ecstasy I can conceive (*MB*, 64–65).

The child Virginia perceives the ebb and flow of the world outside in a half-way state of consciousness.[38] This intermediary dimension of her memory is meta-

---

[37] For the origins of the Aristotelian neologism *enargeia* and its relation to the Platonic conception of *dynamis* see: Hans-Georg Gadamer, "Wort und Bild – 'so wahr, so seiend'", *Gesammelte Werke* Bd. 8 (Tübingen: Mohr, 1993), 386–387.

[38] The character of James, in *To the Lighthouse*, experiences a childhood memory similar to Virginia Woolf's in *A Sketch of the Past*: "the blinds were sucked in and out by the breeze; all was blowing, all was growing; and over all those plates and bowls and tall brandishing red and yellow flowers a very thin yellow veil would be drawn, like a vine leaf, at night. Things became stiller and darker at night. But the leaf-like veil was so fine, that lights lifted it, voices crinkled it; he could see through it a figure stooping, hear, coming close, going away, some dress rustling, some chain tinkling" (*TL*, 185). Another conspicuous parallel can be found in Thomas Mann's *Buddenbrooks* in the description of the first morning of Johann Buddenbrook's holidays at Travemuende. *Buddenbrooks* (Frankfurt: Fischer, 53. Aufl., 2004), 630–631: "Das Zimmer lag in dem gelblichen Tageslicht, das schon durch das gestreifte Rouleau hereinfiel, während doch ringsum noch Alles still war [...] Und dieser sanft belebte Friede erfüllte den kleinen Johann alsbald mit

phorically expressed in the semi-transparent blind. The scene creates its distinct temporality in contrasting the linearity implicit in the threefold repetition of an action – "fills, and fills, and fills" – , with the twice recurring sound of the waves breaking: "one, two, one, two". The narrative progression of the scene itself is therefore paradoxically embedded into a complex of motion and standstill, suggested by the repetitive syntactic pattern, which continuously asserts the presence of the successive impressions in the repeated affirmation of the "it is". The image which gradually gains imaginative presence in memory is never a finished entity, but depends on being remembered time and again, and created in this potentially infinite process of remembrance. Likewise, Woolf's method of "telling the past in installments" involves a concentration on details, and the detachment of the moment of being from the past, in order to set it afloat again in an evolving narrative.

In her second 'first memory' the cyclical rhythm of the waves and the vision of light gradually converge into an experience of wholeness, and transport the child into a quasi-mystical state of heightened perceptual as well as epistemic activity, which culminates in a moment of synaesthetic rapture: "it is almost impossible that I should be here". The text traces the very act of coming into being of the remembered scene within a distinct temporality of aesthetic vision, which makes possible the creation of the image in the moment of being until the becoming of the image equals its state of being.

Woolf resorts to her childhood memories in the nursery, because to her they have acquired a presence and reality on their own: "Those moments – in the nursery, on the road to the beach – can still be more real than the present moment" (*MB*, 67). Her recollection of the past in *A Sketch of the Past*, in which she envisages the past as a vanishing point of scenes and emotions ("I see it – the past – as an avenue lying behind; a long ribbon of scenes, emotions. There at the end of the avenue still, are the garden and the nursery" (*MB*, 67)) is paralleled by her recourse to childhood memories in *The Waves*: "In the beginning there was the nursery" (*W*, 239).

The child's eye view, however, does not merely express nostalgia, but rather becomes a prerequisite for aesthetic creation, for seeing something as if it was for the first time. Revisiting this initial moment provides a foundation for Woolf's writing of memoirs as a distinct form of being in the course of time. For Woolf, the child's eye view presents a unique kind of impression, which gains its strength through phenomenological and formal simplicity.

---

der köstlichen Empfindung jener ruhigen, wohlgepflegten und distinguierten Abgeschiedenheit des Bades, die er so über Alles liebte".

Like Roger Fry, who was fascinated by children's drawings and their perception that is yet unspoiled by habit,[39] Virginia Woolf employs the child's-eye-view in inaugural scenes of fictional world-making. *Mrs. Dalloway* begins on "a morning – fresh as if issued to children on a beach" (*MD*, 3). The enchanted world of childhood described at the beginning of *The Waves* is composed of light and colour, allows for a shifting of signifiers, and expresses a sense of unfamiliarity and wonder when investigating into the singularity of a momentary vision: "This is our world, lit with crescents and stars of light; and great petals half transparent block the openings like purple windows. Everything is strange" (*W*, 12). The children's views are distinguished from ordinary vision by their clarity and their delight in the single, isolated object.[40]

In the early episodes of *The Waves*, the imaginative independence of the children's view, which is not yet reached or tainted by convention, is rendered on a more elegiac note in the episodes concerned with adolescence and middle-age. The six friends revisit scenes from the past, and their meetings mark dialectical moments in time in which union, wholeness and permanence are simultaneously created and suspended. At the farewell dinner for Percival they get together for a last time and their separate memories commonly rooted in childhood are symbolised by the many-petalled "red carnation in a vase", which both conveys the wholeness of the group of friends and its parts ("a whole flower to which every eye brings its own contribution" (*W*, 82)).

The moment of their meeting, referred to as "now", creates a comprehensive and almost synaesthetic wholeness that is sustained by their rendering of individual memories:

'Now let us issue from the darkness of solitude,' said Louis.
'Now let us say, brutally and directly, what is in our minds,' said Neville. 'Our isolation, our preparation is over. The furtive days of secrecy and hiding, the revelations on staircases, moments of terror and ecstasy'.
'Old Mrs. Constable lifted her sponge and warmth poured over us,' said Bernard. 'We became clothes in this changing, this feeling garment of flesh.'
'The boot-boy made love to the scullery-maid in the kitchen garden,' said Susan, 'among the blown-out washing.'
'The breath of wind was like a tiger panting,' said Rhoda.
'The man lay livid with his throat cut in the gutter,' said Neville. 'And going upstairs I could not raise my foot against the immitigable apple tree with its silver leaves held stiff.'

---

39 See for instance "The Artist's Vision", and "The Art of the Bushmen", *Vision and Design*, ed. by J.B. Bullen (New York: Dover Publications, 1981), 32; 60.
40 Harvena Richter conflates the poet's, the painter's and the child's view in Woolf's fiction. Richter, *Virginia Woolf. The Inward Voyage* (Princeton: Princeton UP, 1977), 82.

'The leaf danced in the hedge without anyone to blow it,' said Jinny.
'In the sun-baked corner,' said Louis, 'the petals swam on depths of green.'
'At Elvedon the gardeners swept and swept with their great brooms, and the woman sat at a table writing,' said Bernard.
'From these close-furled balls of string we draw now every filament,' said Louis, 'remembering when we meet' (*W*, 80–81).

The characters are disentangling their individual sensations, imaginations and observations pertaining to their common experiences of the past, the "close-furled balls of string", and extend them into the strands of the present narrative. Louis' and Neville's introductory words "now let us" can be read as incantations summoning into presence the distinct recollections that are to be shared by the congregation of friends.

Even though the narrative form of the polilogue renders temporality as fragmented within the disjoint visions of the separate voices, and conveys the temporal gap between past visions and their present meeting, it is also a quantitative addition of the single recollections, which expands the present moment and presents the gradual evolving of visions into narrative. In the same way as the six voices simulate a paradoxical coexistence of the whole and its parts, they also create a synchronised presence of present and past.

When the death of Percival breaks the continuity between past and present that the characters were earlier trying to preserve, they are overcome by feelings of futility, loneliness and meaninglessness. In the absence of Percival, the characters are separated not only from one another, but also from their common past, which becomes increasingly unreal to them. Even though they try to prevent the past from streaming away into oblivion by revisiting it, they realise that their meetings remain charged with the futile hope to remember: "Barns and summer days in the country, rooms where we sat – all now lie in the unreal world which is gone. My past is cut from me. [...] The past, summer days and rooms where we sat, stream away like burnt paper with red eyes in it. Why meet and resume?" (*W*, 99).

The rhetoric of beginnings with its reliance on minimalist forms of sketches and scenes can be regarded as a strategy in which the text presents itself as a self-contained unit that creates its own temporality through dialectical constellations. Dynamic temporal processes as well as seemingly timeless standstill are rendered through perception in which temporal categories of past and present appear as inherently relational and dependent on individual viewpoints.

Woolf's treatment of beginnings in which something is rendered as if it were seen, experienced, and created for the first time adds newness and change as temporal dimensions pertinent to aesthetic vision. The emphasis on the child's eye view relies on this notion of newness, originality, and innocence as it presents an enquiry into Woolf's recurrent concern with "the thing before it was made anything" (*TL*, 193). The temporality of aesthetic vision in Woolf's works is structured by an anachronistic movement towards imaginary beginnings, in which scenes and images from the past are created 'as if' they appear for the first time. This paradox is created through an immanently reflexive structure of the text. Like *The Waves*, *A Sketch of the Past* creates the temporality of aesthetic vision as a narrative pursuit of wholeness which involves seeing beyond the surface of the present: "I write this partly in order to recover my sense of the present by getting the past to shadow this broken surface. Let me then, like a child advancing with bare feet into a cold river, descend again into that stream" (*MB*, 98).

3.3 *Jacob's Room* and the space of time

Contemporary reviews both praised and criticised *Jacob's Room* for being a segmented novel.[41] Whereas it was appreciated for being Woolf's first experimental work and in this respect for many critics a genuinely Modern one, the more unfavourable reviews accuse Woolf of simply transcribing "fragments she overhears in tube, tram or train" to make a "rag-bag of impressions", to provide "piecemeal references to personages and things"; and generally hold that "no true novel can be built out of a mere accumulation of these notebook entries". [42]

Jacob's Room creates aesthetic vision in spatio-temporal constellations within an overall anachronistic structure. The formal segmentation of the novel corresponds to its enquiry into the aesthetic function of image-related memories that question the notion of memory as representation. Among the seemingly free-floating impressions and images so prolific and irritating to some critics, spatial metaphors of scaffolding, bricks, tombs, skulls and bones abound and describe an inevitable movement of the narrative towards the death of its central character. Figuratively, however, Jacob Flanders is already dead at the beginning of the novel. This structural anachronism in which the text purports to recon-

---

[41] *Virginia Woolf. The Critical Heritage*, 93–115. In a letter to Virginia Woolf, Lytton Strachey writes: "One remembers detail after detail – the pier at Scarborough, the rooks and the dinner-bell, the clergyman's wife on the moors, [...] one's head swirls round and round." Ibid., 93. An anonymous reviewer notes that: "Mrs. Woolf has the art of dividing the continuous and yet making one feel that the stream flows remorselessly" Ibid. 96.; Lewis Bettany's review for the *Daily News* is one of the more unfavourable ones: "Mrs. Woolf's new story, which is so full of parentheses and suppressions, so tedious in its rediscoveries of the obvious, and so marred by its occasional lapses into indelicacy, that I found great difficulty in discovering what it was all about". Ibid. 98.
[42] Ibid., 108; 103; 99.

struct something which it first of all creates makes Jacob's past the present of reading. Hence it is possible to read *Jacob's Room* as a memorial or as an elegy when considering its allusions to Rupert Brooke or Thoby Stephen, or even as a monument enclosing the novel itself in a tomblike space. In the *Recherche* Proust draws the analogy between the archiving mechanisms of the mind, the book and the cemetery, that can also be applied to reading *Jacob's Room*, as he illustrates the link between reading and remembering: "A book is a huge cemetery in which on the majority of the tombs the names are effaced and can no longer be read" (*Remembrance* 3: 940).

Whereas monuments for the most part glorify the culture they memorise in a gesture which conveys grief through pride, *Jacob's Room* precludes historic heroism. Like an empty tomb, as an almost literal equivalent to London's "Cenotaph", *Jacob's Room* centers on an absence and denies the reader access to the internal life of its main character.[43] As such it rather presents a counter-memorial, in which Woolf both explores and interrogates the relation between time, memory and space.[44] In the same vein, the novel inquires into the use of memory when commemorating the past in memorials and monuments. The gesture embodied is twofold and presents the central paradox of *Jacob's Room* in which the urge to memorialise is contrasted with the futility of doing so.

Jacob's absence throughout the novel, and poignantly at its end, causes the anachronistic regress of the narration. In creating Jacob as an inherently elusive character, Woolf employs a principle of character presentation which she later describes in the voice of Clarissa Dalloway: "She would not say of any one in the world now that they were this or were that" (*MD*, 8). The multiple views on Jacob which are portrayed in *Jacob's Room* likewise remain essentially partial, and even their accumulation fails to represent him in a clear-cut picture. Characters observing Jacob thus assert that "[n]obody sees any one as he is" (*JR*, 36), and repeatedly conclude that "[it] is no use trying to sum people up" (*JR*, 37; 214). Since summing a person up would entail arriving at a definite and fixed picture of them as well as holding them captive within it, *Jacob's Room* refutes any attempt at bringing views on Jacob, or anybody else of the characters to a closure. *Jacob's*

---

43 Cf. Robert Regino's reading of *Jacob's Room* in the context of war memorials. "Virginia Woolf and the Technologies of Exploration: *Jacob's Room* as a Counter-Monument", *Woolf and the Art of Exploration. Selected papers from the Fifteenth International Conference on Virginia Woolf*, ed. by Helen Southworth and Elisa Kay Sparks (Clemson: Clemson University Digital Press, 2006), 86–94.

44 Avrom Fleishman suggests that *Jacob's Room* anticipates *Three Guineas*, and in many ways, the novel presents the same argument in fictional form. *Virginia Woolf: a Critical Reading* (Baltimore: Johns Hopkins UP, 1975).

Room makes use of multiple perspectives as a means to illustrate the impossibility to equate seeing and knowing. In the same way as the reader is only given the outward and seemingly random descriptions of the many characters appearing in the novel, they themselves seem to be left to themselves, concerned with their own affairs, and hardly communicating on more than a superficial level: "The proximity of the omnibuses gave the outside passengers an opportunity to stare into each other's faces. Yet few took advantage of it. Each had his own business to think of. Each had his past shut in him like the leaves of a book known to him by heart; and his friends could only read the title" (*JR*, 85).

Likewise, only the surface, the name and title of Jacob are revealed. Single facets of his character are mostly rendered through external focalisation of third person narrators like Jacob's former Latin teacher: "'Now I know that face –' said Reverend Andrew Floyd, coming out of Carter's shop in Piccadilly, 'but who the dickens – ?' and he watched Jacob, turned round to look at him, but could not be sure – 'Oh, Jacob Flanders!' he remembered in a flash. But he was so tall; so unconscious; such a fine young fellow" (*JR*, 243). Jacob's absence from England while he is on his journey in Greece is reflected in Fanny Elmer's attempt to invoke Jacob's presence through pictorial substitutes. She idealises Jacob and nourishes her mental image of him in looking at the sculpture of Odysseus in the British Museum in what comes to regular almost therapeutic intervals:

> Sustained entirely upon picture postcards for the past two months, Fanny's idea of Jacob was more statuesque, noble, and eyeless than ever. To reinforce her vision she had taken to visiting the British Museum, where, keeping her eyes downcast until she was alongside of the battered Ulysses, she opened them and got a fresh shock of Jacob's presence, enough to last her half a day. But this was wearing thin. And she wrote now – poems, letters that were never posted, saw his face in advertisements on hoardings (*JR*, 238).

This kind of self-inflicted, repeated visual shock-therapy undergone by Fanny to call Jacob into being and to refresh her memory not only results in her never sending her letters or poems, but in summoning up ubiquitous after-images of him. Ironically, however, in trying to attach her mental image of Jacob to the fixed entity of a statue in what becomes almost a compulsion to repeat, she confines him to a lifeless effigy. The ambiguity between life and lifelessness in *Jacob's Room* is created in analogous constellations between the visible and the invisible, the present and the absent. Like the Odysseus-statue coming to life for Fanny, images and objects related to Jacob become virtually more alive than he is. Contrary to her intention to fight against oblivion, however, Jacob to her has already become an exhibit in the museum, and a monument of the past that is dead and in this way uncannily immortal.

Jacob's Room treats temporality within a semiotic and metaphorical perspective rather than from the protagonist's point of view. Impressions, images, and image-related memories become a structural device, and serve to establish significant correspondences between temporally and spatially distant elements, and the reader is introduced into this internal frame of reference built on recurring emblematic images. In repeatedly focusing on details and dwelling on single episodes, the text creates a relational network, forges links, and sets visual markers. Emblematic images, in particular, acquire significance when they are linked to the dominant theme of death lurking beneath the surface and provide a mnemonic arrangement of focal points. *Jacob's Room* is interspersed with the appearance of bones and skulls which both serve as reminders of death and the past and as premonitions of the future.

Similar to the boar's head hanging on the wall in *To the Lighthouse* (*TL*, 115) which frightens and fascinates the two children respectively, the image of the skull at the opening of *Jacob's Room* is a paradoxical symbol which constitutes one of Jacob's earliest perceptions as a child roaming the Cornish beach, and which likewise points to Jacob's own death: "There he stood. His face composed itself. He was about to roar when, lying among the black sticks and straw under the cliff, he saw a whole skull – perhaps a cow's skull, a skull, perhaps, with the teeth in it" (*JR*, 7). The finding of the skull presents a disturbing element given within the context of a seemingly peaceful scene on the beach. Like a piece of jetsam, the skull is found next to a pair of lovers, and the juxtaposition of death and love forms a semiotic opposition which builds up the central tension of the novel: "There on the sand not far from the lovers lay the old sheep's skull without its jaw. Clean, white, wind-swept, sand-rubbed, a more unpolluted piece of bone existed nowhere on the coast of Cornwall" (*JR*, 8).

The symbolic combination of life and death is taken up later in the novel when the skull reappears as an ornament in the description of the interior of Jacob's room in Cambridge: "a rose or a ram's skull is carved in the wood. The eighteenth century has its distinction" (*JR*, 94). The emblematic image visually encodes different levels of temporality and presents the central ambivalence of the novel. In exposing the duality of perception, the conflation of both symbols "a rose or a ram's skull" (*JR*, 246) is at once charged with the double notion of *eros* and *thanatos*, and serves as a *memento mori* which supports the analogy between the room and the tomb. The recurrent pattern of significant images not only creates a network of associations that hold the text together, but it also appeals to the reader's memory. The anticipated perspective of the reader in *Jacob's Room* is one of synthesising or unifying through memory, and of creating links between otherwise disparate elements. For the reader, *Jacob's Room* therefore becomes a mnemonic space that is temporally structured by images that add a vertical dimension of symbolism to the linear succession of scenes.

Memory in *Jacob's Room* is described as an ambiguous process of collecting, recollecting, and preserving. It is spatially encoded in the room as the novel's central metonymy. The mnemonic texture of *Jacob's Room* encourages a process of reading as recuperating the absent, the unseen and the overlooked, and of transforming it into a significant, yet momentary whole. As scattered fragmentary impressions circle round him in a kaleidoscopic way ("yet all the while having for centre, for magnet, a young man alone in his room" (JR, 129)), Jacob and his metonymic room attract multiple readings, and the reader also becomes a collector, who catalogues details, lists particularities about characters, and classifies objects in the room, all of which pertain to the aura of absence, an absence which is more of an "uncanny presence".[45]

The movement of the narration accordingly vacillates between the panoramic point of view of an omniscient narrator and the characters' dispersed perspectives. It never reaches beneath the surface and proceeds from one object to the next similar to the movement of sunlight inside a room, which is only able to illuminate the shape of the objects, but not their substance: "Back came the sun, dazzlingly. It fell like an eye upon the stirrups, and then suddenly and yet very gently rested upon the bed, upon the alarum clock, and upon the butterfly box stood open" (JR, 27).

Not unlike the open box from which the butterflies have escaped, Jacob's character forms an epistemological vacuum. Jacob increasingly withdraws from any attempt to be classified by a single view of him, until his final absence poignantly exposes the irretrievable loss of a signifier to which all the signs could formerly relate. The absence of the signifier is complemented by a narrative process of multiplying the signs. Rather than establishing causal relations between the signs to create coherence, the text activates their metonymical potential to present the absent: "One fibre in the wicker armchair creaks, though no one sits there" (JR, 49).

In *Jacob's Room* image- or object-related memories are powerful, yet fallible. The text displays at the same time a distraction of memory through providing numerous possibilities of meaning and relevance, and a concentration of visual memory materialising in emblematic images. Symbolised by material objects, and, above all, the empty room, perceptions, perspectives and memories constitute the symbolic universe of the text, whilst maintaining the balance between the seen and the unseen. Jacob's character epitomises this central ambivalence,

---

[45] Kazan, "Description and the Pictorial in *Jacob's Room*", 711.

in the metonymic image of the black box, which both can be read as a symbol of death and as the 'black box' later known in psychology, representing the unfathomable character of the human mind. Jacob's box, however, is not empty, and contains letters and a pair of trousers:

> Jacob threw them into the black wooden box where he kept his mother's letters, his old flannel trousers, and a note or two with the Cornish postmark. The lid shut upon the truth. This black wooden box, upon which his name was still legible in white paint, stood between the long windows of the sitting-room (*JR*, 93).

In *Jacob's Room*, the narrative follows the structure of a search for what is lost, in the awareness of the futility of any hope of finding it. The motif of a search for the evanescent is metaphorically present in Jacob's habit of catching butterflies and moths.[46] In the same way as both species symbolise the duality of the visual and the unvisual, day and night, life and death, they metaphorically point to the process of reading as collecting fragments (*JR*, 26). Apart from the novel's presentation of collecting on the level of character creation, *Jacob's Room* uses collecting or re-collecting as a metaphor for the vain effort of the novelist to catch life: "It is thus that we live, they say, driven by an unseizable force. They say that the novelists never catch it; that it goes hurtling through their nets and leaves them torn to ribbons. This, they say, is what we live by – this unseizable force" (*JR*, 217). Furthermore, the metaphor of collecting butterflies characterises Jacob as the searcher who cannot be found himself.[47] Like moths circling around light and striving towards it, scattered fragments of perspective, providing clues for the reader, draw him closer to Jacob's character without granting him any final insight apart from the conclusion that final insight cannot be reached.

Like the antiquary or the collector, the novelist strives to disclose the unseen, to order and categorise it. He is, however, confronted with the dilemma that in the very moment of its fixation, the present becomes the past, and life becomes death. In equating the novelist, who engages in the inherently futile task of keeping life – past or present – alive, to the butterfly catcher, who aims at conserving and exhibiting life, the text reveals the deceptive character of preservation in asserting that the exhibit is always either only a part or a substitute of the original, but never the thing itself.

---

46 Harvena Richter, "Hunting the Moth: Virginia Woolf and the Creative Imagination", *Virginia Woolf: Revaluation and Continuity*, 13–28.
47 In *Moments of Being*, Woolf describes how Jack Hills introduced her to Morris' book on butterflies: "He taught us to sugar trees; he gave us his copy of Morris's *Butterflies and Moths*, over which I spent many hours, hunting up our catches among all those pictures of hearts and darts and setaceous Hebrew characters" (*MB*, 104).

The anachronistic temporality of aesthetic vision questions any unambiguous reference, and inaugurates the dynamics of deferral and approximation, in which seeing, like loving, in *Jacob's Room* never means possessing, and the textual processes of search and recollection never arrive at an accurate or reassuring representation.

In *Jacob's Room* the narrative rather subverts the tendency of containment by means of metaphorically exposing methods of confinement that are connected to memory and conservation. The metaphor of boxes and containers set within the context of the theme of death is pervasive in *Jacob's Room*. When Mrs. Flanders searches for her brooch she lost in the moor, the narrator presents the moor as a naturalistic warehouse or treasure chamber:

> The moor accepted everything. Tom Gage cries aloud so long as his tombstone endures. The Roman skeletons are in safe keeping. Betty Flanders' darning needles are safe too and her garnet brooch. And sometimes at mid-day, in the sunshine, the moor seems to hoard these little treasures, like a nurse (JR, 184).

As an equivalent to the moor as a receptacle of a multiplicity of lost material objects, the British Museum is presented as a large mind storing immaterial intellectual goods. In *Jacob's Room*, the museum and the archive are metaphors of memory and artificial storage mechanisms, exhibiting the visible and keeping the unseen in reserve. In *Jacob's Room*, the notion of the archive is employed both as a metaphor and as an institutionalised form of memory.[48] The museum and the archive present examples of monumentalised culture, exhibiting itself for the contemporary world and for posterity. The archive organises collective memory, selects what is worth keeping, conserves cultural heritage and makes knowledge about the past accessible.

In *Jacob's Room*, the British Museum is compared to an exteriorised mind and an archiving mechanism for memory, in which the metaphor of the 'treasure chamber of memory' is transferred to society at large. The British Museum is first of all portrayed as an uncanny and inscrutable self-perpetuating system:

> There is in the British Museum an enormous mind. Consider that Plato is there cheek by jowl with Aristotle; and Shakespeare with Marlowe. This great mind is hoarded beyond the power of any single mind to possess it. [...] The vast mind was sheeted with stone; and each compartment in the depths of it was safe and dry. The night-watchmen, flashing their lanterns over the backs of Plato and Shakespeare, [...] poor, highly respectable

---

48 Michel Foucault, *Archäologie des Wissens* (Frankfurt am Main: Suhrkamp, 1973), 186–188. Michel Foucault regards the archive not merely as a material storage device, but as a system and regulatory mechanism guided by underlying structures of power.

men, with wives and families at Kentish Town, do their best for twenty years to protect Plato and Shakespeare and then are buried at Highgate. Stone lies solid over the British Museum, as bone lies cool over the visions and heat of the brain. Only here the brain is Plato's brain and Shakespeare's; the brain has made pots and statues, great bulls and little jewels, and crossed the river of death this way and that incessantly, seeking some landing, now wrapping the body well for its long sleep; now laying a penny piece on the eyes (JR, 148–149).

The museum resembles a tomb, and the force behind the archiving mechanism remains unknown even to the guardians, who protect it and ensure its existence, but will themselves not be included in the vast mechanism of remembrance.

Jacob's Room criticises the urge to memorialise in national terms. The novel rather explores the intersection of personal memory and history in exposing the failure of ideological or collective constructions of memory as representation. The temporality of aesthetic vision created in terms which are spatial and image-related rather asserts an open and also paradoxical process in which forms and phenomena allow for both a contraction and an extension of temporality according to the individualised span of the moment.

Jacob's Room correspondingly ends with an everyday object submitted to the memory of the reader: the "pair of Jacob's old shoes". Woolf had used shoes and boots as a metonymy for people in *The Voyage Out*: "'I always think that people are so like their boots', said Miss Allan" (*TVO*, 243), and later she employed the image in *To the Lighthouse* in Lily Briscoe's praise of Mr. Ramsay's boots (*TL*, 153). In *The Waves*, the friends mourn for the loss of Percival: "The figure that was robed in beauty is now clothed in ruin. The figure that stood in the grove where the steep-backed hills come down falls in ruin, as I told them when they said they loved his voice on the stair, and his old shoes and moments of being together" (*W*, 104).

Although the pair of old shoes in *Jacob's Room* is reminiscent of the still life of old shoes drawn by Van Gogh[49], the image of Jacob's shoes is not merely the narrative equivalent of a painted still-life. The shoes capture Jacob's life-journey in a poetic image that expresses the duration of time in an instant. Like a painting the shoes metonymically represent Jacob's absence. Heidegger's famous interpretation of Van Gogh's picture in "Die Wahrheit des Kunstwerks" argues that Van Gogh's painting is not a mimetic illustration of an everyday object, but that it illustrates how being comes into the picture. Heidegger's argument can be taken as an extension of the temporal logic in *Jacob's Room*, in which the presence of

---

[49] Martin Heidegger, "Der Ursprung des Kunstwerkes", *Holzwege* (1935–1936), (Frankfurt am Main: Klostermann, 6. Aufl., 1980), 17–24.

the image paradoxically asserts a world through absence – an absence most profoundly marked in death.

The novel, however, does not just end in death but with a question, which expresses the final loss of the signifier as well as the altered nature of the quotidian object, which is taken out of its functional context and made to resemble a work of art. Mrs. Flanders' open question "What am I to do with these?" hands the problem of interpretation over to the reader, and marks aesthetic vision as a performance of temporality which is left to the dynamics of reading as preservation, repetition and renewal. "The continuous present is created only in the act of reading",[50] writes Mark Hussey, and one also realises that what is lost in *Jacob's Room* has never been present to the reader in the first place.

3.4 "Was that the end?" – *Between the Acts* and the paradox of vision in time

Woolf's later works are not only concerned with different experiments in biographical writing, but also with narrative strategies in which vision and temporality materialise into constellations between individual life time and collective history.[51] In addition to her work on the biography of Roger Fry and her own memoir, Woolf was preoccupied with writing what was going to be her last novel, *Between the Acts*. The novel bears close relations to some of her contemporaneous works in terms of form and theme. Some of the childhood recollections she describes in *A Sketch of the Past* reappear as motifs in *Between the*

---

50 Mark Hussey, *The Singing of the Real World*, 124.
51 Woolf began writing the novel, whose working title was 'Pointz Hall' in April 1938. In an entry into her diary on 26 April 1938 she describes her project ("to sketch out a new book") in a similar way to that of *The Waves*, where she experiments with themes and style: "Yet in spite of that here am I sketching out a new book; only dont please impose that huge burden on me again, I implore. Let it be random & tentative; something I can blow of a morning, to relieve myself of Roger: dont, I implore, lay down a scheme; call in all the cosmic immensities; & force my tired & diffident brain to embrace another whole – all parts contributing – not yet awhile. But to amuse myself let me note: why not Poyntzet Hall: a centre: all lit. discussed in connection with real little incongruous living humour; & anything that comes into my head; but "I" rejected: 'We' substituted: to whom at the end there shall be an invocation? "We" ... composed of many different things ... we all life, all art, all waifs & strays – a rambling capricious but somehow unified whole – the present state of my mind? An English country; & a scenic old house – & a terrace where nursemaids walk? & people passing – & a perpetual variety & change from intensity to prose. & facts – & notes; & – but eno'" (*D* V, 135).

Acts.⁵² The novel is not only formally related to the earlier piece of short fiction, "The Moment: Summer's Night", but its transient and "sketchy" nature was one of the reasons why Woolf had initially decided against its publication.⁵³

Although the novel observes the Aristotelian unities of time and place, the narrative trajectory of *Between the Acts* is inherently a temporal arc⁵⁴ in which the idea of in-between-ness is enacted on the temporal level of aesthetic vision. Space and time in *Between the Acts* are simultaneously encoded in different referential contexts as the novel is set between historical remoteness and the proximity of the present, between the two World Wars, between word and image, between the individual and the collective, between nature and artifice and between actors and spectators.

Woolf's method of scene-making in which she relates aesthetic vision and temporality is taken up in 'the play in the play', the 'scenes from English history'. Not unlike *Jacob's Room*, *Between the Acts* is not divided into chapters, but falls into a succession of scenes and episodes of various lengths. The transitions between the early scenes of the novel are marked by their alternately foregrounding either time or place. From the very beginning, the novel shifts between different time frames which correspond to different angles of perspective. From the initial 'moment of a summer's night' inside Pointz Hall, the narrative moves to the description of an aerial view of it in the morning: "Pointz Hall was seen in the light of an early summer morning to be a middle-sized house" (*BA*, 3). At the end of the scene, the narrative returns to the interiour of the house, and focuses on the image of a moment frozen in time: "under a glass case there was a watch that had stopped a bullet on the field of Waterloo" (*BA*, 3). The watch displayed behind the glass case metonymically represents the spatiotemporal construction of the novel, which creates a time and place of relative isolation located between the impact of war and the lifetime of the individual. The momentary suspension of temporality is related to the secluded and empty interior of the house in the "remote village in the very heart of England" (*BA*, 9).

---

52 These include the vision of a flower's completeness, the skeleton of the dog in the swamp and the sheep's thigh bone recovered from the lily pond.
53 Woolf writes to John Lehmann that she has decided against the publication of *Between the Acts*, and she points out that, among other things, the novel was "too slight & sketchy" (*L* VI, 482).
54 Frieder Stadtfeld has noted the correspondence between the time frame of the pageant and the centuries it covers from 15:00 until 19:20 on the day of the performance. "Virginia Woolfs letzter Roman: 'more quintessential than the others'", *Anglia* 91 (1973), 58 n. 5.

The centrality of time and place is defined by the novel's many structural oppositions in which people and places can be two different things at the same time. Pointz Hall is simultaneously referred to as a presently visible shape, and as an event in history at large.[55] Parts of the house such as the larder which once was a chapel indicate a shift between present foreground and past background. Likewise the inhabitants of Pointz Hall are referred to by their real names as well as their nicknames: "She would save a slice for Sunny – his drawing-room name Sung-Yen had undergone a kitchen change into Sunny" (*BA*, 19).

Like the site of the mansion itself, which represents the contrast between nature and the work of man – "Nature had provided a site for a house; man had built his house in a hollow" (*BA*, 5) – the two other main locations of the novel, the barn and the dip of the ground as the stage for the pageant, are encoded in two time frames.

> The Barn to which Lucy had nailed her placard was a great building in the farmyard. It was as old as the church, and built of the same stone, but it had no steeple. It was raised on cones of grey stone at the corners to protect it from rats and damp. Those who had been to Greece always said it reminded them of a temple. Those who had never been to Greece – the majority – admired it all the same (*BA*, 15).

The barn is presented both as a secularised version of the village church and as a monument of ancient Greece. The place for the stage beyond the terrace is equally ambivalent and creates a paradoxical site of imaginary artifice, "the natural stage" (*BA*, 47), against the backdrop of the English countryside. Miss La Trobe's enthusiasm about the spot – "'That's the place for a pageant, Mr. Oliver!' she had exclaimed. [...] 'There the stage; here the audience; and down there among the bushes a perfect dressing-room for the actors'" (*BA*, 35) – reiterates the scene in *A Midsummer Night's Dream* when Peter Quince inspects the place in the wood for the rehearsal of the interlude: "Pat, pat; and here's a marvail's convenient place for our rehearsal. This green plot shall be our stage, this hawthorn brake our tiring-house" (*MND*, 3.1.2–5).

Like Shakespeare's "green plot", which, apart from being the theatrical stage, is at once the enchanted realm of 'Faerieland', the rehearsal stage for the play in the play, and the place of confusion for the lovers, the terrace in *Between the Acts* presents a site of vision in between the real place and the imaginary space, between the timeless infinity of the view and the contemporary position of the

---

[55] Cf. Alexandra Harris on Woolf's celebration of the countryside in *Between the Acts* and Woolf's building of narrative spaces. *Romantic Moderns. English Writers, Artists and the Imagination from Virginia Woolf to John Piper* (London: Thames and Hudson, 2010), 113–114; 261.

audience: "The lawn was as flat as the floor of a theatre. The terrace, rising, made a natural stage. The trees barred the stage like pillars. And the human figure was seen to great advantage against a background of sky" (*BA*, 47).

A Midsummer Night's Dream also provides a model for Woolf's double plot and the idea of the play in the play. Woolf's last novel investigates into the theatre, the annual village pageant as a visual means in which elements of the past may be reinterpreted in the present by an audience. It presents a space in time, into which different levels of temporality converge, and where what is visible can be different things at the same time.[56]

Before the novel turns to the "Scenes from English History" performed by the villagers, it introduces different kinds of individualised temporality. The interaction and collision of the subjective time-frames of the characters is given as a set of discontinuing and momentary overlapping scenes in otherwise incongruous lives. Inspired by reading "An Outline of History", Mrs. Swithin indulges into a daydream about the prehistoric past until her sense of time is suspended, and the vision of the past takes over her perception of the present:

> It took her five seconds in actual time, in mind time ever so much longer, to separate Grace herself, with blue china on a tray, from the leather-covered grunting monster who was about, as the door opened, to demolish a whole tree in the green steaming undergrowth of the primeval forest (*BA*, 4).

For Lucy Swithin, it is not only the return to the past which shapes her vision of the present, but also present sights and sounds inspire her to expand the present moment into the past or the future: "An obliging thrush hopped across the lawn; a coil of pinkish rubber twisted in its beak. Tempted by the sight to continue her imaginative reconstruction of the past, Mrs. Swithin paused; she was given to increasing the bounds of the moment by flights into past or future" (*BA*, 5).

The narrative alternates between the expansion of a single moment within the individual vision or reverie of a character and the subsequent resuming of the plot in the context of another scene.[57] Old Mr. Oliver interrupts his grandson's play (*BA*, 6–7), and is himself interrupted by Isa when he dreams about his youth in India (*BA*, 10).[58]

---

[56] Claudia Olk, "Virginia Woolf's 'Elizabethan Play': *Between the Acts* and *A Midsummer Night's Dream*", *Shakespeare Jahrbuch* 146 (2010), 113–130.

[57] Lucio Ruotolo discusses Isa's romantic disposititon for disharmony and escapism. *The Interrupted Moment. A View of Virginia Woolf's Novels* (Stanford: Stanford UP, 1986), 207–208.

[58] Gillian Beer examines the corresponding disrupted syntactical structure in *Between the Acts*. "Introduction", xxf.

The novel, however, neither adheres to a narrative of teleological progression nor to a cyclical pattern of time, but it presents a structural principle of varied repetition in which characters are both immersed in time and exempt from it. In contrast to Giles, whose sense of time is controlled by causality, Lucy Swithin indulges into the moment and invests it with meaning and history. She brings linear time to a standstill, and instead expands the moment within her imagination by releasing a chain of associations about the components and the origin of quotidian things such as the loaf of bread she is about to cut.

> The cook's hands cut, cut, cut. Whereas Lucy, holding the loaf, held the knife up. Why's stale bread, she mused, easier to cut than fresh? And so skipped, sidelong, from yeast to alcohol; so to fermentation; so to inebriation; so to Bacchus; and lay under purple lamps in a vineyard in Italy, as she had done, often; while Sands heard the clock tick; saw the cat; noted a fly buzz (*BA*, 20).

Lucy Swithin creates an imaginary causality, and the cook, Mrs. Sands, works steadily and mechanically observing time – "cut, cut, cut" – like sand in an hourglass inevitably running its course determined by gravity, Lucy is inspired by what she sees and steps out of actual time when she inquires into its past. When she takes William Dodge on a tour around the house, she embarks on a journey backwards in time, and the succession of rooms they visit reconnects her to her childhood: "Mrs. Swithin stopped by the bed. 'Here,' she said, 'yes, here,' she tapped the counterpane. 'I was born. In this bed'" (*BA*, 43).

Whereas Isa remains entangled in her personal and domestic predicament, Lucy freely moves between time and space. The difference between both women is illustrated in the novel's predominant imagery of birds. The birds associated with Isa – swans with webbed feet, and the faded peacocks on her dressing gown – remain in their respective element and either float on water or stay on ground. Lucy, who stays at Pointz Hall during the summer and spends her winters in Hastings (*BA*, 4), however, is compared to seasonal birds. She likes to look at the swallows which to her represent the return of the same (*BA*, 63), and her brother even refers to her as "sister swallow" (*BA*, 72). After the play, when she looks at the lily pool, she finds herself between two elements, and in "caressing her cross" she asserts the semantic energy residing in paradoxical binary constellations: "Above, the air rushed; beneath was water. She stood between two fluidities, caressing her cross" (*BA*, 127). Her supple sense of time and reality defies any state of being tied down to convention, religion, materiality, or even to her own body: "Really! It was her brother! And his dog! She seemed to see them for the first time. Was it that she had no body? Up in the clouds, like an air ball, her mind touched ground now and then with a shock of surprise" (*BA*, 72).

Lucy is capable of seeing the extraordinary within the ordinary, of reversing time and bringing it to a stop. When she is described as "The old girl with a wisp of white hair flying" (*BA*, 16), she is attributed a similar airy nature as that of the clouds whose movement abides by no particular law, and who seem to dwell in a time and space between eternity and actual time.

> There was a fecklessness, a lack of symmetry and order in the clouds, as they thinned and thickened. Was it their own law, or no law, they obeyed? Some were wisps of white hair merely. One, high up, very distant, had hardened to golden alabaster; was made of immortal marble. Beyond that was blue, pure blue, black blue, blue that had never filtered down; that had escaped registration. It never fell as sun, shadow, or rain upon the world, but disregarded the little coloured ball of earth entirely (*BA*, 13).

The view of the sky presents an image of eternity, immortality and timelessness which transcends emotion, colour and form. From the disinterested orbital vantage point timelessness converges into colourlessness, and in Pointz Hall, the possibility of a limitless extension of the horizontal as well as the vertical view simultaneously threatens, bores and fascinates the different characters. Whereas Mrs. Manresa is tired by the endless repetition of what she sees (*BA*, 41), William Dodge and Lucy Swithin are inspired by the vastness of the view to broaden their minds and make their inner vision correspond to what they see: "Mrs. Swithin and William surveyed the view aloofly, and with detachment. How tempting, how very tempting, to let the view triumph; to reflect its ripple; to let their own minds ripple; to let outlines elongate and pitch over – so – with a sudden jerk" (*BA*, 41).

The relativity of individual time is emphasised when it is seen against history at large: "Only something over a hundred and twenty years the Olivers had been there" (*BA*, 3), and when characters are preoccupied with tracing the etiologies and etymologies of people, buildings and expressions. The concerns of the individuals with time are contrasted by the invocations to timelessness and the eternal. The timelessness of the ever-present view in this respect conveys a sense of beauty, which lies in the immutable. Lucy Swithin finds reassurance in the recurrence of sameness and infinity promised by the view, because it will prevail over their individual lives:

> They looked at the view; they looked at what they knew, to see if what they knew might perhaps be different today. Most days it was the same. 'That's what makes a view so sad,' said Mrs. Swithin, lowering herself into the deck-chair which Giles had brought her. 'And so beautiful. It'll be there,' she nodded at the strip of gauze laid upon the distant fields, 'when we're not' (*BA*, 32).

Lucy Swithin and her brother complement each other in a seemingly infinite process: "But, brother and sister, flesh and blood was not a barrier, but a mist. Nothing changed their affection; no argument; no fact; no truth. What she saw he didn't; what he saw she didn't – and so on, ad infinitum" (*BA*, 15). They inhabit a timeless present in which 'time does not exist' (*BA*, 51).

3.4.1 Vision and silence

In *Between the Acts*, the opposition between word and image is rendered in terms of vision in time. Lucy and Bartholomew's resistance to temporal progression corresponds to their position as members of the audience to the pageant, which is marked by its silence and inaction: "There was nothing for the audience to do. Mrs. Manresa suppressed a yawn. They were silent. They stared at the view, as if something might happen in one of those fields to relieve them of the intolerable burden of sitting silent, doing nothing, in company" (*BA*, 40). The equanimity of the older generation is contrasted by the restlessness of the younger. Whereas Lucy and Bartholomew are contented with being the audience – "'Our part,' said Bartholomew, 'is to be the audience. And a very important part too'" (*BA*, 36); "We remain seated" – "We are the audience" (*BA*, 37) – Isa, Giles, and William – for different reasons, suffer from it. For Giles being forced to remain seated and to merely watch it is dramatised as Promethean agony: "This afternoon he wasn't Giles Oliver come to see the villagers act their annual pageant; manacled to a rock he was, and forced passively to behold indescribable horror" (*BA*, 37), and even during the interval, he "remained like a stake in the tide of the flowing company" (*BA*, 60). The "monstrous inversion", which Giles calls the sight of the snake and the toad caught between life and death, eating and being eaten, presents the standstill of a dilemma, which he resolves in killing both animals: "But it was action. Action relieved him" (*BA*, 62).

Giles' sense of being held captive is shared by Isa and applied to their marriage, in which she feels caged and torn between love and hate:

> Giles glared. With his hands bound tight round his knees he stared at the flat fields. Staring, glaring, he sat silent. Isabella felt prisoned. Through the bars of the prison, through the sleepy haze that deflected them, blunt arrows bruised her; of love, then of hate (*BA*, 41).

The verb 'glare' throughout the novel indicates a way of seeing that implies the frozen, silent, and motionless stance of the viewer. At the beginning of the pageant it is used to describe the audience from Miss La Trobe's perspective: "They glared as if they were exposed to a frost that nipped them and fixed them all at the same level. Only Bond the cowman looked fluid and natural" (*BA*, 48).

The idea of paradox and of a stationary void between two mutually-exclusive alternatives is illustrated in situations of choice and contrasting options. William is undecided about what to do during the interval: "'Shall I,' he murmured, 'go or stay?'" (*BA*, 60), and characters are constantly concerned about the weather: "'And which will it be?' Mrs. Swithin continued. 'Wet or fine?'" (*BA*, 13). Likewise, the Afghan hound is of a twofold nature, which is beyond the reach of human attempts to tame it: "His tail never wagged. He never admitted the ties of domesticity. Either he cringed or he bit. Now his wild yellow eyes gazed at her, gazed at him. He could outstare them both" (*BA*, 10).

One of the most prominent oppositions of the novel is illustrated by the two portraits of a male ancestor and an unknown woman, which convey the legacy of the past and contrast the silence of the nameless female with the 'talk-producing' ancestor, who has a name, which, however, remains unknown to the reader:

> Two pictures hung opposite the window. In real life they had never met, the long lady and the man holding his horse by the rein. The lady was a picture, bought by Oliver because he liked the picture; the man was an ancestor. He had a name. He held the rein in his hand. [...] He was a talk producer, that ancestor. But the lady was a picture (*BA*, 21–22).

The two portraits present opposites in visual and temporal form. Their juxtaposition enables the present viewer to connect the two otherwise unrelated lives of the portrayed – one of them of realistic, the other one of obscure origin – who: "in real life [they] had never met". Apart from their gendering of language and silence, the portraits correspond to different models of temporality. The 'portrait of the lady' identifies the silent image with femininity, the unreferential, and unreal ("the lady was a picture"), and conveys a sense of timelessness similar to the outlasting view overlooking the countryside: "They all looked at the lady. But she looked over their heads, looking at nothing. She led them down green glades into the heart of silence" (*BA*, 30). The analogy of vision, silence and timelessness is contrasted by the link between words, masculinity and ancestral heritage, reflecting the novel's broader concern with temporality and language.

The characters' difficulty to communicate becomes apparent in the elliptic course of their conversations. Rather than finishing Hamlet's soliloquy, which reflects the novel's concern with mutually exclusive alternatives, each of them recalls lines from different Shakespearean soliloquies, which are expressive of their respective plight:

> To be, or not to be, that is the question. Whether 'tis nobler ... Go on!' she nudged Giles, who sat next her. 'Fade far away and quite forget what thou amongst the leaves hast never known ...' Isa supplied the first words that came into her head by way of helping her husband out of his difficulty. 'The weariness, the torture, and the fret ...' William Dodge added, burying the end of his cigarette in a grave between two stones (*BA*, 33).

Giles' inability to complete Hamlet's soliloquy illustrates his dilemma, which he interprets as not having a choice and not being able to act. It is Lucy, who interrupts the indiscriminate amalgamation of quotations, who implicitly reminds the group that they are spectators rather than actors, and advises them to look at what lies beyond words: "'We haven't the words – we haven't the words,' Mrs. Swithin protested. 'Behind the eyes; not on the lips; that's all'" (*BA*, 34). Her appeal to the superiority of the mind and images that lie "behind the eyes" is challenged by her brother's view, who cannot imagine thoughts beyond words: "'Thoughts without words,' her brother mused. 'Can that be?'" (*BA*, 34).

Lucy, however, often communicates without words by looking at another person, such as William Dodge, or by contemplating a view or an object. When she and the others look at the two portraits, she translates the silence of the ancestor's picture into the very words, which to her might have led to the painting of the picture: "'I always feel,' Lucy broke the silence, 'he's saying: 'Paint my dog'" (*BA*, 30).

The thoughts of Lucy and Isa attach themselves to images instead of words. Rather than speaking, Isa prefers to watch in silence: "In all this sound of welcome, protestation, apology and again welcome, there was an element of silence, supplied by Isabella, observing the unknown young man" (*BA*, 23). For Isa, words of poetry transform into images: "words made two rings, perfect rings, that floated them" (*BA*, 2), and when she later reflects on her encounter with Mr. Haines, she fails to do the reverse and translate images into words: "the words he said, handing her a teacup, handing her a tennis racquet, could so attach themselves to a certain spot in her; and thus lie between them like a wire, tingling, tangling, vibrating – she groped, in the depths of the looking glass, for a word" (*BA*, 8).

The elusiveness of language in *Between the Acts* is not only reflected in the characters' search for words, or the fugitive nature of a moment in time, but also within a temporal pattern of continuation and onward movement in which words can be exhausted, used up, and like the nurses steadily "trundling" the perambulator and "rolling words", words are wearing thin and leave only faint sensations of taste and colour:

> The nurses after breakfast were trundling the perambulator up and down the terrace; and as they trundled they were talking – not shaping pellets of information or handing ideas from one to another, but rolling words, like sweets on their tongues; which as they thinned to transparency, gave off pink, green, and sweetness (*BA*, 5).

The novel's critique of conventional language is expressed within the chronological model of time of the pageant. Even though history is presented as a linear progression of scenes, words are mainly linked to the idea of repetition as a kind of eternal recurrence based on natural cycles as in the repeated song of the villagers *"the earth is always the same, summer and winter and spring; and spring and winter again; ploughing and sowing, eating and growing; time passes. ...* The wind blew the words away" (*BA*, 78).

For the most part of the pageant, words do not reach the audience (*BA*, 48), voices peter out (*BA*, 59), actors forget their lines (*BA*, 53), and words are being blown away by the wind (*BA*, 77). Miss La Trobe only hears "scraps and fragments" of the conversation when the audience is assembling (*BA*, 75). During the pageant, the visual impact of the scene is given prominence over words, which are either inaudible, forgotten, or about which the narrator repeatedly insists that: "It didn't matter what the words were; or who sang what" (*BA*, 58).

The temporal linearity of sentences or songs is continuously broken, and the sound of words appears equally ephemeral as that of music. The contrast between sound and silence, however, is cast into a modulated progression in which time inverts itself when silences give way to sounds, and sounds drown into the silence that precedes them.

When the Reverend Streatfield offers his verbose summary of the pageant's meaning, La Trobe, whose play he is summarising, remains conspicuously "invisible": "O Lord, protect and preserve us from words the defilers, from words the impure! What need have we of words to remind us? Must I be Thomas, you Jane?" (*BA*, 117).

The impurity of words he refers to reveals a profound skepticism about language in general and can also be read as a comment on the use of words in contemporary war propaganda. In mounting the soapbox, where previously characters of the pageant had stood and delivered their speeches, the Reverend unwittingly becomes part of the performance, and adds an element to history becoming histrionic. At the end of the pageant, the Reverend has "no further use for words" (*BA*, 120). His closing words of thanks do not succeed in creating unity, but they are "cut in two" (*BA*, 119) by the appearance of the planes.

Like in the early scenes of the novel, the temporality of aesthetic vision expressed in the pageant is essentially one of alternation between fixity and flux, between pictorial stasis and narrative motion, achieved by the contraction of the narrative into the formal unity of the scene, and its dissolution, or "dispersal" during the intervals. Motion and standstill, however, do not provide stable categories into which parts of the novel can be clearly divided. The scenes of the pageant convey stasis and progression at the same time, and the description of the audience is equally ambivalent when it expresses both standstill and motion in pictorial terms: "Soon the lawns were floating with little moving islands of coloured dresses. Yet some of the audience remained seated" (*BA*, 93). The paradoxical image of the "moving island" not only resolves the novel's opposition between motion and standstill, but it also reverberates in the analogous contrast between land and water. As a synonym for England, the island marks the uncertain state of the country in the present,[59] and is a paradoxical symbol of the insularity of Pointz Hall in 'the heart of the country'. The audience moreover epitomises both the stasis, isolation and dryness of an island, and the collective fluidity of the stream, when it inundates the lawns and when it gathers together again at the end of the interval: "The audience was streaming back to the terrace" (*BA*, 97). The indistinct clusters of people moving during the interval pictorially express a moment in time when both the larger state of the nation, and the state of the individual are linked by a shared condition of non-attachment: "Yet somehow they felt – how could one put it – a little not quite here or there. As if the play had jerked the ball out of the cup; as if what I call myself was still floating unattached, and didn't settle. Not quite themselves, they felt" (*BA*, 93).

The structure of the narrative itself creates scenes from the pageant as islands in the stream of the historical meta-narrative within an overall temporality fluctuating between acts and intervals. In the performance of the annual pageant, the time passing in the novel is cast into scenes within a play about the passing of historical time, in which the unity of the scene is orchestrated into a larger historical context.[60] The reader is constantly made aware of more than one dimension of time, and enabled to correlate them. Reading time interacts with the time of the narration and the received ideas of historical time represented in the scenes. Scenes appear as signatures of temporality, and the scenic arrangement of the novel turns the reader into a spectator and a part of the audience.

In addition to temporal condensation and flux, transhistorical timelessness lingers above the present time of the novel and the presentation of immanent time in the performance, and makes it possible to relate as well as to question the impact of the past on the present and the future. In constantly combining small, contracted units of time with larger expanding ones, the novel stresses their mutual dependence and reveals the paradoxical simultaneity of temporal distance and immediacy.

Playing on historical remoteness and history made recognisable in the present-day, the pageant brings forth a hermeneutic interplay of comparison, interrelation, and differentiation. During the play, temporal oppositions are defined visually as dialectical opposites which govern the performance. The stage

---

59 Gillian Beer, "The Island and the Aeroplane: the Case of Virginia Woolf", *Nation and Narration*, ed. by Homi Bhabha (London: Routledge, 1990), 266.

60 Frieder Stadtfeld notes the increasing proximity of epic and dramatic parts towards the end of the novel. "Virginia Woolfs letzter Roman: 'more quintessential than the others'", 63ff.

appears as a place between past, present, and future, between the singular vision of the individual and the timelessness of the view. The "Scenes from English History" not only interrupt the narrative flow of the novel and create an intermediary realm within the linear narration, but, in presenting fragments of history, they also refute the idea of chronological progression in the service of an overall teleological history. Indicative of the novel's resistance to linear models, it is once again Lucy Swithin who interrupts the course of the play by her arrival: "But there was an interruption. 'O,' Miss La Trobe growled behind her tree, 'the torture of these interruptions!' 'Sorry I'm so late,' said Mrs. Swithin" (*BA*, 49).

The village pageant stages its own historicity in a metadramatic mode, and imitates the historical development of dramatic forms. Drawing on the medieval Mystery Plays, the prologue of the pageant underlines the effect of temporal remoteness in directing the audience's attention to history made visible, emphasising what can and should be seen on stage. The archaic register used by the allegorised figure of England gives further emphasis to her appeal to the audience to willingly suspend their historical distance, and make two temporal levels overlap.

> *Come hither for our festival* (she continued)
> *This is a pageant, all may see*
> *Drawn from our island history*
> *England am I. . . .* (*BA*, 47).

Although seeing is meant to equal believing in the theatrical illusion of historical distance, historical identity remains an illusion never to be achieved. The audience's comments interrupt the words spoken on stage and constantly transport the reader back into the present of the narrative time of the novel. Time inverts itself in the interaction between the play and the audience, and what was foreground becomes background, and what is background rises to the surface. This movement between narrative time and the time of the narration once again takes up the analogy to the double plot in *A Midsummer Night's Dream* where during the performance of the mechanicals' play at the court of Athens, Theseus, Hippolyta and the 'lovers' cannot refrain from intervening, and from destroying the efforts at creating theatrical illusion by their witticisms. This not only exasperates Peter Quince's actors as it does Miss La Trobe, but also involves the reader/spectator as a third party to link the words of the play with the comments of the audience, and grants that despite its relative remoteness the action still has a bearing on the present.

In the pageant's attempts at creating the illusion of historicity by using stereotypes, and catering to conventionalised expectations of the audience, the visibility of the performance marks the dissolution of historical time, and expresses the dilemma that the present view can no longer capture the past. Theatrical illusion can neither be built up nor maintained, and the pageant is conspicuous by neither having a recognisable beginning nor a distinct ending. Instead, it starts and finishes with questions and observations by the narrator: "So it was the play then. Or was it the prologue?" (*BA*, 47); "Was that the end? The actors were reluctant to go. They lingered; they mingled" (*BA*, 121).

The scenes of the pageant are signatures of the temporality of aesthetic vision in that they provide a visual means to express that neither a sense of historical teleology nor the continuity of time can be regained. Aesthetic vision brings forth a temporality which resists received models of teleological progress. Moreover, the novel's distinct temporality is incompatible with unifying or harmonising constructions of time. Rather than continuity, the scenes of the pageant emphasise discontinuity and non-identity, and, in doing so, they disclose the character of delusion inherent in any construction of seamless historical continuity.

Consequently, Miss La Trobe's desperate struggle for a cathartic effect on the audience by communicating her vision fails: "Hadn't she, for twenty-five minutes, made them see? A vision imparted was relief from agony … for one moment … one moment. Then the music petered out on the last word *we*. […] She hadn't made them see. It was a failure, another damned failure! As usual. Her vision escaped her" (*BA*, 61).

La Trobe relies on the impact of the theatre's visuality to bring about insight. In her effort to "make them see, douche them with present time" (*BA*, 111) she is confronted by the dilemma of how to convey the present moment without making it realistic. She detects one of the shortcomings of her enterprise and believes that it was: "'Reality too strong,' she murmured" (*BA*, 111). Ironically, the sudden rainfall which literally grants her her wish, and which stops as unexpectedly as it came, presents an even stronger element of reality intervening into the course of the pageant: "Down it poured like all the people in the world weeping. Tears. Tears. Tears" (*BA*, 111). The anthropomorphic rain not only presents one of the many instances in the novel when nature takes over the course of events, and overcomes the division between mankind and nature, but it also answers the recurrent uncertainty about the weather, in uniting opposites and demonstrating that, in the end, it was both "wet and fine".

3.4.2 The rhythm of vision in time

Other than planned by La Trobe, things in the pageant take their own course, and the repetition of "tears" not only emphasises the impact of the present as an elegiac moment of recognition, but it also corresponds to the novel's expansion of the moment by means of threefold repetitions: from the futility expressed by the beating of time of the dying butterfly: "beat, beat, beat" (*BA*, 9); "never, never, never" (*BA*, 10) to the central "Empty, empty, empty; silent, silent, silent" (*BA*, 22) of the room, and the "chuff, chuff, chuff", and the "tick, tick, tick" of the machine during the pageant. The triadic sequences of these repetitions create a cyclical rhythm of musical time, which is present both in the inanimate machines and in nature, when for instance the swallows dance a waltz (*BA*, 113).

The 'time-machine' and the gramophone representing this rhythm are used to indicate the passing of time, and provide both continuity and a sense of unity between individual time and the collective time expressed in the pageant. Like the musical and the mechanical rhythm time produces momentary cohesion: "Time was passing. How long would time hold them together?" (*BA*, 94).

The threefold rhythm is used to overcome mutually exclusive alternatives. In bringing together the audience and the play, time as music also intensifies the characters' vision, and contributes to a harmony between sight and sound: "Music wakes us. Music makes us see the hidden, join the broken. Look and listen" (*BA*, 75). The simultaneity of vision and sound is expressed when the scenery is perceived as a musical score in which swallows transform into notes and trees into bars:

> Real swallows. Retreating and advancing. And the trees, O the trees, how gravely and sedately like senators in council, or the spaced pillars of some cathedral church. . . . Yes, they barred the music, and massed and hoarded; and prevented what was fluid from overflowing (*BA*, 113).

The view of the scenery in terms of a naturalised order creates a pictorial and musical equivalent to the paradox of motion and stasis, word and image, language and silence.

In the pageant, music in many ways is an organising principle and a means of providing continuity. At times when the visual impact of the play does not accomplish the consistency La Trobe desires, she turns to music as a last resort to bridge gaps, to simulate continuity, and to make the audience return to their seats, to watch and be silent: "Down came her hand peremptorily 'Music, music,' she signalled" (*BA*, 76).

Likewise, when theatrical illusion fails, and nothing can either be seen or heard on stage, nature, once again, takes up a part in the play. As an acoustic counterpart to the rain, the choric sounds of the cows contrast the present with the primeval, the mechanical with the natural, they endow the play with emotion, and provide a link between the scenes: "From cow after cow came the same yearning bellow. The whole world was filled with dumb yearning. It was the primeval voice sounding loud in the ear of the present moment. [...] The cows annihilated the gap; bridged the distance; filled the emptiness and continued the emotion" (*BA*, 87). The course of the pageant, however, is mainly governed by inanimate and anonymous sounds. The gramophone generally determines the movement of the audience between the acts and preserves the continuity of the pageant: "Only the tick tick of the gramophone held them together" (*BA*, 95).

Formally, the term interval is used both in the dramatic and the musical sense. The first interval is introduced by the repeated chant of the gramophone "*dispersed are we*" (*BA*, 59/60). Until the audience eventually leaves their seats, the thoughts of the single characters rhythmically alternate with the "wailing" and "moaning" of the gramophone. Mrs. Manresa's suggestion "'Follow, follow, follow me. . . . Oh Mr. Parker, what a pleasure to see you here! I'm for tea'" (*BA*, 60) is followed by Isa's reiterating the "Dispersed are we" (*BA*, 60). The rhyme contradicts the theme of dispersal, formally connects the individuals to each other, and paradoxically unites them in their collective dispersal.

When William Dodge wonders if he should "follow, follow, follow the dispersing company?", the "dispersed are we" both interrupts his thoughts and links them to the rhythm of the music. Likewise, Cobbet of Cobbs Corner, who otherwise conceives of time according to the rhythm in which he waters his plants (*BA*, 68), uses a threefold rhythm when he asks himself about Miss La Trobe's intentions, "'What was in her mind, eh? What idea lay behind, eh? What made her indue the antique with this glamour – this sham lure, and set' 'em climbing, climbing, climbing up the monkey puzzle tree?'" (*BA*, 60). Once again, "monkey puzzle tree" rhymes with the succeeding "dispersed are we". Each character thus contributes both to the dispersal, and to the "we" which holds the rhyme together and creates unity in disparity.

Whereas the other characters seem to be connected to the movement of the crowd and the ebb and flow of the music, Giles is exempt from it: "Giles remained like a stake in the tide of the flowing company" (*BA*, 60). His thoughts neither follow nor precede the "dispersed are we". His motionless, isolated, and self-contained stance is expressed when the narrator produces the rhyme between "wood" and "stood": "'Follow?' He kicked his chair back. 'Whom? Where?' He stubbed his light tennis shoes on the wood. 'Nowhere. Anywhere.' Stark still he stood" (*BA*, 60).

The repeated interventions of the gramophone present an element in a ritualised, mock-liturgical structure of the interval, in which the collective provides a response to the individual and conveys the sense of unity in disparity. The alternation of the rhythm is brought to a closure when Lucy Swithin bids her brother to depart from the scene with her: "'Bart, my dear, come with me. . . . D'you remember, when we were children, the play we acted in the nursery?'" (*BA*, 60). Lucy's "nursery" rhymes with "come with me", but is not immediately followed by a "dispersed are we". Instead, her brother reminisces about their childhood. Unlike other members of the audience, who either follow the crowd, wonder about the play, or remain unsure about what to do at all, Lucy and Bartholomew both relate the play to their past when they compare it to their childhood games, and also to the future, when Bart acknowledges that for them "the game's over" (*BA*, 60). Their distancing themselves from the scene is given further emphasis by the presence of the reporter who notes down their names. Mr. Page, whose name alludes both to a servant and the printed page of a newspaper documenting the present, creates a fleeting sense of the present as being already the past.

The paradoxical union in disparity between forward and backward movement in time is reflected in the ways in which sentences of different meaning resonate with each other in rhythm, and the narrative takes on the rhythm of poetry. The progression of time, which Isa describes as an endless, enduring, interchangeable, and possibly futile course is 'echoed' by Mr. Oliver's repetition of the nursery rhyme:

> 'This year, last year, next year, never,' Isa murmured.
> 'Tinker, tailor, soldier, sailor,' Bartholomew echoed (*BA*, 135).

The rhythm of the nursery rhyme entwines narrative progression and temporal regress, and the passage transports Isa forwards to an endless future and Oliver backwards to childhood. The tripartite rhythm of repetitions and phrases in *Between the Acts* is expressive of the simultaneous presence of a tripartite structure of temporality.

For Lucy and Bartholomew, the end of the novel suggests both the idea of return and of continuation: Lucy returns to her book: "It was time to read now, her *Outline* of History. But she had lost her place. She turned the pages looking at pictures – mammoths, mastodons, prehistoric birds. Then she found the page where she had stopped" (*BA*, 135). For Lucy, the temporal gap created in the second half of the novel by the performance is recast as merely an interruption in her reading. In her final appearance in the novel, she finishes a chapter "quickly, guiltily, like a child who will be told to go to bed before the end of the chapter" (*BA*, 135). The end of the chapter in the outline of history again suggests both a backward movement into prehistory, and a forward movement in the process of reading.

At the end, the hope invested into music and rhythm only temporarily relieves La Trobe's anxiety and eventually does not succeed in creating unity. Neither do the nursery rhymes appease the uneasiness of the audience, who, before the pageant turns to its final scene "the present time. Ourselves", is made to endure a time of waiting for the end. The dramatic display of the present, in which the audience finds itself "in limbo", in a temporal vacuum between past and present, is emphasised by the absence of music, and the inexorable ticking of the time-machine:

> All their nerves were on edge. They sat exposed. The machine ticked. There was no music. The horns of cars on the high road were heard. And the swish of trees. They were neither one thing nor the other; neither Victorians nor themselves. They were suspended, without being, in limbo. Tick, tick, tick went the machine (*BA*, 110).

Rather than with the expected "Grand Ensemble, round the Union Jack" (*BA*, 98), the play ends on the "distorting and upsetting and utterly unfair" (*BA*, 114) ensemble of the audience reflected by the fragments of glass: "And the audience saw themselves, not whole by any means, but at any rate sitting still" (*BA*, 115).

> The view repeated in its own way what the tune was saying. The sun was sinking; the colours were merging; and the view was saying how after toil men rest from their labours; how coolness comes; reason prevails; and having unharnessed the team from the plough, neighbours dig in cottage gardens and lean over cottage gates. The cows, making a step forward, then standing still, were saying the same thing to perfection. Folded in this triple melody, the audience sat gazing (*BA*, 83–84).

Sight and sound merge into the general dissonant uproar when the sounds of cows and dogs provide a background for the audience's reaction towards their fleeting images, which are finally completed by the actors appearing on stage. The visual impact of the mirrors creates the present as an orchestration of fragments of presence, and is further sustained by the temporary ending of time, which recalls the image of the watch in the glass case from the beginning of the novel: "The hands of the clock had stopped at the present moment. It was now. Ourselves" (*BA*, 115).

The division between actors and audience, between present and past is visualised as the wall of civilisation, which is addressed in similar terms as the wall that tragically separates the lovers Pyramus and Thisbe in *A Midsummer Night's Dream*: "*Look at ourselves, ladies and gentlemen! Then at the wall; and ask how's this wall, the great wall, which we call, perhaps miscall, civilization, to be built by* (here the mirrors flicked and flashed) *orts, scraps and fragments like ourselves?*" (*BA*, 116).

Suggesting separation and unity at the same time, the wall, made out of scraps and fragments, prepares for a gradual building up of cohesion among the audience. After the momentary suspension of time, the fragments are recombined and re-arranged into a kaleidoscopic whole at the sound of three notes following one another: "Like quicksilver sliding, filings magnetized, the distracted united. The tune began; the first note meant a second; the second a third" (*BA*, 117).

When the audience is about to leave, the anonymous voice of the loudspeaker asking for contemplation and self-recognition provides a further contraction of time for the audience when it looks at itself in the mirrors. Time is dissociated from rhythm and condensed into minimal units of words: "*before we go* . . . (Those who had risen sat down) . . . *let's talk in words of one syllable, without larding, stuffing or cant. Let's break the rhythm and forget the rhyme. And calmly consider ourselves*" (*BA*, 115).

The passage refers back to an earlier one in the novel where an unidentifiable voice is heard practicing scales in which words of one syllable consisting of three letters are the origins out of which phrases and songs can be composed: "the separate letters formed one word 'Dog'. Then a phrase. It was a simple tune, another voice speaking" (*BA*, 73). The rhythm of musical time is finally broken, when the sound of the gramophone subsides and leaves it open whether unity or dispersal will prevail: "The gramophone gurgled *Unity – Dispersity*. It gurgled *Un . . dis* . . . And ceased" (*BA*, 124).

After the play, the sound of church bells takes over and ends the rhythm of the gramophone, and for Isa the silence in the absence of another note is paralleled by the change of the stage back into being a spot of grass:

> The church bells always stopped, leaving you to ask: Won't there be another note? Isa, half-way across the lawn, listened. . . . Ding, dong, ding . . . There was not going to be another note. The congregation was assembled, on their knees, in the church. The service was beginning. The play was over; swallows skimmed the grass that had been the stage (*BA*, 128).

Corresponding to the triadic sequences of rhythm, the novel develops its temporality within a triadic structure between past, present, and future, in which the paradox of binary oppositions gives rise to a third element, between the oppositions of language and silence, between word and image, and between love and hate.

The threefold structure of repetitions is sustained by the use of monosyllabic, three letter-words, nursery rhymes, scales and wordplays on "cat", "A.B.C." (*BA*, 71), and "Isa". The novel's recurrent pattern of three elements and the number three is most closely linked to Isa's character. Isa is thirty-nine years old, and in the first scene of the novel she finds herself on a three-cornered chair (*BA*, 2), and later faces a three-folded mirror (*BA*, 7). In her initial description, her pigtails and the faded dressing-gown are mentioned three times (*BA*, 2), and the beginning of the novel marks the third time she meets Haines (*BA*, 2). When the play, which keeps 'running' in Isa's head (*BA*, 70), makes her wonder about its meaning, she finds that it does not tell her anything she did not know already and analytically starts thinking in dualisms:

> Did the plot matter? She shifted and looked over her right shoulder. The plot was only there to beget emotion. There were only two emotions: love; and hate. There was no need to puzzle out the plot. Perhaps Miss La Trobe meant that when she cut this knot in the centre? Don't bother about the plot: the plot's nothing (*BA*, 56).

Nevertheless, Isa cannot entirely escape from the play. When she tries to break away from the plot which, apart from being "nothing" to her is mere "verbiage, repetition" (*BA*, 57), she is incapable of doing so. Her silent interruption of a love scene is not only itself a repetition, but casts herself into the role of an actress, when it echoes a line from *A Midsummer Night's Dream* in which Egeus' interrupts and silences Lysander's attempt at an explanation:[61] "It was enough. Enough. Enough" (*BA*, 57).

When the death of an old woman on stage is shown, Isa wishes to take her place and becomes aware of the third element superseding love and hate: "She fell back lifeless. The crowd drew away. Peace, let her pass. She to whom all's one now, summer or winter. Peace was the third emotion. Love. Hate. Peace. Three emotions made the ply of human life" (*BA*, 57). Isa's thoughts about death, and her desire for time to have a stop is expressed when in reflecting her life, she restates the last line from *The Waves*, "The waves broke on the shore" (*W*, 199), which marks the death of Bernard: "'Dispersed are we,' Isabella followed her, humming. 'All is over. The wave has broken. Left us stranded, high and dry. Single, separate on the shingle. Broken is the three-fold ply …'" (*BA*, 60). After the pageant, Isa who only remembers "orts, scraps and fragments" (*BA*, 133) from it, becomes aware of her own isolation, and can no longer connect the three emotions creating the "ply of human life".

Like the mechanicals' play in *A Midsummer Night's Dream*, Miss La Trobe's pageant does not have an epilogue. Instead, her contemplating another play at the end of the day can be read as an epilogue to *Between the Acts*, one which, however, is incapable of producing an ending. In a state similar to that described by Puck in his final appeal to the audience: "If we shadows have offended, /Think but this, and all is mended:/ That you have but slumbered here/ while these visions did appear" (*MND* 5.1. 402–405), for La Trobe words and visions rise to the surface of her mind: "Then something rose to the surface. 'I should group them,' she murmured, 'here.' It would be midnight; there would be two figures, half concealed by a rock. The curtain would rise. What would the first words be? The words escaped her" (*BA*, 130).

The scene she composes prefigures the last scene of the novel, and provides it with a second, if open ending, when Isa and Giles are alone, and inadvertently

---

[61] Egeus: "Enough, enough, my lord; you have enough – " (*MND*, 4. 1. 154).

become actors in the yet unwritten play. Unlike the words she has used in the pageant, unconventional language, words which are not merely descriptive, taken from literary sources, or indicative of historical evidence, gain importance for her: "Words without meaning – wonderful words" (*BA*, 131). Rather than a horizontal linearity, these words provide a vertical model of time rising to the surface of the characters' minds (*BA*, 53) in the here and now. The verticality of time which has been symbolically present in the lily pond is individualised when the water world of the lily pond and its mud illustrate La Trobe's creative process. Like the mysterious pond with its "black cushion of mud" (*BA*, 26) the "fertile mud" of La Trobe's imagination makes words rise to the surface (*BA*, 131). Half-conscious and no longer seeing clearly, she imagines the time, place and characters of a scene, and, after an interruption caused by the starlings settling on a tree,[62] she is able to hear their words:

> The cheap clock ticked; smoke obscured the pictures. [...] She no longer saw them, yet they upheld her, sitting arms akimbo with her glass before her. There was the high ground at midnight; there the rock; and two scarcely perceptible figures. Suddenly the tree was pelted with starlings. She set down her glass. She heard the first words (*BA*, 131).

Similar to "The Moment: Summer's Night", at the end of *Between the Acts*, aesthetic vision takes place in-between the extremes at the moment when visual perception is about to fade in the dusk. La Trobe only gains her aesthetic vision of a play to come when she loses sight of her surroundings, and when she is able to depart from historical reference: "There was no longer a view – no Folly, no spire of Bolney Minster. It was land merely, no land in particular. She put down her case and stood looking at the land. Then something rose to the surface" (*BA*, 130).

In the twilight Isa likewise looks out of the window at the scenery disappearing from sight, and the pageant disappearing from her memory: "she watched the pageant fade. The flowers flashed before they faded. She watched them flash" (*BA*, 134). She longs for a release from her dilemma of being caught in-between two emotions by a future La Trobe appearing out of the bushes: "Love and hate – how they tore her asunder! Surely it was time someone invented a new plot, or that the author came out from the bushes..." (*BA*, 134).

---

62 The image of starlings prompting artistic vision is likewise used in *To the Lighthouse*: "All of this danced up and down, like a company of gnats, each separate, but all marvelously controlled in an invisible elastic net – danced up and down in Lily's mind, in and about the branches of the pear tree, where still hung in effigy the scrubbed kitchen table, symbol of her profound respect for Mr. Ramsay's mind, until her thought which had spun quicker and quicker exploded of its own intensity; she felt released; a shot went off close at hand, and there came, flying from its fragments, frightened, effusive, tumultuous, a flock of starlings" (*TL*, 25).

In her relation with Giles, Isa, who previously "had not spoken to him, not one word. Nor looked at him either" (*BA*, 69), is granted her wish, when, at the end of the novel, both of them obtain the opportunity to act their hitherto "unacted parts" (*BA*, 95, 121, 128). The last scene of the novel balances its main opposition between language and silence, man and woman, when word and image fall into one in the final sentence: "Then the curtain rose, they spoke" (*BA*, 136). In the creation of this new play, however, also a new audience is constituted: the reader, and the future, which Isa had claimed for her generation is not suspended, but postponed into the future of the respective "now" created in the present of reading.

The remaining third element in a paradox, exceeding love and hate, which Isa longs for, and which in the narrative present of *Between the Acts* might be peace, is transferred to a future beyond the time of the novel. Unlike T.S. Eliot's "The Waste Land", which gestures towards a more reconciliatory ending in its threefold repetition of "shantih", "the peace which passeth understanding",[63] *Between the Acts* does not offer a final resolution, and abstains from prophesying a peaceful future.

---

63 T.S. Eliot, *Collected Poems 1909–1962* (London, Boston: Faber & Faber, 1963), 79; 86.

4 The Poetry of Aesthetic Vision in *The Waves*

The paradigmatic tension between the desire to reach unity or fulfilment and the need to defer the moment of final union is crucial to the narrative temporality of aesthetic vision. This paradoxical dynamics in which opposites define one another and are integrated into a synaesthetic perspective also provides a vantage point from which to approach the role of vision in *The Waves* where the novel's theme reflects Woolf's poetic method. The continuous movement of flux and reflux, of creation and renewal and the defiance of finality inherent in Woolf's process of writing finds a metaphorical and structural analogue in the recursive movement of the waves. Woolf adapted the title of her novel from the first line of Shakespeare's sonnet: "Like as the waves make towards the pebbled shore", which not only encapsulates the nexus of time, death and art that threads its way through the novel,[1] but which also indicates the merging of perspectives and genres that Woolf experimented with in *The Waves*.

When she was writing *The Waves*, Woolf intensely explored her own creative practice: "I want to watch & see how the idea at first occurs. I want to trace my own process" (*D* III, 113). The challenge of writing *The Waves* is perhaps best described in a letter to Ethel Smith, where Woolf calls *The Waves* "an impossible book" (*L* IV, 187). The impossibility she addresses refers to literature's attempt to mimetically render the conditions of being and consciousness, and the inherently doomed impetus of the novelist 'to catch life' in an all-encompassing mode. In "Modern Fiction" Woolf points to the way in which Russian fiction presents this impossibility imbricated in life as the very subject of what she considers a "hopeless interrogation" between writer and reader: "It is the sense that there is no answer, that if honestly examined life presents question after question which must be left to sound on and on after the story is over in hopeless interrogation that fills us with a deep, and finally it may be with a resentful, despair" (*CE* II, 109).[2]

---

[1] Bernard refers to the sonnets: "I too will press the flowers between the pages of Shakespeare's sonnets" (*W*, 57), and repeats the line in the scene at Hampton Court (*W*, 140); "Like a long wave, like a roll of heavy waters, he went over me, his devastating presence – dragging me open, laying bare the pebbles on the shore of my soul" (*W*, 57). Bernard's monologues are saturated with lines of poetry. He identifies himself with Lord Byron (*W*, 53) and cites the sonnet "Let me not to the marriage of true minds" in his final soliloquy as part of his private repertoire of phrases (*W*, 173).
[2] Criticism has been alert to the novel's self-inflicted impossibilities, and sometimes censured the aesthetic achievement of *The Waves*. Alex Zwerdling reads *The Waves* as a dead end of experimental prose. *Virginia Woolf and the Real World* (Berkeley: U of California Press, 1986), 12. Franz K. Stanzel speaks of it as an attempt that is technically paralysed. "Die Erzählsituation in

Woolf, however, does not despair, but in her conclusion to "Modern Fiction" asserts that the impossibility to represent is a condition for the multiple possibilities of her art. She conceives of the writer's creative process in images of water, infinity, and a limitless horizon that will become crucial to *The Waves*: "they [English and Russian fiction] flood us with a view of the infinite possibilities of the art and remind us that there is no limit to the horizon, and that nothing – no 'method', no experiment, even the wildest – is forbidden, but only falsity and pretence" (*CE* II, 110).

The Waves, initially named *The Moths*,[3] presents such an experiment with the expanding possibilities of vision in narrative and method. The novel is not merely a manifesto of Modernism, or a "warehouse" for key Modernist narrative techniques, but it is dedicated to the unconventional, the unfinished, and the not yet made that sets out to achieve the impossible and invents a form for itself. *The Waves* interacts with contemporary discourses on form and perception in art, and it uses vision to present a poetic reflection on the possibility of creation through language that goes beyond narrative and combines a variety of literary forms.[4] The novel therefore dispenses with traditional elements of plot. Its structural alternation between the *Interludes* and the episodes encompasses both the notion of Impressionist fixity and narrative flux that results in a modulated, recursive process of reading.

Virginia Woolfs *Jacob's Room, Mrs. Dalloway* und *To the Lighthouse*", *Germanisch-Romanische Monatsschrift*, 35 (1954), 196. Similar to James Naremore (*The World Without a Self*), Mark Hussey dismisses *The Waves* as an aesthetic failure, which in his view is "useful as a storehouse of typical ideas, but not more than this. It is a kind of warehouse in which are found the materials from which novels such as *To the Lighthouse* or *Between the Acts* may be created". *The Singing of the Real World*, 82. Upon completing *The Waves*, Woolf wrote to Clive Bell: "I have finished my book [*The Waves*] – yes – but it is a failure. Too difficult: too jerky: too inchoate altogether. But what's the point of writing if one doesn't make a fool of oneself?" (*L* II, 330).

3 In the first draft of her novel, Woolf considered different possible titles: "The Moths? or the life of anyone, life in general, or, moments of being, or the waves". *Virginia Woolf. The Waves. The two Holograph Drafts*, transcribed and ed. by J.W. Graham (Toronto: U of Toronto Press, 1976), 28. Harvena Richter interprets the moth and the butterfly as metaphors for the central contrast between visibility and invisibility in *The Waves*. Harvena Richter, "Hunting the Moth: Virginia Woolf and the Creative Imagination", *Virginia Woolf. Revaluation and Continuity*, ed. by Ralph Freedmann (Berkeley et al: U of California P, 1980), 13. *The Waves* appeared in two versions. The first one was begun on 10. September 1929 and finished on 10. April 1930. The second version was created between February und May 1931. The corrected typescript went into print in June 1931.

4 Harold Nicholson in his early review of the novel remarks that "[i]t expands the lyrical note which lurks always as the undertone to her writings into something antiphonal, sacerdotal, vatic. There is a note in this book which has never been heard in European literature". *The Critical Heritage*, 266.

The wave-like movement of becoming and receding is metonymical for the novel's poetic texture that draws on dialectical constellations on a number of levels. Through the use of vision, *The Waves* negotiates the relations between the whole and its constituent parts, between impression and form, between the unity and the separation of characters into privacy, and between the text and the reader.

The first part of this chapter is thus concerned with the notion of aesthetic possibility that emerges from the impossibility to represent, and it investigates into the dialectical relation between impression and form in the *Interludes*. The second part examines privacy as a poetic mode and a textual strategy that brings into play models of performance and spectatorship.

4.1 Visibility and form in the *Interludes*

The Waves is founded on an aesthetic interest in the creation of a narrative reality *en miniature*. In an entry into her diary of November 1928, Virginia Woolf adumbrates her ideas for a new novel: "The idea has come to me that what I want to do is to saturate every atom. I mean to eliminate all waste, deadness, superfluity: to give the moment whole; whatever it includes" (*D* III, 209).[5] The paradoxical image of the atom reflects Woolf's concern with minimal forms, and provides a model for the relation between the whole and its parts that is negotiated throughout the novel. The idea of saturation and the metaphor of the atom denoting indivisible and yet fissionable matter also creates a parallel between her conception of her new novel and a scientific experiment.[6]

Woolf designed her novel as a new departure in narrative, which was inspired by the question of "how the whole is held together" (*TL*, 160) that she had pursued in *To the Lighthouse*. She describes her own method in the writer's advice she offers in "A Letter to a Young Poet" (1932):

---

[5] In a letter to Roger Fry, Woolf describes the effect of Proust's style as 'saturated': "Oh if I could write like that! I cry. And at the moment such is the astonishing vibration and saturation and intensification that he procures – there's something sexual in it" (*L* II, 525).

[6] T.S. Eliot creates a similar parallel in "Tradition and the Individual Talent", where he defines the process of depersonalisation in the relation between poetry and the poet, and states that "It is in this depersonalisation that art may be said to approach the condition of science". Eliot describes the activity of the poet's mind in terms of a scientific experiment in which it becomes a "receptacle for seizing and storing up numberless [...] particles", and where in an intensively artistic process of concentration and combination "the fusion takes place, that counts". "Tradition and the Individual Talent", 53; 55.

> That perhaps is your task – to find the relation between things that seem incompatible yet have a mysterious affinity, to absorb every experience that comes your way fearlessly and saturate it completely so that your poem is a whole, not a fragment; to re-think human life into poetry and so give us tragedy again and comedy by means of characters not spun out at length in the novelist's way, but condensed and synthesized in the poet's way (*CE* II, 191).

The problem that Woolf's aesthetics persistently pursues is a problem of relations,[7] in which the holistic notion of unity appears as a regulative idea that consists of and is defined by binary oppositions. It is concerned with the epistemological dualism between the visible and the invisible, the processes of understanding and observation between subject and object, and with the metonymical unity between the whole, the atom, and its parts.[8]

Woolf's aesthetics is replete with notion of the momentary, the single fleeting impression and its relation to a larger concept of form. When she describes her idea of *The Waves*, Woolf conceives of the moment as "a combination of thought; sensation; the voice of the sea" (*D* III, 209). She writes *The Waves* in a phase of extensive critical reflection about the development of literature in opposition to traditional ways of representation.[9] Her critique of the legacy of realism and representation in *The Waves* therefore also manifests itself as a narrative inquiry into processes of vision as they are prominent in contemporary art forms, above all Impressionism. Gombrich characterises the program of Impressionism from 1860 onwards: "If we trust our eyes, and not our preconceived ideas of what things ought to look like according to academic rules, we shall make the most exciting discoveries".[10] Impressionism did not break with the tradition of representation, but aimed at a depiction of reality that was founded on an act of faith in the mimetic potential of visual perception. This inherently positivist fidelity to

---

[7] The question as to when and how unity can be thought of as unity is discussed in analytical philosophy under the epithet 'holism'. In the aftermath of Quine's theories, holism was further investigated by Sellars, Davidson and Brandom. Verena Mayer, *Semantischer Holismus* (Berlin: Akademie, 1997).
[8] Rutherford constructed his model of the atom in analogy to the planetary system, in which the nucleus determined the orbit of the electrons. Bohr, by contrast, applied Max Planck's theory of quanta to the movement of the electrons around a circle, in which they change from one orbit to the next in quantum leaps. An important addition to Bohr's model was Erwin Schrödinger's definition of the quantum particles as standing waves. For analogies between models in the natural sciences and narrative techniques see: Catherine N. Hayles, *The Cosmic Web. Scientific Field Models and Literary Strategies in the Twentieth Century* (Ithaca, London: Cornell UP, 1984).
[9] "Women and Fiction" (1929), "Phases of Fiction" (1929) and *A Room of One's Own* (1929) are crucial to Woolf's theoretical reflection about future forms of writing.
[10] E.H. Gombrich, *The Story of Art* (Oxford: Phaidon, 14th ed, 1984), 406.

the accuracy of perception instigated the Impressionist preoccupation with the effects of sunlight on objects, and hence with colour.[11]

Light and shade were essential to the rendition of an impression of colour and could serve to indicate time and atmosphere. Claude Monet in particular experimented with the serial presentation of one, almost unchanged motif – such as his famous haystacks or the view of Rouen cathedral – at different times of the day or the year. Monet himself uses the term series, and describes his twofold aim to affect the sense perceptions of the viewer, and to present his experience that exceeds mere receptive visual perception.[12] He does not aim at a scientific examination of sunlight at successive times of the day nor does he adhere to an exact temporal sequence, but rather offers a study of varieties.

Woolf-scholarship of the 1970s and 1980s was strongly interested in the influence of the plastic arts and the formalist aesthetics of Roger Fry on her novels.[13] This tendency established itself in analyses of their use of imagery, or in formal comparisons of artistic technique. The *Interludes* in *The Waves* were habitually regarded as analogues to Impressionist paintings and as artistic representations of detailed perceptions. Jack F. Steward compares Woolf's narrative technique in the *Interludes* with the style of Cézanne and draws further parallels between them and the paintings of Seurat, Kandinsky and Monet.[14] Indeed, the nine *Interludes* can loosely be read as descriptions of the same scene, which depicts the course of the sun on a day by the sea. In the early stages of the novel, Woolf conceived of the *Interludes* to connect parts of the plot and also to form a background to it: "The interludes are very difficult, yet I think essential; so as to bridge & also give a background – the sea; insensitive nature – I dont know" (*D* III, 285).

The first *Interlude*, or rather the prologue of the novel, describes a sunrise over the sea that recalls the book of Genesis.[15] The sun separates the sea from

---

11 Renate Brosch analyses the analogies between impressionistic painting and narrative discourse in the 19th century: Renate Brosch, *Krisen des Sehens. Henry James und die Veränderung der Wahrnehmung im 19. Jahrhundert* (Tübingen: Stauffenburg, 2000), 282ff.
12 James Rubin, *Impressionism* (London: Phaidon, 2001), 348.
13 Diane Gillespie and Leslie Hankins, *Virginia Woolf and the Arts* (New York: Pace UP, 1997); Marianna Torgovnick, *The Visual Arts, Pictorialism and the Novel* (Princeton: Princeton UP, 1985); Allen McLaurin, *Virginia Woolf. The Echoes Enslaved* (Cambridge: CUP, 1973); Perry Meisel, *The Absent Father: Virginia Woolf and Walter Pater* (New Haven: Yale UP, 1980); Jesse Matz, *Literary Impressionism and Modernist Aesthetics* (Cambridge: CUP, 2001).
14 Jack Stewart, "Spatial Form and Color in *The Waves*", *TCL* 28, 1 (1982), 86–107.
15 Jane Marcus offers an alternative interpretation, and reads *The Waves* as an anti-imperialist text. She interprets the *Interludes* from a postcolonial perspective as ritualised Hindu prayers to the sun. "'Britannia Rules *The Waves*'", *Decolonizing Tradition: New Views of Twentieth-Century 'British' Literary Canons*, ed. by Karen Lawrence (Urbana: U of Illinois Press, 1992), 136–162.

the sky and awakens animals and plants to life. It is metaphorically related to the divine light, but also to the lamp, the romantic symbol of the artistic imagination,[16] which illuminates a room and makes quotidian objects appear in unfamiliar colours, until eventually the voices of the six characters rise out of nothingness. The text does not follow a traditional plot, but it is determined by a rhythm, which, according to Woolf, should be "in harmony with the painters'" (*D* III, 316).

In the *Interludes*, not unlike the serial paintings of Monet, the effect of time passing is crucial to the appearance of the world. Changes in time are presented as changes in the intensity of sunlight and colour.[17] Differences in form and colour are indicated in changes of perspective.[18] Instead of exploring the Impressionist potential of fiction, however, *The Waves* marks a departure from the positivist optimism inherent in Impressionism. Roger Fry in *Vision and Design* finds fault with the exaggerated "fidelity to appearance" (*VD*, 19) of Impressionism and he criticises the superficiality and formlessness of its artistic vision: "some of them [the painters] reduced the artistic vision to a continuous patchwork or mosaic of coloured patches without architectural framework or structural coherence" (*VD*, 11).[19] Form, design and structure were of course central principles in Fry's conception of Post-Impressionism, and Quentin Bell, in his inaugural lecture on Roger Fry describes the altered status of the artist in Fry's theory: "these painters whom Fry himself christened the 'Post-Impressionists' were able to restore the artist to his old position as a designer and not a mere observer".[20]

Both Woolf and Fry consider the neglect of formal principles as one of the major shortcomings of Impressionism. In *To the Lighthouse*, the appearance of the rather complacent painter Mr. Paunceforte is therefore also used as a parody of how conventional expectations can bring about an inflationary Impressionistic style: "Since Mr. Paunceforte had been there, three years before, all the pictures

---

[16] M.H. Abrams, *The Mirror and the Lamp. Romantic Theory and the Critical Tradition* (London, Oxford: OUP, 1971 [1953]).
[17] The sheer frequency of adjectives of colour in the *Interludes* evokes impressions of colour. Distinct colours or clusters of colours dominate single *Interludes*. The fifth *Interlude* alone uses 42 adjectives of colour to describe the setting at mid-day, and nine to present dusk. Woolf's narrative interest in colours is expressed in her short fiction, such as "Blue and Green" (*CSFWV*, 142–145).
[18] The second *Interlude* is dominated by green. It starts with the combination of green and blue: "*Blue waves, green waves*", and gradually uses lighter colours before it again turns to green: "*green – emerald – green*" (*W*, 16).
[19] Fry excludes Monet and Cézanne from his criticism of conventional Impressionism and its disregard of principles of form.
[20] Quentin Bell, "*Roger Fry*". *Inaugural Lecture delivered in the University of Leeds 2nd December 1963* (Leeds: Leeds UP, 1964), 11.

were like that, she said, green and grey, with lemon-coloured sailing-boats, and pink women on the beach" (*TL*, 13).

Woolf's criticism of early Impressionism was directed against its exclusive commitment to sense impressions and its separation of impression and form. Woolf instead was concerned with relating appearance to form, and to her Fry's formalist, and Post-Impressionist aesthetics presented an integrative model of artistic vision that combined theoretical reflection and sensibility: "While he [Fry] was arguing about the theory of art in the abstract his eye was ranging over the picture...Then there was a moment of fusion, of comprehension...how was it done? By the union, it seemed to me, of two different qualities, his reason and his sensibility" (*CE* IV, 89). Fry argued against an unmediated reception of impressions, and his theory of art focused on the transformation of sense impressions through art. To him the paintings of Cézanne exemplified this ideal: "an art based on passionate study of actual life, but ending in a complete transformation of its data".[21] According to Fry, Cézanne managed to create the link between the "infinite complexity of experience" and "the most simple and logical relations".[22]

Fry's understanding of Post-Impressionism aims at a modification of impressions in combining them with principles of form. In Fry's aesthetic reflections the question of unity is essentially one of the relation between impression and form, in which particles of reality and atomised impressions can be mediated through an underlying 'pattern'.[23] His aesthetics attempts to balance the lack of form in Impressionism by pronouncing a Post-Impressionist practice that he traces from 'vision' to 'design'. He describes his ideal of a synthesis of mimesis and design in what he names 'significant form', where form emerges as an aesthetic reality behind appearance. Fry however emphasises that the kind of unity between form and impression that is so crucial to 'significant form' is itself invisible: "But we must consider that the unity is here essentially poetic and imaginative, and not visual".[24] The merely absorbing eye, the 'pure eye' of Impressionism would

---

21 Roger Fry, *Cézanne. A Study of His Development* (London: The Hogarth Press, 1927), 87.
22 Ibid., 70.
23 For Woolf's conception of reality and her notion of the 'pattern' see: Vera Nünning, *Die Ästhetik Virginia Woolfs* (Frankfurt am Main: Lang, 1990), 46f. Perry Meisel identifies the methodological search for form as Woolf's main objective in narrative: "The classic and enduring question for Woolf, of course, is the question of what form or 'design', as she puts it in 'Modern Fiction,' can 'resemble the vision in our minds,' what method is right to express 'what we wish to express' (*CE* II, 105, 108), with the free expression of temperament the ruling standard in her very conception of writing". Meisel, *The Absent Father: Virginia Woolf and Walter Pater*, 76.
24 Roger Fry, "Introduction", *Discourses on Art by Sir Joshua Reynolds* (London: Seely & Co. Ltd., 1905), xvii.

be incapable of recognising and appreciating what Woolf likewise calls "the pattern", or "the more obscure angles and relationships" (*CE* IV, 157). Form as such remains timeless and abstract, and it would be impossible to make it visible. Woolf similarly considers form as inherently invisible, and maintains: we may not be "in a position to perceive the form itself" (*CE* II, 124).

Invisibility figures as a narrative possibility of creating form, and the invisibility of formal principles was not only discussed in contemporary art history, but in the natural sciences and in philosophical epistemology as well. While art history and the visual media were interested in the potentialities of the visible, epistemology and physics increasingly approached the invisible. As Ann Banfield has shown,[25] the numerous developments in analytical philosophy and the natural sciences at the beginning of the 20th century provided for new fields of metaphors and new semantic potentialities for narrative that effected ways of perceiving reality, and also altered the field from which the metaphors, such as the atom, could be taken.

What to some critics appears as a superficial and Impressionist effect of the *Interludes* is therefore not an unmediated, imitative description, but it is rather sustained by formal and invisible structures. The novel redefines fictional form in terms of metaphor and pattern. In the *Interludes*, form is not only metaphorically present as shapes and lines, such as the "*dark line*" (*W*, 1), and asserts a geometrical form behind the visible surface, but it also refers to the form of the narrative itself. The novel's first sentence: "*The sun had not yet risen*" (*W*, 1), expresses a state of anticipation, and introduces the notion of the yet uncreated, "the thing itself before it was made anything" (*TL*, 193). The seascape that then is created in the course of the text consists of metaphorical surface materiality that is presented as "*slightly creased as if a cloth had wrinkles in it*" (*W*, 1). The momentary impression of this surface, however, is structured by an invisible, underlying perpetual rhythm of the waves that not only combines sight and sound, but in its movement of rising and falling, of 'pausing and drawing out' again introduces the anthropomorphic comparison to the unconscious breathing of a sleeper. Animate and inanimate nature, materiality and the immaterial are fused and captured in the many similes ("*as if a cloth*", "*like a sleeper*", "*as if the white sediment*", "*as if the arm*" (*W*, 1)) that invoke a variety of possible referents and mark the semiotic tension between the approximation and retreat of the poetic image. The scene exceeds denotative description and follows a dramatic structure that culminates in the moment of the risen sun, which emphasises the correlation of

---

[25] Ann Banfield, *The Phantom Table. Woolf, Fry, Russell and the Epistemology of Modernism* (Cambridge: CUP, 2001).

the whole and its parts when *"the fibres of the bonfire were fused into one haze, one incandescence which lifted the weight of the woollen grey sky on top of it and turned it to a million atoms of soft blue"* (*W*, 1). The divisions between form and impression, surface and depth likewise fade when the surface of the sea and also the leaves in the garden become transparent in the all-pervading light. Other than presenting a mere analogue to an Impressionist painting or faithfully rendering empirical perceptual experience, the text uses vision to multiply its references to sense impressions in a way that reflects on experience. It likewise provides a critique of ways of representing vision and reveals the limitations of any exclusively Impressionist or empiricist representation in modelling a fictional world through language where the empiricist reference to reality is counter-balanced by the reference to art. Vision becomes a function of the text that engages the readers in analysing their perception. The novel reflects on vision, it teaches us how to see it, and it insists that we see it in several ways at once.

The *Interludes*, however, appeal to more than just the visual sense, and they also present smell, rhythm and sound. Similar to the dynamics between opacity and transparency, invisible form and visible surface that are presented in the first *Interlude*, in the third *Interlude*, the momentary convergence of separation and choric reunion emerges in the song of the birds: *"the birds that had sung erratically and spasmodically in the dawn on that tree, on that bush, now sang together in chorus, shrill and sharp; now together, as if conscious of companionship, now alone as if to the pale blue sky"* (*W*, 46).

The *Interludes* continually modify the relation between the visible and the invisible, and create a dynamics in which particles merge and disperse again. They correlate angles of perspective which either reduce or magnify the focus of the narrative, and reveal the principle of relation and relativity, which Woolf programmatically describes in "Modern Fiction": "Let us not take it for granted that life exists more fully in what is commonly thought big than in what is commonly thought small" (*CE* II, 107).

The third *Interlude* presents the sunlit and visible world and also its counterpart, the unlit, invisible and phantom world below the sea and underneath the plants. Correspondingly, it mediates between the panoramic view of the sea and the sky and the birds' eye view, which similar to the perspective of the snail in "Kew Gardens", creates a microcosm of possible viewpoints indicated by the repeated use of the suggestive words "perhaps" and "or":

> their eyes glancing, and their heads turned this way, that way; aware, awake; intensely conscious of one thing, one object in particular. Perhaps it was a snail shell, rising in the grass like a grey cathedral, a swelling building burnt with dark rings and shadowed green by the grass. Or perhaps they saw the splendour of the flowers making a light of flowing purple over the beds, through which dark tunnels of purple shade were driven between the stalks. Or they

> *fixed their gaze on the small bright apple leaves, dancing yet withheld, stiffly sparkling among the pink-tipped blossoms. Or they saw the rain drop on the hedge, pendent but not falling, with a whole house bent in it, and towering elms; or, gazing straight at the sun, their eyes became gold beads* (W, 47).

The magnifying view of the birds' eyes fixes objects, reshapes and relativises their proportions. The *Interludes* not only describe the effects of sunlight on objects, but create aesthetic vision which transforms the world of objects into an imaginary one, and brings out features of it which have remained hitherto unseen: "*A plate was like a white lake. A knife looked like a dagger of ice*" (W, 71). Unlike an Impressionist study of varieties of the same object, the transformative gaze of the narrator repeatedly focuses on the views of the sea, the house and the garden, and in the fourth *Interlude* the scene temporarily widens when the course of sunlight is followed to more remote places: "*It lit up the smooth gilt mosque, the frail pink-and-white card houses of the southern village, and the long-breasted, white-haired women who knelt in the river bed beating wrinkled cloths upon stones*" (W, 97).

Form and substance define one another in a paradoxical movement, which alternates between the formation and the concomitant dissolution of outlines. Whereas the early sunlight "*hardens the rocks*", and lays "*sharp stripes of shadow on the grass and the edges of chairs and tables*" (W, 16), objects appear fluid and formless in the vague light of the morning – "*everything became softly amorphous as if the china of the plate flowed and the steel of the knife were liquid*" (W, 11), – at midday, however, they are separated from each other and their distinct form becomes visible: "*[the sun] began to bring out circles and lines*" (W, 47), and in the evening sun are "*lined with shadows*", "*lengthened, swollen and made portentous*" (W, 139).

The recursive temporality of the *Interludes* describes both the creation and the un-creation of form when in the ninth *Interlude* "*sky and sea were indistinguishable*" (W, 157) again, and when a metaphorical sea of darkness inundates the visible world: "*Darkness rolled its waves along grassy rides and over the wrinkled skin of the turf, enveloping the solitary thorn tree and the empty snail shells at its foot*" (W, 159).

The narrative strategies employed in the *Interludes* both evoke and refute mimetic representation, and rely on the invisible notion of form as a counter discourse to Impressionism. *The Waves* indeed transforms the Impressionist gaze in providing it with formal principles, and it undermines the invisible realism of logical empiricism, in creating a formally consistent narrative reality that does not entirely jettison its relation to the describable world. Rather than in the empirical world, however, it is in language, in its reflexive, imaginative, and fluid dimension that *The Waves* finds its narrative ontology.

The *Interludes* are therefore not mere visual analogues to Impressionist paintings. Essentially, they do not even describe the course of the sun on a single day, but rather offer an ekphrastic emulation of perception, which reflects on systems of representation. Aesthetic vision in the *Interludes* becomes a model of how language creates the aesthetic object. Image and text interact and go beyond the boundaries of production and reproduction. The text becomes the realm in which the image appears, and the image becomes the horizon against which the text constitutes itself.[26] This movement of transgression describes a process in which the poetic image strives towards the dynamics of narrative and the narrative text towards the more static condition of the image. What Woolf had described in "Modern Fiction" as the "view of the infinite possibilities of the art [that] remind us that there is no limit to the horizon" (*CE* II, 110) is no longer a matter of poetic assertion, but materialises in the text.

The structure and composition of *The Waves* comprises elements of the threefold process Woolf had described in "Modern Fiction", though not in exactly the same linear succession. Imperceptible impressions are not merely passively registered, but provided with a sense of order ("let us record the atoms as they fall upon the mind in the order in which they fall" (*CE* II, 107)), before, in a second step, their underlying pattern is revealed ("let us trace the pattern, however disconnected and incoherent in appearance, which each sight or incident scores upon the consciousness" (*CE* II, 107)). Pattern and impression, however, are in constant need to be rearranged, and can never be arrested into a static unit. *The Waves* performs this process in its regular structural change between the *Interludes* and the episodes, in which the reflection of form provides a link between the *Interludes* and the novel as a whole, which Woolf called her "abstract mystical eyeless book" (*D* III, 203).

4.2 The "little language" and the private view

The aesthetic impossibility to represent life corresponds to the impossibility of creating any kind of lasting unity between characters. *The Waves* displays this double impossibility, and explores aesthetic vision as a dynamic process that is sustained by the transitory and delicate relation between the visible and the invisible, the self and its other, the separation and merging of voices and views.

---

26 The term 'horizon' is used in Husserl's sense of 'Sinnhorizont' that accompanies processes of understanding. In *The Waves* it metaphorically refers to the visual divide between two elements: air and sea.

Similar to Woolf's earlier novels her aesthetic point of departure in *The Waves* evolves out of discontent with the current state of fiction, and its obeisance to conventional restrictions in presenting character that had preoccupied Woolf when she was planning *Mrs. Dalloway*: "all this I did because there was no convention ready to my hand to establish a link between your mind and my mind".[27] Early on, Lucio Ruotolo describes Woolf's distinct aesthetic objective in creating characters and establishing relations between them: "Virginia Woolf urges the modern writer to face a human dimension that both underlies and transcends 'the fabric of things', to look beneath conventional behaviour into a private world each of us possesses".[28]

As Emily Dalgarno notes, Woolf often engages readers and characters in a game of I-spy in foregrounding the difference and exclusiveness of individual views: "A sense of conflict is often represented by Woolf as the inability of two persons to see the same object in the same way".[29] In "Mr. Bennett and Mrs. Brown", this partiality of perspective becomes a principle of character creation: "You see one thing in character, and I another" (*CE* I, 325).

The narrator in *Jacob's Room* likewise articulates the insurmountable gap between internal and external ways of seeing: "nobody sees anyone as he is" (*JR*, 36), which is also resonant in *Mrs. Dalloway*,[30] *Between the Acts*, and *The Waves*. Whereas Lucy Swithin and Bartholomew Oliver in *Between the Acts* complement each other's way of seeing – "What she saw he didn't, what he saw, she didn't" (*BA*, 15), Bernard in *The Waves* regrets that vision cannot be shared – "'But unfortunately, what I see [...] you do not see'" (*W*, 159) – , and that seeing remains essentially subjective and limited – "A contrast. That I see and Neville does not see; that I feel and Neville does not feel" (*W*, 59).

Processes of vision, of seeing, and observing become crucial to establishing relationships between characters. They do not exclusively gesture towards oneness, the transgression of boundaries, and the union of opposites, but leave open a space in-between, in which perspectives do not merge into a borderless flow of thoughts between characters, but in which both difference and a sense of separation are equally maintained. The dialectical movement of unity and dif-

---

27 Virginia Woolf "Mrs Dalloway Fragments". Holograph pages in notebook dated Hogarth House, Richmond Jan 7, 1924, 107. BERG.
28 Ruotolo, *Six Existential Heroes. The Politics of Faith*, 17.
29 Emily Dalgarno, *Virginia Woolf and the Visible World* (Cambridge: CUP, 2001), 2.
30 Deirdre Gunnison stresses the importance of the reader to complement and complete the image or scene rendered in the text: "'Each of course saw something different': *Mrs. Dalloway* and the experience of the novel", *Virginia Woolf Bulletin*, 6 (Jan. 2001), 23.

ference that had governed the dynamics of impression and form is also at work on the level of characters in *The Waves*. The characters' thoughts and consciousnesses in *The Waves* are hence not just permanently floating together, but also separating into selfhood and privacy.

The relation between a public, objectified view and the subjective privacy of vision therefore constitutes another organising paradox of Woolf's aesthetics. It both enables the reader to capture narrative reality and to read a character, and it expresses the impossibility of the very attempt. The discursive turn towards privacy can be regarded as another counter-movement to conventional representation where the notion of privacy becomes a mode of aesthetic vision that describes a fluid process of both approximation and withdrawal. The elusive pattern of the connection to and the detachment from the aesthetic object in the *Interludes* corresponds to the ways in which the relation between language and the world and between the characters is presented in the episodes. The narrator's vision of nature in the *Interludes* is therefore linked to the perspectives of the six characters in the episodes. The first episode can be read as a new beginning of the novel, which starts with the creation of a world through language. The morning scene in the garden in which the children describe their impressions is reminiscent of "the morning fresh, as if issued to children on a beach" (*MD*, 3) at the beginning of *Mrs. Dalloway*.

> 'I see a ring,' said Bernard, 'hanging above me. It quivers and hangs in a loop of light.'
> 'I see a slab of pale yellow,' said Susan, 'spreading away until it meets a purple stripe.'
> 'I hear a sound,' said Rhoda, 'cheep, chirp; cheep chirp; going up and down.'
> 'I see a globe,' said Neville, 'hanging down in a drop against the enormous flanks of some hill.'
> 'I see a crimson tassel,' said Jinny, 'twisted with gold threads.'
> 'I hear something stamping,' said Louis, 'A great beast's foot is chained. It stamps, and stamps, and stamps' (*W*, 2).

This second beginning of the novel at the same time evokes and frustrates expectations of Impressionist representation, or the straightforward communication of mental images.[31] Like the first *Interlude*, however, it presents a semiotic rendering of perception. In what may seem as a polilogue, in which the children describe what they see, it is impossible to say whether the six voices are speaking about the same thing, whether they describe nature or rather a work of art, or

---

31 Gabriele Schwab considers *The Waves* "one of the most esoteric texts of our century". She likewise interprets this passage as an "esoteric literary language game". *Entgrenzungen und Entgrenzungsmythen: Zur Subjektivität im modernen Roman* (Stuttgart: Steiner, 1987), 94.

if they communicate at all. The passage does not indicate whether the children participate in a game of words denoting synaesthetic processes of signification, or whether they simply play "I spy". Whereas the anaphoras "I see" or "I hear" suggest unison of the voices, the use of the first person respectively separates the speakers.

The idea of circularity and repetition that is suggested by the alternating voices is symbolised by "the ring" or "the globe", and it is counterbalanced by the notion of linearity and progression in the onomatopoetic references to hearing. What the children see or hear is not tied to any visual or auditory referent, but it establishes recurrent leitmotifs of the novel that become associated with the respective voices. In contrast to Bernard, Neville and Susan, who say they see material objects, Louis and Rhoda are connected through their hearing the sounds of animals.

The novel's second invocation of beginnings in minimalist scenic constellations becomes a basis for the creation of a dialogical narrative reality out of the intimacy of a childhood-scene that is created in the children's use of language ("In the beginning there was the nursery" (*W*, 239)). The language in which they utter their impressions is what the text calls "some little language" (*W*, 159). Minimalist forms and poetic language had figured prominently in *To the Lighthouse* and also in *Jacob's Room*, where the relation between perception, consciousness and pre-discursive layers of imagery in children's vision had been conceived of as: "a private code, a secret language" (*TL*, 10). The insufficiency and failure of conventional language to convey her thoughts and the whole of her emotions is described in *To the Lighthouse* by Lily Briscoe, who deems it impossible to find the right words:

> And she wanted to say not one thing, but everything. Little words that broke up the thought and dismembered it said nothing. 'About life, about death; about Mrs. Ramsay' – no, she thought, one could say nothing to nobody. The urgency of the moment always missed its mark. Words fluttered sideways and struck the object inches too low. Then one gave it up; then the idea sunk back again; then one became like most middle-aged people, cautious, furtive, with wrinkles between the eyes and a look of perpetual apprehension (*TL*, 178).

In *Between the Acts*, the hope Miss LaTrobe invests into dramatic creation likewise relies on "words of one syllable" (*BA*, 115), and in *Mrs. Dalloway* the anonymous singer produces sounds "without direction, vigour, beginning or end, running weakly and shrilly and with an absence of all human meaning" (*MD*, 88).

The concern for the yet unmade with "Things [that] quiver as if not yet in being" (*W*, 77), and people's "unacted parts" pervades not only *Between the Acts* and Lily Briscoe's artistic vision in *To the Lighthouse*,[32] but it is also prominent in the reflection of language and vision in *The Waves*: "It is better to look at a rose, or to read Shakespeare as I read him here in Shaftesbury Avenue. [...] This is poetry if we do not write it" (*W*, 130).

The "little language" describes the fragility of aesthetic vision in providing visions of things before they are named, or conventionally made into anything. Neville, who believes that "speech is false" (*W*, 90), voices his nominalist belief that: "Nothing should be named lest by so doing we change it. Let it exist, this bank, this beauty, and I, for one instant, steeped in pleasure" (*W*, 52). For Neville, who like Bernard and Louis considers himself a poet, poetry is not created by the classification of phenomena outside the mind, and he conceives of it as an internal rhythm of the waves: "Now begins to rise in me the familiar rhythm; words that have lain dormant now lift, now toss their crests, and fall and rise, and fall and rise again. I am a poet, yes" (*W*, 52). The recurrent rise and fall of the waves that marks Neville's retreat into his mind, also describes his need for a continuous return to privacy: "But by some inscrutable law of my being sovereignty and the possession of power will not be enough; I shall always push through curtains to privacy, and want some whispered words alone" (*W*, 38).

The language of the children departs from poetical conventions, and this is why it becomes poetic in the original sense of the word. In the realm of privacy, language becomes saturated in itself and does not find any referent outside itself. The "little language" refers to pre-discursive stages of poetry, to minimalist dramatic utterances, and also to the formlessness of prose: "'Heaven be praised,' I said, 'we need not whip this prose into poetry. The little language is enough'" (*W*, 176). "The little language" relates the characters to one another, and creates not only their privacy, but also a private system of reference: "They speak now without troubling to finish their sentences. They talk a little language such as lovers use" (*W*, 93). The characters' intimate exchange is compared to the secret, elliptic language of lovers: "a little language such as lovers use, broken words" (*W*, 159). Like the language of the children, the language of the lovers builds on mutual understanding. In *The Waves* the lovers Louis and Rhoda are connected by their secret code and appear as conspirators and spies: "Louis and Rhoda, the conspirators, the spies at table, who take notes" (*W*, 185). The language of the lovers remains exclusively accessible in the realm of privacy, and the narrator is

---

32 "What she wished to get hold of was that very jar on the nerves, the thing itself before it has been made anything" (*TL*, 193). Cam likewise describes the world of her thoughts: "the dark, the slumberous shapes in her mind; shapes of a world not realised but turning in their darkness, catching here and there, a spark of light" (*TL*, 189).

cast into a position, in which he is only capable to describe, but not to replicate it: "Listen Rhoda (for we are conspirators, with our hands on the cold urn), to the casual, quick, exciting voice of action, of hounds running on the scent. They speak now without troubling to finish their sentences. They talk a little language such as lovers use" (*W*, 93).

The "little language" abstains from completion or wholeness, and differs from the sequential phrase-making that is characteristic of Bernard. In order to gain reassurance, Bernard creates sequences, sentences, and phrases, and alphabetically records them in his book of phrases: "As it is, finding sequences everywhere, I cannot bear the pressure of solitude. When I cannot see words curling like rings of smoke round me I am in darkness – I am nothing" (*W*, 86). In his final soliloquy, Bernard recapitulates his endeavours as a writer, and acknowledges that the finding of a true story is an ever receding goal: "I have made up thousands of stories, I have filled innumerable notebooks with phrases to be used when I have found the true story, the one story to which all these phrases refer. But I have never yet found that story. And I begin to ask, Are there stories?" (*W*, 124). The limitation of phrase-making reveals the imperfection of life, which resists finite representation: "I said life had been imperfect, an unfinished phrase" (*W*, 190). He recognises the failure of merely collecting phrases from experience and of reapplying them to life assuming that they represent it, and it is only when he conceives of himself as the shadowy existence of a self without a self that he imagines a "new world" (*W*, 192). Towards the end of the novel he gradually returns to his almost prelapsarian state of a poet's language, and is "unable to speak save in a child's words of one syllable; without shelter from phrases" (*W*, 192).

The notion of privacy is formally reflected in minimal scenes of observation and corresponds to the use of private, unconventional language. The novel perhaps anticipates the critique of the shortcomings of conventional language in *Between the Acts*, and investigates into the possibility of a language of privacy. Between characters the private code becomes a means of relating the visible of a simulated impression to the invisibility of its effect on consciousness.

Privacy constructs a train of thought which leads through language, and relates vision and consciousness as a kind of private language. The language of the children is characterised by its simple propositions, which allude to their pictorial equivalent, the picture book to which the friends come back at the end of the novel and attempt to revisit their past: "let us turn over these scenes as children turn over the pages of a picture-book and the nurse says, pointing: 'That's a cow. That's a boat'" (*W*, 159). [33]

---

[33] In the first half of the 20th century philosophy and linguistics prominently contributed to the

Other than the children's more private and arbitrary acts of naming, however, the nurse's instructions rely on established systems of reference between sign and signifier. In creating its world through language, *The Waves* refers to a level of imagistic thought, which marks language as devoid of conventional form and meaning.

Woolf was familiar with contemporary philosophical and linguistic debates on language, meaning and privacy such as Bertrand Russell's argument that privacy in the proper sense of the word would refer to the impossibility to express the condition of the real.[34] She writes to Ethel Smith: "I can't altogether lay hands on my meaning. The other thing anyhow interests me much more – the impossibility of one person understanding another" (*L* II, 372). Woolf's interest in this impossibility, however, becomes a possibility of fiction. In her essay "Craftsmanship – Words fail me", she examines the creative potentialities of language, argues against a functional conception of language and maintains that words "hate being useful, that it is in their nature not to express one simple statement but a thousand possibilities" (*CE* II, 246).

In "Letter to a Young Poet", Woolf refers to a similar kind of possibility when she describes the task of the poet who conveys his private vision and challenges pre-conceived perception:

> The poet is trying honestly and exactly to describe a world that has perhaps no existence except for one particular person at one particular moment. And the more sincere he is in

---

discourse of privacy. Bertrand Russell for instance also engages in the general debate, which proliferated in Cambridge circles. Russell distinguishes between public and private language, and defines private language as a kind of language that is governed by a set of rules which can only be grasped by the speakers by way of introspection. The private language is highly subjective, depends on the individual capacity for receiving sense impressions, and is used to articulate the way in which things appear to the speaker. The public language, by contrast, would be a generalisation of private visions in a shared public space. Bertrand Russell classifies the reduction of language to formal propositions inherent in the childrens' language such as: "This is here", "This is now" (*W*, 12) as "atomic propositions". They refer to the subjective naming of objects and states of mind without claiming to describe the actual existence of what they name, or purporting to be objectively provable. Atomic propositions rather provide a combination of content and register which is indifferent to any truth value. Banfield discusses Russell's theory of 'atomic propositions' in depth. *The Phantom Table*, 302ff.

34 Bertrand Russell distinguishes between the appearance of an object in a private space and its public reality. Cf. *The Problems of Philosophy* (London: 1912), 46f: "Again, different people see the same object as of different shapes, according to their point of view. [...] The real space is public, the apparent space is private to the percipient. In different people's private spaces the same object seems to have different shapes; thus the real space, in which it has its real shape, must be different from the private spaces".

keeping to the precise outline of the roses and cabbages of his private universe, the more he puzzles us who have agreed in a lazy spirit of compromise to see roses and cabbages as they are seen, more or less, by the twenty-six passengers on the outside of an omnibus (*CE* II, 189).

In exploring the possibilities of language in poetry, Woolf invokes privacy as a condition for writing, and creates an analogy between the self and words:

> [W]hen words are pinned down they fold their winds and die. Finally and most emphatically, words, like ourselves, in order to live at ease, need privacy. Undoubtedly they like us to think and they like us to feel, before we use them; but they also like us to pause; to become unconscious. Our unconsciousness is their privacy; our darkness their light.[35]

Privacy serves as a category to describe the text as well as a mode of narration that balances the impersonal with the personal and the external with the internal without pretending to arrive at a final synthesis. Woolf's novels draw on the notion of privacy to express the need of the individual to remain inviolate. In the same way as Bernard realises that "stories that follow people into their private rooms are difficult" (*W*, 31), Mrs. Ramsay acknowledges the elusiveness of her character and its resistance to ever be fully revealed: "she took a look at life, for she had a clear sense of it there, something real, something private, which she shared neither with her children nor with her husband" (*TL*, 59). Likewise, in *Mrs. Dalloway*, fanaticism, love and psychiatry are considered to be dangerous for "the privacy of the soul": "love and religion would destroy that, whatever it was, the privacy of the soul" (*MD*, 139).

In her essay on Montaigne Woolf discusses the necessity of this retreat into privacy as the soul's freedom to explore and experiment: "Without other guide, and without precedent, undoubtedly it is far more difficult to live well the private life than the public. [...] But it is an art; and the very material in which it works is variable and complex and infinitely mysterious – human nature" (*CR* I, 64). Woolf reads Montaigne's essays both as a praise of privacy and as an "attempt to communicate a soul" (*CR* I, 64): "'C'est une vie exquise, celle qui se maintient en ordre jusques en son privé'" (*CR* I, 64).

In the same way as the impossibility to represent privacy warrants the independence of the text, the private life of the self, and the necessary aesthetic impossibility to lastingly unite inner and outer perspective preserve the freedom

---

[35] Virginia Woolf, "Craftsmanship – Words fail me", delivered Thursday, April 20th, 1937, 6–8. BERG. (*CE* II, 251).

of the individual mind. To Woolf Montaigne is an example of this sovereignty of the creative self:

> The laws are mere conventions, utterly unable to keep touch with the vast variety and turmoil of human impulses; habits and customs are a convenience devised for the support of timid natures who dare not allow their souls free play. But we, who have a private life and hold it infinitely the dearest of our possessions, suspect nothing so much as an attitude. Directly we begin to protest, to attitudinise, to lay down laws, we perish. [...] Let us simmer over our incalculable cauldron, our enthralling confusion, our hotch-potch of impulses, our perpetual miracle – for the soul throws up wonders every second. Movement and change are the essence of our being; rigidity is death; conformity is death: let us say what comes into our heads, repeat ourselves, contradict ourselves, fling out the wildest nonsense, and follow the most fantastic fancies without caring what the world does or thinks or says (*CR* I, 63).

Privacy becomes an aesthetic possibility in that it implies the presence of a remainder, of something which cannot be directly or entirely grasped. It describes an intermediate state between characters and between the reader and the aesthetic object. The relation between unity and difference pertaining to it creates a reflexive retreat of the subject towards itself, in which privacy becomes a mode of self-reflection in the formation of the aesthetic subject.

In "Mr. Bennet and Mrs. Brown" Woolf envisions this fictional reality of the private view when she discusses the creation of character: "To be 'real'," a character must have

> the power to make you think not merely of itself, but of all sorts of things through its eyes – of religion, of love, or war, of peace, of family life, of balls in country towns, of sunsets, moonrises, the immortality of the soul. [...] And in all these novels all these great novelists have brought us to see whatever they wish us to see through some character. Otherwise, they would not be novelists; but poets, historians, or pamphleteers (*CE* I, 325–326).

In *The Waves*, characters have a similar function: "Everything that happens in *The Waves* happens through someone". Gillian Beer writes: "Their senses are the medium as much as their opinions".[36] In "Mr. Bennet and Mrs. Brown", Woolf further stresses that the gaze indeed is not isolated or solipsistic, but mutual when she writes: "I believe that all novels begin with an old lady in the corner opposite" (*CE* I, 324). In *Mrs. Dalloway* the 'old lady opposite' (*MD*, 139) becomes a symbol of "the privacy of the soul". *The Waves* similarly relies on the formation of opposites and mutuality. In scenes of intersubjective exchange and retreat into

---

[36] Gillian Beer, "Introduction", *The Waves* (London: Vintage, 2000), xviii.

privacy the novel presents both the characters' subjective consciousnesses, and the shifting relations between them.

The six characters form a private nucleus. In the first episode of the novel, the first words spoken by Bernard refer to the ring as a leitmotif and a structural element of the novel.[37] Schematically, the outer ring of *The Waves* describes the cyclical sequence of the hours of the day, whereas the inner ring refers to the constellation of characters around the absent other of Percival. The idea of communion and oneness suggested by the ring is paralleled by the leitmotif of the red carnation: "A single flower as we sat here waiting, ... – a whole flower to which every eye brings its own contribution" (*W*, 82). "Every eye" in this passage does not only refer to the eye of the observer, but also to the single characters to whom "I" becomes almost a name which is interchangeable, and which is alternately taken up by the single voices: "I am not one person; I am many people; I do not altogether know who I am – Jinny, Susan, Neville, Rhoda or Louis; or how to distinguish my life from theirs" (*W*, 185). In referring to themselves as "I", the characters both join the inner ring, and become indistinguishable from one another, and assert their separate subjectivity: "For this is not one life; nor do I always know if I am man or woman, Bernard or Neville, Louis, Susan, Jinny, or Rhoda – so strange is the contact of one with another" (*W*, 188). The pronoun "I" is at once inclusive and exclusive for the characters, but it does not refer to anything outside them.

Each of the characters, however, has a different way of relating to the group of friends, and to life in general. Bernard, the writer, approaches what he sees by inventing stories about it in a similar way as Woolf had described it in "Mr. Bennett and Mrs. Brown". In a train compartment, it is the presence of others which inspires him to invent stories about them: "But if I find myself in company with other people, words at once make smoke rings – see how phrases at once begin to wreathe off my lips" (*W*, 42). Bernard not only constantly observes, but also constantly creates what he sees in phrases. Whereas Neville relies on introspection, Bernard permanently needs opposites to create stories and also to create himself. He is both a creator of words and is himself created by them:

> But I only come into existence when the plumber, or the horse-dealer, or whoever it may be, says something which sets me alight. [...] For they bring me into existence as certainly as you do. [...] I am made and remade continually. Different people draw different words from me (*W*, 88).

Bernard believes that "We are creators" (*W*, 96), and like him all of the characters create themselves through private visions expressed in minimal declarative

---

[37] Marilyn Tanger, "Looking at *The Waves* through the Symbol of the Ring", *VWQ* III, 4 (1974), 241.

propositions like "This is", "I am", or "There is Jinny" (*W*, 78), "That is Bernard" (*W*, 79). Their monological statements, however, imply the possibility of communication in the same way as their creation of themselves relies on mutual exchange: "'Let me then create you. (You have done as much for me.) [...] 'Am I right? Have I read the little gesture of your left hand correctly?'" (*W*, 54).

Like the characters' reciprocal visions and creations of themselves, narrative reality in *The Waves* never describes a stable state of being, but is continuously formed through shifting references. These shifts are sustained by the interchange of unification and dispersal. Despite the close ties between the six friends, single characters like Rhoda or Louis feel left out from their inner circle: "What the fissure through which one sees disaster? The circle is unbroken; the harmony complete. Here is the central rhythm; here the common mainspring. I watch it expand, contract; and then expand again. Yet I am not included" (*W*, 60).

Even though Bernard does not sense separation between himself and others ("I do not believe in separation. We are not single" (*W*, 43)), he also believes that "A good phrase, however, seems to me to have an independent existence. Yet I think it is likely that the best are made in solitude" (*W*, 43). Bernard expresses the ambivalence of the writer's public and private self: "I am not one and simple, but complex and many. Bernard, in public, bubbles; in private, is secretive" (*W*, 48). He both needs to be exposed to impressions and to "the illumination of other people's eyes" (*W*, 75), and to retreat into solitude. Bernard is torn between the desire to immerse himself into a union with others, and the need of detachment, and yet he realises that his longing to unite and to understand is bound to remain unfulfilled:

> to indulge impossible desires to embrace the whole world with the arms of understanding – impossible to those who act. Am I not, as I walk, trembling with the strange oscillations and vibrations of sympathy, which, unmoored as I am from a private being, bid me embrace these engrossed flocks (*W*, 74).

The dynamics of attachment and separation between characters is likewise reflected in the structure of the novel. The characters' uniting and dispersing, and their alternately assuming and discarding identities describes a cyclical movement analogous the kaleidoscope:[38] "Meeting and parting, we assemble different forms,

---

[38] The kaleidoscope was invented in 1815 by Sir David Brewster, who regarded it as a combination of beauty, symmetry and productivity. Jonathan Crary, *Techniques of the Observer* (Cambridge, Mass.: MIT Press, 1991), 116. In "The Captain's Death Bed", Woolf creates a parallel between the activity of the mind and the kaleidoscope: "[T]he Captain's mind is like a kaleidoscope"(*CE* I, 179).

make different patterns" (*W*, 112). Their monologues follow a kaleidoscopic pattern of repetition, and fragments of the single characters' speeches resurface in Bernard's final soliloquy. The rhythmic modulations between the amalgamation and dispersal of parts create constellations between characters as well as the transition from one speaker to the next in a serial process of change in perspective.

The novel's alternation between the *Interludes*, the narrative and dialogic passages likewise follows a cyclical and kaleidoscopic rhythm that marks the interplay between form and substance, and between solidity and flux. The combination of sense impressions inside the kaleidoscope is transitory and variable, and yet symmetrical as changes in colour and form are reflected between the mirrors. The arrangement of particles and fragments inside the kaleidoscope, their breaking apart and reuniting is contingent and without any stable referent. The notion of perception inherent in the kaleidoscope hence is one of permanent change and renewal, in which each configuration of fragments marks only a temporary state, and never a definite image.

In his final soliloquy, Bernard sums up his life, as well as the shifting constellation between characters: "Was this, then, this streaming away mixed with Susan, Jinny, Neville, Rhoda, Louis, a sort of death? A new assembly of elements? Some hint of what was to come?" (*W*, 187). The assembly, dispersal and re-assembly of characters is reflected in their view of themselves. It is particularly Louis and Rhoda, who are paradoxically united in their feeling of fragmentation. Whereas Louis is able to gather the fragments – "my shattered mind is pieced together by some sudden perception" (*W*, 23) – Rhoda fails to reconnect the fragments of her being: "I am broken into separate pieces; I am no longer one" (*W*, 69).

The novel evokes the visual analogy to the kaleidoscope and the mosaic to express the movement of its structure and imagery. In the second *Interlude*, the garden is described as a "*mosaic of single sparks*": "*the dew dancing on the tips of the flowers and leaves made the garden like a mosaic of single sparks not yet formed into one whole*" (*W*, 16). When the image returns in Bernard's final soliloquy it suggests cyclical renewal and the continuous presence of the uncreated (*W*, 165). At the end of his monologue, Bernard does not resign to fate, but overcomes his lethargy, and is ready to continue the ongoing endeavours of the writer to create a new whole out of kaleidoscopic pieces:

> It is the effort and the struggle, it is the perpetual warfare, it is the shattering and piecing together – this is the daily battle, defeat or victory, the absorbing pursuit. The trees, scattered, put on order; the thick green of the leaves thinned itself to a dancing light. I netted them under with a sudden phrase. I retrieved them from formlessness with words (*W*, 191).

The idea of "piecing together" is guided by a holistic notion of order that corresponds to the process of narration as it is reflected in the kaleidoscopic structure of the novel:

> Let us again pretend that life is a solid substance, shaped like a globe, which we turn about in our fingers. Let us pretend that we can make out a plain and logical story, so that when one matter is dispatched – love for instance – we go on, in an orderly manner, to the next (*W*, 178).

Within the 'orderly manner' in which the isolation of impressions or characters alternates with their unification, privacy, created in minimal dialogical scenes, provides a momentary element of pause: "The leaves now are thick in country lanes, sheep cough in the damp fields; but here in your room we are dry. We talk privately. The fire leaps and sinks, making some knob bright" (*W*, 55). The private conversation provides a sense of structure and order in the characters' lives: "After quarrelling and reconciliation I need privacy – to be alone with you, to set this hubbub in order" (*W*, 119). The text mentions this privacy between characters but does not expose it nor does it venture beyond the single character's minds: "It does not matter what I say. Crowding, like a fluttering bird, one sentence crosses the empty space between us. It settles on his lips. I fill my glass again. I drink. The veils drop between us. I am admitted to the warmth and privacy of another soul" (*W*, 67).

In referring to its own status as language, the text withdraws from depicting the other, and instead uses the metaphors of the bird and the veil to release the reader's imagination. Private visions relate internal and external perspectives, and mark the intimacy of intersubjective exchange. Privacy is a state only momentarily reached by the characters. Visions in private are vulnerable and sensitive, and the text stages its own ways of refraining from the intrusion into another's privacy. The children for instance try to imagine their teachers in their private rooms (*W*, 27; 30–31), but, at the same time, caution themselves not to go too far: "But stories that follow people into their private rooms are difficult" (*W*, 31).

Privacy is a term for the impossible and unattainable, and yet it also evokes its opposite, the need to communicate, the need for the public, and the need for reflection. The notion of privacy as a means of defining the self both attracts and deters the characters, and as much as they express their need for closeness, a permanent retreat into privacy would mean a threatening confinement. Rhoda desires to break free from privacy,[39] and defiantly indulges in anonymity: "Now I

---

[39] Susan Gorsky, "The Central Shadow:' Characterization in *The Waves*", *Modern Fiction Studies*, 18 (1972), 47.

will walk down Oxford Street envisaging a world rent by lightning; [...] I like the passing of face and face and face, deformed, indifferent. I am sick of prettiness; I am sick of privacy. I ride rough waters and shall sink with no one to save me" (*W*, 104–105).

Bernard likewise voices the ambivalence of privacy, and expresses the insight that he only becomes aware of himself when parts of his character are visible to others: "The truth is that I am not one of those who find their satisfaction in one person, or in infinity. The private room bores me, also the sky. My being only glitters when all its facets are exposed to many people" (*W*, 123).

The characters' self depends on relationships. The notion of an other remains a narrative necessity, and a character's introspection is inextricably linked to their need to be seen by somebody else. Privacy enables characters like Bernard to expand the idea of his self by dividing it into a private and a public self, which makes it possible for him to acquire a performative sense of himself in which he is able to perceive himself as an other: "But *you* understand, *you*, my self, who always comes at a call" (*W*, 49).

In *The Waves* the character of Percival is an invisible other who cannot be reached, who recedes and eventually disappears, but who remains a magnetic core in the text to which the other characters are repeatedly drawn in order to re-define themselves. In being invisible, Percival is a lacuna, an imaginative point of reference, and a centre of privacy to which Neville and Bernard, in particular, return to create themselves. Bernard realises that in order to be a poet, and to make phrases, he needs the silence of Percival: "I recover what he was to me: my opposite" (*W*, 102). The loss of Percival is in part also a loss of Bernard's self and his ability to write poetry, and he suffers because he is no longer able to share what he sees with anyone: "I see sights that make me weep. For they cannot be imparted. Hence our loneliness; hence our desolation. I turn to that spot in my mind and find it empty. My own infirmities oppress me. There is no longer him to oppose them" (*W*, 102).

In his final monologue then Bernard takes the place of his opposite, Percival, and notices that in the process he himself becomes increasingly invisible. Unseen even by his friends, he leads the shadowy existence of a phantom: "And I, too, am dim to my friends and unknown; a phantom, sometimes seen, often not" (*W*, 184).

Bernard's soliloquy becomes a dialogue in which he remains both within and outside of his self, and in which minimalist units of speech are rendered within equally minimalist scenes of observation in which he reflects about himself and his friends. His immersion into the past is presented in the expansion of his viewpoint, which includes the lives of others "I am not one person; I am many people; I do not altogether know who I am – Jinny, Susan, Neville, Rhoda, or Louis; or how to distinguish my life from theirs" (*W*, 185). Bernard's extension of his self when looking into the past, however, is counterbalanced by the contraction of it when he speaks about himself in his present phantom-like state. Although unity with the others continues to remain a possibility to him, he realises that he can never lastingly reach it: "We saw for a moment laid out among us the body of the complete human being whom we have failed to be, but at the same time, cannot forget. All that we might have been we saw" (*W*, 185).

Privacy marks the impossibility of positivist immediacy as well as the impossibility to lastingly unite one's gaze with that of an other. *The Waves*, which Woolf calls "the playpoem" presents this dialogic process in terms of performance. Bernard increasingly sees life as role-play, and expresses his need for an audience: "Also I like to find the pageant of existence roaring, in a theatre for instance" (*W*, 181). He addresses an implicit spectator when he describes the asymmetry in observing himself and at the same time being observed by the person opposite him. His attempt to adopt the perspective of the other results in his descriptions of a sequence of objective observations that take the form of stage directions and resume the game of I spy:

> But unfortunately, what I see (this globe, full of figures) you do not see. You see me, sitting at a table opposite you, a rather heavy, elderly man, grey at the temples. You see me take my napkin and unfold it. You see me pour myself out a glass of wine. And you see behind me the door opening, and people passing. But in order to make you understand, to give you my life, I must tell you a story – [...] I begin to long for some little language such as lovers use, broken words, inarticulate words, like the shuffling of feet on the pavement (*W*, 159).

Sight alone does not convey privacy, knowledge or understanding, and Bernard longs for "a little language" to relate the story of his life to his opposite. The difference between the character's inner view of the self and the spectator's gaze illustrates the impossibility of visual perception to equate the internal and the external viewpoint.

> I, who had been thinking myself so vast, a temple, a church, a whole universe, unconfined and capable of being everywhere on the verge of things and here too, am now nothing but what you see – an elderly man, rather heavy, grey above the ears, who (I see myself in the glass) leans one elbow on the table, and holds in his left hand a glass of old brandy (*W*, 196).

The characters' views of themselves are frequently rendered in images of infinite expansion and saturation: "Immeasurably receptive, holding everything, trembling with fullness, yet clear, contained – so my being seems" (*W*, 195). Compared to the immensity of the character's being, the perception of their outward appearance by the reader/spectator remains deficient and unavoidably reductive: "I am merely 'Neville' to you, who see the narrow limits of my life and the line it cannot pass. But to myself I am immeasurable; a net whose fibres pass imperceptibly beneath the world" (*W*, 142).

The visible outside of a character is ambivalent, because it marks a boundary to the observer. When this boundary dissolves characters are confronted with the danger of losing themselves and containing nothing. In *The Waves*, characters are aware of the division within themselves and they compare themselves to actors. In his soliloquy Bernard interprets his existence in terms of Greek theatre, in which speakers are absorbed by the chorus and in which the actor can both experience the immersion into the chorus and detach himself from it.

> The sound of the chorus came across the water and I felt leap up that old impulse, which has moved me all my life, to be thrown up and down on the roar of other people's voices, singing the same song; to be tossed up and down on the roar of almost senseless merriment, sentiment, triumph, desire (*W*, 187).

The relation between the chorus and the actor further illustrates the inclusion of an individual perspective into a more general horizon. The chorus describes this dialectical state of the subject as an observer and as the observed, which is mediated by the musical and at the same time wave-like rhythm. Woolf uses choric figures of women like Mrs. McNab in *To the Lighthouse* and the old woman singing with a "voice of no age or sex, the voice of an ancient spring spouting from the earth" (*MD*, 88) in *Mrs. Dalloway*. Both women remain highly ambiguous. Mrs. McNab who, like a classical chorus, relates terrible events like the World War or the death of Mrs. Ramsay, nevertheless works towards the recreation of the summerhouse, and the old woman in the street is a counterpart to Peter Walsh, and yet she includes him in the quest for love and unity. Like Peter Walsh, Septimus Smith also encounters a choric opposite when he hears the London sparrows singing "freshly and piercingly in Greek words" about "life beyond a river where the dead walk, how there is no death" (*MD*, 26). The birdsong, and the broken, reduced syllables uttered by the woman in her "singing of love" (*MD*, 89), which to Peter Walsh mark an "absence of all human meaning" (*MD*, 88), constitute a "little language" to create the self in the absence of an other.[40] This self, as Clarissa Dalloway meditates, is not tied to appearances, but relies on an unseen part which can take up many different roles:

---

[40] Hillis Miller has identified the origin of the woman's song in Richard Strauß' "Allerseelen", which refers to the reunion with the dead. *Fiction and Repetition: Seven English Novels* (Oxford: Basil Blackwell, 1982), 190.

that since our apparitions, the part of us which appears, are so momentary compared with the other, the unseen part of us, which spreads wide, the unseen might survive, be recovered somehow attached to this person or that, or even haunting certain places, after death. Perhaps – perhaps (*MD*, 167).

The theatrical sense of the self as actor and spectator, and the ability to be both inside and outside of one's consciousness is equally endorsed by Bernard. Although Neville had told him: "But you are not Ajax or Percival" (*W*, 119), Bernard in the end takes up the roles of both. Like Rhoda, who, when contemplating death, had thought about Ophelia[41] as a model, Bernard, in his gradually drawing to his own absence and invisibility, becomes a substitute for the absent Percival, and finally takes up the role of Ajax when he borrows the words of the Greek hero: "Ὦ θάνατε θάνατε"[42] to unheroically fling himself towards death (*W*, 198). To create as well as to uncreate himself, Bernard needs an opposite in the same way in which he needs, as it seems, a text through which to assert the immortality of an other.

The privacy of aesthetic vision, and the privacy of language become dialectical modes of expression that relate the reader to the text and the characters to each other, and yet imply the impossibility of maintaining a lasting relation between the self and the other. The dynamics between unity and withdrawal is expressed in the building up and the concomitant suspension of the formal confines of monologue and dialogue in a dramatic setting which involves the reader as spectator. In *The Waves* Woolf experiments with language in the way in which she had envisioned it in "On not knowing Greek", where she emphasises the poetic potential of the chorus:

> The intolerable restrictions of the drama could be loosened, however, if a means could be found by which what was general and poetic, comment, not action, could be freed without interrupting the movement of the whole. It is this that the choruses supply; the old men and women who take no active part in the drama, the undifferentiated voices who sing like birds in the pauses of the wind; who can comment, or sum up, or allow the poet to speak

---

41 Rhoda describes her vision of her own death-scene analogous to *Hamlet* 4. 7. 166–183. "Who then comes with me? Flowers only, the cow-bind and the moonlight-coloured May. Gathering them loosely in a sheaf I made of them a garland and gave them – Oh, to whom? We launch out now over the precipice. Beneath us lie the lights of the herring fleet. The cliffs vanish. Rippling small, rippling grey, innumerable waves spread beneath us. I touch nothing. I see nothing. We may sink and settle on the waves. The sea will drum in my ears. The white petals will be darkened with sea water. They will float for a moment and then sink. Rolling me over the waves will shoulder me under. Everything falls in a tremendous shower, dissolving me" (*W*, 137).
42 Sophocles, *Ajax*, l. 854.

himself or supply, by contrast, another side to his conception. Always in imaginative literature, where characters speak for themselves and the author has no part, the need of that voice is making itself felt (*CE* I, 5–6).

In *The Waves* Woolf has found the poetic means to redefine the aesthetic possibility of the voice to express the singular and the general, and to both connect to an opposite and to stay apart from it. The discourse of privacy in *The Waves* likewise depends on the difference between world and self, the singular and the common voice, between the visible and the invisible particularly when it calls this distinction into question.

The novel's composition follows a hermeneutical logic, in which Impressionist visibility and formal narrative invisibility are positioned as composites that mutually shape each other. In relying on the notion of impossibility of a final synthesis or all-encompassing unity, the aesthetic creation of vision in narrative is revealed as a potentially interminable, dynamic process that involves the poetic creation of vision through language and the dramatic performance of a self in need of an other.[43] The aesthetic impossibility of privacy balances distance and closeness, the microscopic and the macroscopic view, the unseen and the unsaid. *The Waves* simultaneously denies and affirms the possibility of creating meaningful relations between the self and others.

The ideal of unity proposed by Woolf therefore is not a predetermined kind of harmony initiated by the author, but describes an ideal that is ultimately not to be reached. It is created in the process of writing, which is founded on processes of selection and fission. As she describes it in her interpretation of Montaigne "it is life that becomes more and more absorbing as death draws near, one's self, one's soul, every fact of existence" (*CE* III, 25). It is the sense of finality and the impossible that reinforces the intensity of singular impressions. At the end of *The Waves*, the structural notion of return is re-established in the novel's closing metaphor in which nature, and impressions of sight and sound again take over the role of the chorus, when "*The waves broke on the shore*" (*W*, 199).

In describing a seemingly paradoxical world in which the evanescent strives towards the ever lasting, and the ever lasting only comes into existence in the ephemerality of the moment, Woolf's works aspire to include the readers' experience. They create and uphold the objective of unity, and yet, formally reveal its

---

[43] Hans Robert Jauss takes up Gadamer's theory, and describes the impossibility of a complete melting of the horizons in hermeneutics, which marks understanding as an infinite process. *Ästhetische Erfahrung und literarische Hermeneutik* (Frankfurt am Main: Suhrkamp, 1982), 27.

indebtedness to partiality and difference, and imply that lasting unity is in itself a fiction.

In *The Waves*, the privacy of vision marks the transition from aesthetic vision into *poiesis*, in which the impossibility to represent describes the condition of possibility for literary creation. The privacy of aesthetic vision serves as a paradigm of this poetic creation, in which the beholder partakes in the construction of the aesthetic object.

Conclusion

> Among the writers there are two kinds: there are the priests who take you by the hand and lead you straight up to the mystery; there are the laymen who imbed their doctrines in flesh and blood, and make a complete model of the world without excluding the bad or laying stress upon the good. [...] There can be no more forcible presentation than this where all actions and passions are represented, and instead of being solemnly exhorted we are left to stray and stare and make out a meaning for ourselves (*CR* I, 17).

Woolf, like Chaucer to whom she refers, would have considered herself a laywoman. She did not adhere to any hegemonic philosophical school or stay dogmatically faithful to any critical approach. Likewise, she did not embrace any single conception of vision and the visual. Vision in this study has proved a fertile category to explore her aesthetics, which emerges out of a continuous quest into the elusive processes of vision in narrative, and the resistance to the impulse to draw on visual perception as the source of unmediated experience and clearly referential meaning. Instead, her works present an engagement with the complex acts of seeing and simultaneously, with the invention of aesthetic vision in narrative.

Woolf devised an aesthetics which challenged the prevailing forms and discourses on vision, and, more profoundly, the solely epistemological function of sight. Her criticism of conventional modes of seeing goes hand in hand with a criticism of traditional views on reality, and her aesthetics presents a critique of empirical sight and expresses a loss of faith into the exactitude of objectivist epistemology.

Woolf's aesthetics of vision is clearly distinct from the Edwardian observation. It destabilises the representational logic between the original and its reproduction, and disappoints readers who expect vision to conform to their notions of mimesis. As a textual strategy to elicit and then thwart the readers' expectations, aesthetic vision rather becomes a means to reconsider given notions of representation and the criteria with which to evaluate conventional modes of such representation.

Woolf's treatment of vision discovers the fluid interactions between the subject and the object of the gaze. Her fiction conveys an inherently dynamic and relational conception of the image in which dissolution and concentration of impressions and perceptual fragments alternate and cannot be expected to amalgamate into one consistent picture.

The ways in which Woolf's literary aesthetics conceptualises sight describe processes of seeing and perception as processes of differentiation and distancing. The differentiation into metaphorically and semantically distinct ways of seeing implies the necessity for her characters and also her readers to adopt various standpoints and perspectives.

Woolf's aesthetics of vision is therefore sustained by opposites and paradoxes. What seems to underlie her works as a persistent duality is the potentiality of aesthetic vision to divide itself in order to create new relations between immediacy and abstraction, between subject and object, between time and timelessness, the universal and the particular, and within the aesthetic subject itself. It is an art of transition, which does not necessarily diminish, or take the edge off the extremes, but which is about finding links to create a momentary whole, of metaphorically making the reader 'see' one thing in terms of another, and of suggesting ways in which to renew and revise one's angle of vision.

Virginia Woolf's novels are marked by a characteristic tension in their presentation and their assessment of vision. They on the one hand offer a reappraisal of the potential of phenomenal and quotidian sight, the perception of details and the immediacy of impressions, and, on the other hand, they limit the scope of bodily sight as an exclusive prerequisite of aesthetic creation.

The dynamic interplay between sensuous and non-sensuous vision creates a structural movement of Woolf's aesthetics of vision which both evokes and refutes the visible as a referent. Woolf's aesthetics relies on the difference between the immediate, sensuous and visible impression, and an abstract, ideal – a decidedly unvisual vision. Her characters like Mrs Dalloway both expose themselves to the quotidian world of impressions and retreat from it, and their way of seeing is always compounded by their way of relating to the invisible. In *Mrs Dalloway*, the text itself poses as a metaphor of the gaze when it presents a character's way of seeing.

The difference between phenomenological immediacy and abstraction, between ordinary sight and traumatic visions, and between the merely receptive and the analytical, or artistic gaze is fundamental to Woolf's many creations of character-constellations in *Mrs Dalloway*, *To the Lighthouse* and *The Voyage Out*. Woolf's semantics of seeing provides models for the relationship between characters and the fictional world of the novel, and she uses the division of the gaze into eye and brain to occasionally polemicise against the contemporary media scene. Woolf's treatment of vision sets itself against merely receptive and normative concepts of it. The narrative differentiation into ways of seeing counters the notion of a totalising and objectified view of the world, and instead explores the dynamics of narrative perspective.

This narrative concern with seeing and being can be extended to Woolf's interest in Greek philosophy, literature and paradigms emerging from Platonism. Woolf's aesthetics of vision owes more to the Platonist dissociation between immanence and ideality than to contemporary ontology. Platonist themes and constellations provided a basis for Woolf's inquiry into the functions of light and colour, and the immanence of *eros* as an aesthetic strategy. Woolf at the same time uses Platonist notions and modifies them. As becomes apparent in the dinner scene in *To the Lighthouse* as an analogy to the *Symposion*, the dynamics of desire and creation are transformed into the immanence of the text within an altogether anti-Platonist stance. The inverted notion of the divided gaze and the double image has been identified as a structural principle of the novel in which Lily's completion of the painting in the absence of Mrs. Ramsay coincides with James' confrontation with the immediate presence of the lighthouse.

Aesthetic vision is a means of encountering perceptual as well as textual boundaries. These not only imply the formal necessity of distance and mediate between an inner and an outer view, but they foreground their respective materiality as a way of reflecting on the aesthetic possibilities of the text. Moreover, the text absorbs the materiality it presents as part of the poetic texture of the novel. Glass and fabric are used to describe different modes of presentation and the different kinds of aesthetic experience related to them. Windows, mirrors, and the veil present symbolic materiality, and create distinct viewing situations connected to it. The overall trajectory between transparency and opacity also refers to the metanarrative functions of textual materiality. Whereas the window dwells on the dual notion of transparency and distance and becomes only transparent in pointing to something impenetrable beyond itself, the mirror is used as a means of challenging the adequacy of vision when it comes to realism and empirical accuracy.

The sense of the interchange between surface and depth conveyed by symbolic materiality has proved a flexible and suggestive paradigm for the discussion of windows, mirrors and the veil. As modalities of the gaze that are tied to a specific materiality, they present a further strategy of immanent reflection and the creation of aesthetic perception in which the resistance to material presence facilitates the creation of narrative modes of perception. The 'veil of words' or the 'veil in the text' as it is prominently discussed in contemporary aesthetic discourse was used in both Woolf's aesthetics and her novels as a way in which the text presents its own materiality. The notions of the diaphanous, the semi-transparent, as well as blurred vision and seeing through tears provide textual strategies to negotiate the perceptual dynamics of desire and loss, and to create images for the experience of the imaginary. As it has been shown, aesthetic experience is not secondary to the text, but it is created in the structural and material modalities of the gaze.

Aesthetic vision and modernist concerns with temporality are distinctly linked by a dialectical interplay in which vision releases temporal processes, and where temporality induces new kinds of vision. The ways in which Woolf's short stories like "The Moment: Summer's Night" anatomise the present moment mark temporal relations as malleable fictional categories, which undermine notions of presence and representation. The temporality of aesthetic vision relies on minimalist categories such as the moment that correspond to the perspective of the child's eye view and to formal narrative units such as the sketch and the scene. Woolf's autobiographical text "A Sketch of the Past" provides an example for this correlation because it connects the idea of openness inherent in the notion of the sketch with a narrative strategy in which the text performs its own temporality as an anachronistic process related to beginnings and original visions. Linearity in narrative is replaced by discontinuity, and temporal relations are rendered in terms of anticipatory, unfolding visions and structural anachronisms pointing back to imaginary beginnings.

The temporality of aesthetic vision is predominantly rendered in figures of the mode of achronicity, paradoxes and parallelisms. Similar to the narrative dynamics that resides in textual materiality, the temporality of aesthetic vision is sustained by a dynamic progress between approximation and retreat. It reveals the semantic energies of the image which release a dynamics of perspectives and standpoints. Woolf's novels, as for instance *Jacob's Room*, mediate between past and present, presence and absence, and use image-related memories to reveal textual structures of retrieval and retreat. In *Jacob's Room*, which undermines the notion of memory as representation, images created by memory are treated in spatio-temporal terms and become as intangible as the remembered character, scene or object. Perceptual details, objects and emblems build up the mnemonic network of the novel and induce a process of reading that can be conceived of in terms of collecting and archiving. Objects of everyday reality become distancing devices, and things reveal themselves in new ways. They become containers of a distinct temporality which describes the ambiguity residing in the expansion and contraction of possible reference, and between the urge to represent and the futility of doing so. Whereas *Jacob's Room* is marked by the central character's absence, the notion of presence in *Mrs Dalloway* relies on a doubly-encoded presence which evokes a dual vision of past and present, and likewise describes the pervasiveness of the two levels of time. *To the Lighthouse* presents the notion of an immanent temporality of aesthetic vision as a modulated process which alternates between the suspension and the expansion of temporality. The aesthetic temporality of *To the Lighthouse* relies on processes of inversion between subject and object, foreground and background in which past, present and future are treated as analogous to the tripartite structure of Lily's painting.

In *Between the Acts*, the paradox of vision in time is negotiated in the novel's many temporalised oppositions. The individualised temporalities of single characters interact with their perceptions and create a narrative process in which moments and scenes are expanded, interrupted, or re-contextualised. As in *Mrs Dalloway*, many of the characters live in more than one time, and they have difficulty in distinguishing imaginary from actual presence. The novel juxtaposes models of linear and cyclical temporality in order to situate the temporality of the novel between the paradoxical notions of time and timelessness, vision and silence. The play in the play likewise describes a temporality which alternates between motion and standstill and is conveyed both in the pictorial stasis of a scene and the progression of the dramatic plot. In analogy to the structural unit of the scene, the interval is used in both the dramatic and the musical sense, and in *Between the Acts* the temporality of aesthetic vision is sustained by a triadic rhythm that provides both temporal unity and dispersal. The novel further treats the figure of paradox in its constellations that centre on threefold models of verbal, musical and conceptual rhythm.

Modernist texts generate new ways of seeing. Fiction not only intimately participated in the ambivalent contemporary preoccupation with visual perception, but creates distinct kinds of vision. In the ways in which it is conceptualised in Woolf's works, aesthetic vision is both a poetical reflection about the possibilities of narrative creation, and a reflection on altered ways of aesthetic experience.

The argumentative trajectory created in this study has identified the processes of distancing from immediate perception in its semantic and phenomenological, its formal, spatial, temporal and intersubjective terms. Whereas the first three parts have investigated into the narrative potentialities of aesthetic vision, the last part of this study focuses on the notion of privacy as aesthetic possibility, and marks a return to the construction of the aesthetic subject through language. Woolf's aesthetics ascribes a special privilege to privacy, a concept with which the ideas of solitude, creativity and intimacy continue to be commonly associated. *The Waves*, however, conceives of privacy as an intersubjective mode which is founded on the division of the inner gaze and enables the viewer to see the self as an 'other'. This ambiguity within the self is explored in the characters' ways of dramatising their existence as actors, spectators and parts of a tragic chorus.

The discourse of privacy in *The Waves* gains its relevance against the background of a hermeneutics of the gaze, in which the novel expresses its critique of scientific knowledge and impressionistic representation. In a strategy in which the text both suggests and refutes unambiguous reference to discourses of vision, it not only engages in a process of raising and deflating the readers' expectations, but in creating new structures of perception which rely on a kaleidoscopic movement of separation and recombination of scenes, images and perspectives.

In their reflection on phenomena and the experience of the visual Woolf's critical and fictional works offer a new and original presentation of perception as an aesthetic phenomenon. It is sustained by a generative dynamics which actualises the potentiality of an unattainable state and essentially aims at the aesthetic productivity of the beholder.

Bibliography

Texts and Editions

Aristotle. *De Anima*. Ed. by William D. Ross. Oxford: Clarendon, 1998.
Aristotle. *De Sensu et Sensibili and De memoria*. Text and transl. with introduction and commentary by G.R.T. Ross. Cambridge: CUP, 1906.
Chaucer, Geoffrey. *The Riverside Chaucer*. Ed. by Larry D. Benson. 3rd ed. Oxford: OUP, 1987.
Conrad, Joseph. *Heart of Darkness*. Harmondsworth: Penguin, 1994.
Conrad, Joseph. *The Nigger of the 'Narcissus'*. London: Dent, 1964.
Eliot, T.S. *Selected Essays by T.S. Eliot*. London: Faber & Faber, 1932.
Eliot, T.S. *The Sacred Wood. Essays on Poetry and Criticism*. London: Methuen, 1957.
Eliot, T.S. *Collected Poems 1909–1962*. London: Faber & Faber, 1963.
James, Henry. *The Portrait of a Lady*. Oxford: Everyman, 1999.
James, Henry. *Daisy Miller and Other Stories*. Ware: Wordsworth, 1994.
Joyce, James. *Ulysses*. Ed. by Hans Walter Gabler. London: The Bodley Head, 2002.
Joyce, James. *A Portrait of the Artist as a Young Man*. London: Grafton, 1988.
Mann, Thomas. *Buddenbrooks. Verfall einer Familie*. Frankfurt am Main: S. Fischer, 53. Aufl., 2004.
Proust, Marcel. *Swann's Way*, I. Transl. by C.K. Scott Moncrieff. London: Chatto and Windus, 1966.
Plato. *Platonis Opera I-VI*. Ed. by Johannes Burnet. Oxford: OUP, 1989.
Plotinus, *Enneads*. Transl. by A.H. Armstrong. Loeb Classical Library. Cambridge, Mass.: Harvard UP, 1966–1988.
Quintilian, Marcus Fabius. *De Institutione Oratoria*. Libri duodecim. Hildesheim: Olms, 1969.
Shakespeare, William. *The Riverside Shakespeare*. Boston: Houghton Mifflin, 1974.
Sophocles. *Works*. Ed. and transl. by Hugh Lloyd-Jones. Cambridge, Mass: Harvard UP, 1994.
Woolf, Virginia. *A Room of One's Own*. London: The Hogarth Press, 1949. [1929]
Woolf, Virginia. *Between the Acts*. London: Vintage, 2000. [1941]
Woolf, Virginia. *Books and Portraits. Some Further Selections from the Literary and Biographical Writings of Virginia Woolf*. Ed. and with a Pref. by Mary Lyon. New York, London: Harcourt Brace Jovanovich, 1977.
Woolf, Virginia. *The Captain's Death Bed and Other Essays*. New York: Harcourt Brace, 1950.
Woolf, Virginia. *Carlyle's House and Other Sketches*. Ed. by David Bradshaw. London: Hesperus, 2003.
Woolf, Virginia. *Collected Essays I-IV*. London: The Hogarth Press, 1966–1967.
Woolf, Virginia. *The Common Reader*. London: The Hogarth Press, 1948. [1925]
Woolf, Virginia. *The Common Reader: Second Series*. London: The Hogarth Press, 1948. [1932]
Woolf, Virginia. *The Complete Shorter Fiction of Virginia Woolf*. Ed. by Susan Dick. San Diego/ New York: Harcourt, 1989.
Woolf, Virginia. "Craftsmanship – Words fail me". Typescript. BERG Collection.
Woolf, Virginia. *The Diary of Virginia Woolf* I-V. Ed. by Anne Olivier Bell und Andrew McNeillie. New York: Harcourt Brace Jovanovich, 1977–1980.
Woolf, Virginia. *The Death of the Moth and Other Essays*. London: The Hogarth Press, 1947. [1942]
Woolf, Virginia. *Granite and Rainbow*. London: The Hogarth Press, 1958.

Woolf, Virginia. Holograph Notes. Nov. 9, 1922-Aug, 2, 1923. BERG.
Woolf, Virginia. *Three Guineas*. London: The Hogarth Press, 1968. [1938]
Woolf, Virginia. *Jacob's Room*. Oxford: OUP, 1992. [1922]
Woolf, Virginia. Jacob's Room. Holograph unsigned dated April 15, 1920-March 12, 1922. BERG.
Woolf, Virginia. "The Leaning Tower – Some Modern Tendencies". Typescript. BERG Collection.
Woolf, Virginia. *The Letters of Virginia Woolf I-VI*. Ed. by Nigel Nicolson and Joanne Trautmann. New York/London: Harcourt Brace Jovanovich, 1975–1980.
Woolf, Virginia. *To the Lighthouse*. New York, London: Harcourt Brace Jovanovich, 1989. [1927]
Woolf, Virginia. *Moments of Being: Unpublished Autobiographical Writings*. Ed. by Jeanne Schulkind. Sussex: Sussex UP, 1976.
Woolf, Virginia. *The Moment and Other Essays of Virginia Woolf*. San Diego: Harcourt Brace, 1975. [1947]
Woolf, Virginia. "Moments of Vision". *TLS*, No. 853, London, 1918, 243.
Woolf, Virginia. *Mrs Dalloway*. Harmondsworth: Penguin, 1992. [1925]
Woolf, Virginia. "Mrs Dalloway, Fragments". Holograph pages in a notebook dated Hogarth House Richmond, January 7. BERG Collection.
Woolf, Virginia. "Mrs Dalloway Holograph Notes", Nov. 9, 1922; Feb 26, 1923.BERG.
Woolf, Virginia. *Night and Day*. Ed. with an introd. by Suzanne Raitt. Oxford: OUP, 1999. [1919]
Woolf, Virginia. Notes for Writing. Holograph notebook, unsigned, dated March 1922- March 1925. BERG.
Woolf, Virginia. *Orlando*. Ed. by J.H. Stape. Oxford: Blackwell, 1994. [1929]
Woolf, Virginia. *A Passionate Apprentice. The Early Journals of Virginia Woolf 1897–1909*. Ed. by Mitchell A. Leaska. London, 1990.
Woolf, Virginia. "Reviewing." With a note by Leonard Woolf. London: The Hogarth Press, 1939.
Woolf, Virginia. *Roger Fry. A Biography*. San Diego/New York/London: Harcourt Brace Jovanovich, 1940.
Woolf, Virginia. Thoughts when beginning a book to be called perhaps At Home: or The Party. Oct 16th, 1922. BERG.
Woolf, Virginia. Travel and Literary Notebook 1906–1909. BL ADD. MS 61837.
Woolf, Virginia. Typescript A Sketch of the Past I, 14 June–15 Nov 1940. BL ADD. MS 61973.
Woolf, Virginia. *The Voyage Out*. Ed. and introd. by Jane Wheare. Harmondsworth: Penguin, 1992. [1915]
Woolf, Virginia. *A Writer's Diary: Being Extracts from the Diary of Virginia Woolf*. Ed. by Leonard Woolf. New York: Harcourt, 1954.
Woolf, Virginia. *Walter Sickert. A Conversation*. London: The Hogarth Press, 1934.
Woolf, Virginia. *The Waves*. London: Vintage, 2000. [1931]
Woolf, Virginia. *The Waves*. The Two Holograph Drafts. Ed. and transcribed by J.W. Graham. Toronto: U of Toronto Press, 1976.
Woolf, Virginia. *The Years*. Ed. and introd. by Jeri Johnson. Harmondsworth: Penguin, 1998. [1937]

Secondary Sources

Abel, Elizabeth. *Virginia Woolf and the Fictions of Psychoanalysis*. Chicago: U of Chicago Press, 1989.
Abrams, M.H. *The Mirror and the Lamp. Romantic Theory and the Critical Tradition*. London, Oxford: OUP, 1971 [1953].
Addison, Joseph. "Pleasures of the Imagination". *The Spectator*, 416 (1712). Ed. by G. Gregory Smith in 4 vols, vol 3. New York: Everyman, w.Y. 73–77.
Adorno, Theodor W. *Ästhetische Theorie*. Gesamtausgabe Bd. 7. Hrsg. von G. Adorno und R. Tiedemann. Frankfurt am Main: Suhrkamp, 1970.
Alt, Christina. *Virginia Woolf and the Study of Nature*. Cambridge: CUP, 2010.
Apter, T. E. *Virginia Woolf. A Study of her Novels*. London: Macmillan, 1979.
Assmann, Aleida. "Obsession der Zeit in der englischen Moderne". *Zeit und Roman*. Hrsg. von Martin Middeke, Würzburg: Königshausen & Neumann: 2002. 253–273.
Assmann, Aleida und Jan. *Schleier und Schwelle I–III*. München: Fink, 1998.
Assmann, Aleida. "Einführung: Geheimnis und Offenbarung". *Schleier und Schwelle II. Geheimnis und Offenbarung*. München: Fink, 1998. 7–14.
Auerbach, Erich. *Mimesis. The Representation of Reality in Western Literature*. Transl. by Willard R. Trask. Princeton: Princeton UP, 1953.
Bachelard, Gaston. *The Poetics of Space. The Classic Look at How We Experience Intimate Places*. Transl. by Maria Jolas. Ed. by John R. Stilgoe. Boston: Beacon Press, 1994.
Bal, Mieke. *Reading "Rembrandt". Beyond the Word-Image Opposition: The Northrop Frye Lectures in Literary Theory*. Cambridge: CUP, 1991.
Baldanza, Frank. "Virginia Woolf's 'Moments of Being'". *Modern Fiction Studies*, 2 (1956), 78–93.
Banfield, Ann. *The Phantom Table. Woolf, Fry, Russell and the Epistemology of Modernism*. Cambridge: CUP, 2001.
Banfield, Ann. "Time Passes. Virginia Woolf, Postimpressionism and Cambridge Time". *Poetics Today*, 24 (2003), 471–516.
Barasch, Moshe. "Der Schleier. Das Geheimnis in den Bildvorstellungen der Spätantike". *Schleier und Schwelle II. Geheimnis und Offenbarung*. Hrsg. von Jan und Aleida Assmann. München: Fink, 1998. 179–201.
Bazin, Nancy. *Virginia Woolf and the Androgynous Vision*. New Brunswick, N.J.: Rutgers UP, 1973.
Beer, Gillian. "The Island and the Aeroplane: The Case of Virginia Woolf". *Nation and Narration*. Ed. by Homi Bhaba. London: Routledge, 1990. 265–290.
Beer, Gillian. *Virginia Woolf: The Common Ground. Essays by Gillian Beer*. Edinburgh: Edinburgh UP, 1996.
Beer, Gillian. "Introduction". *The Waves*. London: Vintage, 2000. xiii–xx.
Beierwaltes, Werner, "Plotins Metaphysik des Lichtes", *Die Philosophie des Neuplatonismus*. Hrsg. von Clemens Zintzen. Darmstadt: WB, 1977. 75–117.
Beja, Morris. "Matches Struck in the Dark: Virginia Woolf's Moments of Vision". *Critical Quarterly*, 6 (1964), 137–152.
Bell, Clive. *Art*. London: Chatto & Windus, 1914.
Bell, Clive. *Proust*. London: The Hogarth Press, 1928.
Bell, Quentin. *Bloomsbury*. London: The Hogarth Press, 1968.
Bell, Quentin. *Virginia Woolf: A Biography*. 2 vols. London: The Hogarth Press, 1972–1973.

Bell, Quentin. *Roger Fry*. Inaugural Lecture Delivered in the University of Leeds 2nd December 1963. Leeds: Leeds UP, 1964.
Belting, Hans. "Vorwort zu einer Anthropologie des Bildes". *Der zweite Blick: Bildgeschichte und Bildreflexion*. Hrsg. von Hans Belting und Dietmar Kamper. München: Fink, 2000. 7–11.
Belting, Hans. *Bildanthropologie*. München: Fink, 2001.
Benjamin, Walter. *Gesammelte Schriften*. I-VII. Hrsg. von Rolf Tiedemann und Herrmann Schweppenhäuser. Frankfurt am Main: Suhrkamp, 1991.
Benjamin, Walter. *The Arcades Project*. Transl. by Howard Eiland and Kevin McLaughlin. Cambridge, Mass.: Belknap Press, 1999.
Bensch, Georg. *Vom Kunstwerk zum ästhetischen Objekt. Zur Geschichte der phänomenologischen Ästhetik*. München: Fink, 1994.
Bergson, Henri. *Matière et mémoire. Essai sur la relation du corps à l'esprit*. Paris: PUF, 1962.
Bettinger, Elfi. *Das umkämpfte Bild. Zur Metapher bei Virginia Woolf*. Stuttgart, Weimar: Metzler, 1993.
Bettinger, Elfi. "Jacob Out of Focus. Virginia Woolfs experimentelles Erzählen zwischen Lyrik und Prosa". *Erzählen und Erzähltheorie im 20. Jahrhundert. Festschrift für Wilhelm Füger*. Hrsg. von Jörg Helbig. Heidelberg: Winter, 2001. 321–339.
Bishop, Edward L. "The Shaping of *Jacob's Room*: Woolf's Manuscript Revisions". *Twentieth Century Literature*, 32 (1986), 115–135.
Bishop, Edward L. *Virginia Woolf*. London: Macmillan, 1991.
Bishop, Edward L. *Virginia Woolf's Jacob's Room. The Holograph Draft*. Transcribed and ed. by Edward L. Bishop. New York: Pace UP, 1998.
Blotner, Joseph L. "Mythic Patterns in To the Lighthouse". *PMLA*, 71 (1956), 547–562.
Blumenberg, Hans. *Lebenszeit und Weltzeit*. Frankfurt am Main: Suhrkamp, 1986.
Blumenberg, Hans. *Paradigmen zu einer Metaphorologie*. Frankfurt am Main: Suhrkamp, 1998.
Blumenberg, Hans. *Ästhetische und Metaphorologische Schriften*. Auswahl und Nachwort von Anselm Haverkamp. Frankfurt am Main: Suhrkamp, 2001.
Boeckhorst, Peter te. *Das literarische Leitmotiv und seine Funktionen in Romanen von Aldous Huxley, Virginia Woolf and James Joyce*. Frankfurt am Main: Lang, 1987.
Boehm, Gottfried. "Im Horizont der Zeit. Heideggers Werkbegriff und die Kunst der Moderne". *Kunst und Technik. Gedächtnisschrift zum 100. Geburtstag von Martin Heidegger*. Hrsg. von Walter Biemel und Friedrich-Wilhelm v. Herrmann. Frankfurt am Main: Klostermann, 1989. 255–287.
Boehm, Gottfried. "Die Wiederkehr der Bilder". *Was ist ein Bild?* Hrsg. von Gottfried Boehm. München: Fink, 1994. 11–38.
Boehm, Gottfried. *Was ist ein Bild?* München: Fink, 1994.
Boehm, Gottfried und Helmut Pfotenhauer. Hrsg. *Beschreibungskunst, Kunstbeschreibung: Ekphrasis von der Antike bis zur Gegenwart*. München: Fink, 1995.
Boehm, Gottfried, Gabriele Brandstetter und Achatz von Müll. Hrsg. *Figur und Figuration: Studien zu Wahrnehmung und Wissen*. Paderborn: Fink, 2006.
Bohrer, Karl Heinz. *Plötzlichkeit. Zum Augenblick des ästhetischen Scheins*. Frankfurt am Main: Suhrkamp, 1981.
Bohrer, Karl Heinz. *Das absolute Präsens. Die Semantik ästhetischer Zeit*. Frankfurt am Main: Suhrkamp, 1994.
Bohrer, Karl Heinz. "Utopie des 'Augenblicks' und Fiktionalität. Die Subjektivierung der Zeit in der modernen Literatur". *Zeit und Roman. Zeiterfahrung im historischen Wandel und

ästhetischer Paradigmenwechsel vom sechzehnten Jahrhundert bis zur Postmoderne. Hrsg. von Martin Middeke. Würzburg: Königshausen & Neumann, 2002. 215–252.
Bohrer, Karl Heinz. *Ekstasen der Zeit. Augenblick, Gegenwart, Erinnerung*. München, Wien: Hanser, 2003.
Bradbury, Malcolm and James McFarlane. Eds. *Modernism. A Guide to European Literature 1890–1930*. London: Penguin, 1991.
Brivic, Sheldon. "The Veil of Signs: Perception as Language in Joyce's *Ulysses*", ELH, 57 (1990), 737–755.
Brosch, Renate. *Krisen des Sehens. Henry James und die Veränderung der Wahrnehmung im 19. Jahrhundert*. Tübingen: Stauffenburg, 2000.
Brosch, Renate. "Verbalizing the Visual: Ekphrasis as a Commentary on Modes of Representation". *Mediale Performanzen: Historische Konzepte und Perspektiven*. Hrsg. von Jutta Eming, Annette Jael Lehmann and Irmgard Maassen. Freiburg im Breisgau: Rombach, 2002. 103–123.
Brosch, Renate. Hrsg. *Ikono/Philo/Logie: Wechselspiele von Texten und Bildern*. Berlin: Trafo, 2004.
Buck-Morss, Susan. *The Dialectics of Seeing: Walter Benjamin and the Arcades Project*. Cambridge, Mass.: MIT Press, 1991.
Bullen, J.B. Ed. *Post-Impressionists in England*. London and New York: Routledge, 1988.
Butler, Christopher. *Early Modernism: Literature, Music and Painting in Europe, 1900–1916*. Oxford: Clarendon Press, 1994.
Cassirer, Ernst. "Mythischer, ästhetischer und theoretischer Raum". *Landschaft und Raum in der Erzählkunst*. Hrsg. von Alexander Ritter. Darmstadt: WB, 1975. 17–35.
Cassirer, Ernst. *Philosophie der Symbolischen Formen I: Die Sprache*. Text und Anm. bearb. v. Claus Rosenkranz. *Gesammelte Werke*. Hrsg. von Birgit Recki. Bd. 11. Darmstadt: WB, 1953.
Cassirer, Ernst. *Philosophie der Symbolischen Formen III: Phänomenologie der Erkenntnis*. Text u. Anm. bearb. von Julia Clemens. *Gesammelte Werke*. Hrsg. von Birgit Recki. Bd. 13. Darmstadt: WB, 2002.
A Catalogue of Books from the Library of Leonard and Virginia Woolf: Taken from Monks House, Rodmell, Sussex and 24 Victoria Square, London and now in the Possession of Washington State University, Pullman USA. Brighton: Holleyman and Treacher, 1978.
Caughie, Pamela L. *Virginia Woolf in the Age of Mechanical Reproduction*. New York: Garland, 2000.
Caws, Mary Ann. *The Eye in the Text: Essays on Perception; Mannerist to Modern*. Princeton: Princeton UP, 1981.
Caws, Mary Ann. *Reading Frames in Modern Fiction*. Princeton: Princeton UP, 1985.
Caws, Mary Ann and Nicola Luckhurst. Eds. *The Reception of Virginia Woolf in Europe*. London: Continuum, 2002.
Church, Margaret. "Concepts of Time in the Novels of Virginia Woolf and Aldous Huxley". MFS, (1955), 19–24.
Cohn, Dorrit. *Transparent Minds: Narrative Modes for Presenting Consciousness in Fiction*. Princeton: Princeton UP, 1978.
Crary, Jonathan. *Techniques of the Observer*. Cambridge, Mass.: MIT Press, 1991.
Cuddy-Keane, Melba. "Virginia Woolf and the Varieties of Historicist Experience", *Virginia Woolf and the Essay*. Ed. by Beth Carole Rosenberg and Jeanne Dubino. New York: St. Martins, 1997. 59–77.
Dalgarno, Emily. *Virginia Woolf and the Visible World*. Cambridge: CUP, 2001.

Dalsimer, Katherine. *Virginia Woolf: Becoming a Writer*. New Haven, London: Yale UP, 2001.
Danius, Sara. *The Senses of Modernism. Technology, Perception, and Aesthetics*. Ithaca: Cornell UP, 2002.
Delattre, Floris. *Le roman psychologique de Virginia Woolf*. Paris: J. Vrin, 1932.
Deleuze, Gilles. *Cinéma 2. L'image-temps*. Paris: Minuit, 1985.
Deleuze, Gilles. *Différence et Répétition*. Paris: PUF, 11ème ed. 2003.
Denvir, Bernard. *Post-Impressionism*. London: Thames and Hudson, 1992.
Deppman, Hsiu-Chuang. "Rereading the Mirror Image: Looking-glasses, Gender and Mimeticism in Virginia Woolf's Writing". *Journal of Narrative Theory*, 31 (2001), 31–64.
Didi-Huberman, Georges. *Devant le Temps. Histoire de l'art et anachronisme des images*. Paris: Minuit, 2000.
Drucker, Johanna. *Theorizing Modernism. Visual Art and the Critical Tradition*. New York: Columbia UP, 1994.
Dunn, Jane. *A Very Close Conspiracy: Vanessa Bell and Virginia Woolf*. Boston: Little Brown, 1990.
Elias, Norbert. *Über die Zeit. Arbeiten zur Wissenssoziologie II*. Frankfurt am Main: Suhrkamp, 1990.
Erzgräber, Willi. "Nachimpressionistische Anschauungen über Kompositionstechnik und Farbsymbolik in Virginia Woolfs Roman *To the Lighthouse*", *Miscellanea Anglo-Americana: Festschrift für Helmut Viebrock*. Hrsg. von Kuno Schumann, Armin Paul Frank und Wilhelm Hortmann. München: Pressler, 1974. 148–183.
Erzgräber, Willi. "'The Moment of Vision' im Modernen Englischen Roman". *Augenblick und Zeitpunkt. Studien zur Zeitstruktur und Zeitmetaphorik in Kunst und Wissenschaften*. Hrsg. von Christian Thomsen und Hans Holländer. Darmstadt: WB, 1984. 361–389.
Fischer-Lichte, Erika. "Ästhetische Erfahrung als Schwellenerfahrung". *Dimensionen ästhetischer Erfahrung*. Hrsg. von Joachim Küpper und Christoph Menke. Frankfurt am Main: Suhrkamp, 2003. 138–161.
Fleishman, Avrom. *Virginia Woolf: A Critical Reading*. Baltimore: Johns Hopkins UP, 1975.
Foucault, Michel. *Archäologie des Wissens*. Frankfurt am Main: Suhrkamp, 1973.
Foucault, Michel. *Überwachen und Strafen*. Frankfurt am Main: Suhrkamp, 1976.
Fowler, Rowena. "Moments and Metamorphoses: Virginia Woolf's Greece". *Comparative Literature*, 51 (1999), 215–242.
Fox, Meghan. "'The Vision must be perpetually remade': An Examination of Ethical and Aesthetic Revisions in *To the Lighthouse*". *Woolf Editing/Editing Woolf. Selected Papers from the Eighteenth Annual Conference on Virginia Woolf*. Ed. by Eleanor McNees and Sara Veglahn. Clemson: Clemson University Digital Press, 2009. 18–27.
Francis, Herbert, E. Jr. "Virginia Woolf and 'The Moment'". *Emory University Quarterly*, XVI (1960), 139–151.
Frank, Joseph. "Spatial Form in Modern Literature". *Critiques and Essays in Criticism*. Ed. by R. W. Stallman. N.Y.: Ronald Press, 1949. 315–328.
Frenk, Joachim. Ed. *Spatial Change in English Literature*. Trier: WVT, 2000.
Friedman, Norman. "The Waters of Annihilation: Double Vision in *To the Lighthouse*". *Journal of English Literary History*, 22 (1955), 61–79.
Froula, Christine. *Virginia Woolf and the Bloomsbury Avant-Garde: War, Civilization, Modernity*. New York: Columbia UP, 2007.
Fry, Roger. "Introduction". *Discourses on Art by Sir Joshua Reynolds*. London: Seeley & Co. Ltd., 1905.

Fry, Roger. *Cézanne. A Study of His Development*. London: The Hogarth Press, 1927.
Fry, Roger. *The Letters of Roger Fry II*. Ed. by Denys Sutton. London: Chatto & Windus, 1972.
Fry, Roger. *Vision and Design*. London: Chatto & Windus, 1927.
Gadamer, Hans-Georg. *Wahrheit und Methode. Grundzüge einer philosophischen Hermeneutik.* Gesammelte Werke Bd. 1, Tübingen: Mohr, 6. Aufl., 1990.
Gadamer, Hans-Georg. "Wort und Bild – 'so wahr, so seiend'". *Gesammelte Werke*. Bd. 8. Tübingen: Mohr, 1993. 373–399.
Genette, Gérard. *Narrative Discourse Revisited*. Ithaca: Cornell UP, 1988.
Gillespie, Diane. *The Sisters' Arts: The Writing and Painting of Virginia Woolf and Vanessa Bell.* New York: Syracuse UP, 1988.
Gillespie, Diane and Leslie Hankins. Eds. *The Multiple Muses of Virginia Woolf.* Columbia: U of Missouri Press, 1993.
Gillespie, Diane and Leslie Hankins. Eds. *Virginia Woolf and the Arts*. New York: Pace UP, 1997.
Goffman, Irving. *Frame Analysis*. Cambridge, Mass.: Harvard UP, 1974.
Goldman, Jane. *The Feminist Aesthetics of Virginia Woolf: Modernism, Postimpressionism and the Politics of the Visual*. Cambridge: CUP, 1998.
Goldman, Mark. "Virginia Woolf and the Critic as Reader". *PMLA*, 80 (1965), 275–284.
Goldman, Mark. *The Reader's Art: Virginia Woolf as a Literary Critic*. The Hague & Paris: Mouton, 1976.
Gombrich, E.H. *The Story of Art*. Oxford: Phaidon 14th ed., 1984.
Gorsky, Susan. "'The Central Shadow:' Characterization in *The Waves*". *MFS*, 18 (1972), 38–52.
Gorsky, Susan. *The Central Shadow: Dualism in Form and Meaning in The Waves*. Ann Arbor: Univ. Microfilms, 1970.
Grabes, Herbert. "Schreiben in der Zeit gegen die Zeit". *Zeit und Roman. Zeiterfahrung im historischen Wandel und ästhetischer Paradigmenwechsel vom sechzehnten Jahrhundert bis zur Postmoderne*. Hrsg. Von Martin Middeke. Würzburg: Königshausen & Neumann, 2002. 313–332.
Gumbrecht, Hans Ulrich. *The Production of Presence. What Meaning Cannot Convey*. Stanford: Stanford UP, 2004.
Gunnison, Deirdre. "'Each of course saw something different'. *Mrs. Dalloway* and the Experience of the Novel". *Virginia Woolf Bulletin*. Woolf Society of Great Britain, 6 (2001), 23–29.
Habermas, Jürgen. "Das Zeitbewußtsein der Moderne und ihr Bedürfnis nach Selbstvergewisserung". *Der Philosophische Diskurs der Moderne. Zwölf Vorlesungen*. Frankfurt am Main: Suhrkamp, 1989. 9–34.
Habermas, Jürgen. *Die Moderne, ein unvollendetes Projekt. Philosophisch-Politische Aufsätze.* Leipzig: Reclam, 3. Auflage, 1994.
Hafley, James. *The Glass Roof: Virginia Woolf as Novelist*. Berkeley: U of California Press, 1954.
Hankins, Leslie. "'Across the Screen of my Brain': Virginia Woolf's 'The Cinema' and Film Forums of the Twenties". *The Multiple Muses of Virginia Woolf*. Ed. by Diane Gillespie and Leslie Hankins. Columbia: U of Missouri Press, 1993.
Harris, Alexandra. *Virginia Woolf*. London: Thames & Hudson, 2011.
Harris, Alexandra. *Romantic Moderns. English Writers, Artists and the Imagination from Virginia Woolf to John Piper*. London: Thames and Hudson, 2010.
Hartley, Lodwick. "Of Time and Mrs. Woolf". *Sewanee Review*, XLVII (1939), 235–241.
Hartmann, Geoffrey. "Virginia's Web". *Chicago Review*, 14 (1961), 20–32.

Hayles, Catherine N. *The Cosmic Web. Scientific Field Models and Literary Strategies in the Twentieth Century*. Ithaca, London: Cornell UP, 1984.

Heffernan, James. *Space, Time, Image, Sign: Essays on Literature and the Visual Arts*. Frankfurt am Main et al.: Lang, 1987.

Heffernan, James. *Museum of Words: The Poetics of Ekphrasis from Homer to Ashbery*. Chicago: U of Chicago Press, 1993.

Heidegger, Martin. *Being and Time*. Transl. by John Macquarrie and Edward Robinson. New York: Harper & Row, 1962.

Heidegger, Martin. "Der Ursprung des Kunstwerks", *Holzwege* (1935–1936). Frankfurt am Main: Klostermann, 6. Auflage, 1980. 17–24.

Heidegger, Martin. *Sein und Zeit*. Tübingen: Niemeyer, 1986.

Heidegger, Martin. "Zeit und Sein". *Zur Sache des Denkens*. Tübingen, 3. Aufl, 1988, 1–25.

Heilbrun, Carolyn G. *Toward a Recognition of Androgyny*. New York: Harper, 1973.

Henry, Holly. *Virginia Woolf and the Discourse of Science. The Aesthetics of Astronomy*. Cambridge: CUP, 2003.

Hirsh, Elizabeth. "Writing as Spatial Historiography: Woolf's *Roger Fry* and National Identity". *Mapping the Self: Space, Identity, Discourse in British Auto/Biography*. Ed. by Frédéric Regard. Saint-Etienne: Publications de l'Université de Saint-Etienne, 2003. 203–216.

Holmes, Gordon. "Disturbances of Visual Space Perception", *The British Medical Journal*, 2 (1919), 230–233.

Holtby, Winifred. *Virginia Woolf*. London: Wishart & Co., 1932.

Humm, Maggie. *Modernist Women and Visual Cultures: Virginia Woolf, Vanessa Bell, Photography and Cinema*. New Brunswick: Rutgers UP, 2003.

Humm, Maggie. *Snapshots of Bloomsbury: The Private Lives of Virginia Woolf and Vanessa Bell*. New Brunswick, NJ: Rutgers University Press, 2006.

Humm, Maggie. Ed. *The Edinburgh Companion to Virginia Woolf and the Arts*. Edinburgh UP, 2010.

Humm, Maggie. "Virginia Woolf and the Arts". *The Edinburgh Companion to Virginia Woolf and the Arts*. Ed. by Maggie Humm. Edinburgh: Edinburgh UP, 2010, 1–4.

Humm, Maggie. "Virginia Woolf and visual culture", *The Cambridge Companion to Virginia Woolf*. Ed. by Susan Sellers. 2nd ed. Cambridge: CUP, 2010. 214–230.

Husserl, Edmund. *Zur Phänomenologie des inneren Zeitbewußtseins* (1893–1917). Hrsg. von R. Boehm, Husserliana X. Hamburg: Meiner, 1985.

Husserl, Edmund. *Analysen zur passiven Synthesis. Aus Vorlesungs- und Forschungsmanuskripten 1918–1926*. Hrsg. von M. Fleischer, Husserliana IX. Den Haag: Nijoff, 1966.

Husserl, Edmund. *Experience and Judgment*. Transl. by James S. Churchill and Karl Ameriks. Evanston: Northwestern UP, 1973.

Hussey, Mark. *The Singing of the Real World: the Philosophy of Virginia Woolf's Fiction*. Columbus: Ohio State UP, 1986.

Hussey, Mark. *Virginia Woolf A-Z: A Comprehensive Reference for Students, Teachers and Common Readers to her Life, Work, and Critical Reception*. New York: Facts on File, 1995.

Hussey, Mark, Vara Neverow, and Jane Lilienfeld. Eds. *Virginia Woolf: Emerging Perspectives*. New York: Pace, 1994.

Ingarden, Roman. "Das Bild". *Untersuchungen zur Ontologie der Kunst. Musikwerk – Bild, Architektur, Film*. Tübingen: Niemeyer, 1962. 137–253.

Ingarden, Roman. *Das literarische Kunstwerk*. Tübingen: Niemeyer: 2. Auflage, 1960.

Ingarden, Roman. *Erlebnis, Kunstwerk und Wert. Vorträge zur Ästhetik 1937–1967*. Tübingen: Niemeyer, 1969.
Iser, Wolfgang. *The Act of Reading. A Theory of Aesthetic Response*. Baltimore: Johns Hopkins UP, 1978.
Iser, Wolfgang. *Walter Pater. The Aesthetic Moment*. Cambridge: CUP, 1987 [1960].
Iser, Wolfgang. "Von der Gegenwärtigkeit des Ästhetischen". *Dimensionen ästhetischer Erfahrung*. Hrsg. von Joachim Küpper und Christoph Menke. Frankfurt am Main: Suhrkamp, 2003. 176–202.
Jacobs, Karen. *The Eye's Mind. Literary Modernism and Visual Culture*. Ithaca, London: Cornell UP, 2001.
Jameson, Fredric. *Signatures of the Visible*. New York: Routledge, 1990.
Jauss, Hans-Robert. *Ästhetische Erfahrung und literarische Hermeneutik*. Frankfurt am Main: Suhrkamp, 1982.
Jauss, Hans-Robert. *Zeit und Erinnerung in Marcel Prousts À la Recherche du Temps Perdu. Ein Beitrag zur Theorie des Romans*. Frankfurt am Main: Suhrkamp, 1986.
Jay, Martin. "Scopic Regimes of Modernity." *Vision and Visuality*. Ed. by Hal Foster. Seattle: Bay, 1988. 3–28.
Jay, Martin. "The Rise of Hermeneutics and the Crisis of Ocularcentrism". *Poetics Today*, 9 (1988), 307–326.
Jay, Martin. "The Disenchantment of the Eye: Surrealism and the Crisis of Ocularcentrism". *Visual Anthropology Review*, 7 (1991), 15–38.
Jay, Martin. *Downcast Eyes: The Denigration of Vision in Twentieth-Century French Thought*. Berkeley: U of California Press, 1993.
Jenks, Christopher. *Visual Culture*. London, New York: Routledge, 1995.
Kablitz, Andreas, Wulf Oesterreicher und Rainer Warning. Hrsg. *Zeit und Text. Philosophische, kulturanthropologische, literarhistorische und linguistische Beiträge*. München: Fink, 2003.
Kant, Immanuel. *Die Kritik der Reinen Vernunft*. Hamburg: Meiner, 1956.
Kazan, Francesca. "Description and the Pictorial in *Jacob's Room*". *ELH*, 55 (1988), 701–719.
Kermode, Frank. *The Sense of an Ending: Studies in the Theory of Fiction*. Oxford: OUP, 1967.
Kern, Stephen. *The Culture of Time and Space 1880–1918*. Cambridge, Mass.: Harvard UP, 1983.
Kestner, Joseph. *The Spatiality of the Novel*. Detroit: Wayne State UP, 1978.
Kierkegaard, Sören. *Der Augenblick. Aufsätze und Schriften des letzten Streits*. Übers. von Hayo Gerdes. Gesammelte Werke Abt. 34. Hrsg. von Emanuel Hirsch. Gütersloh: Mohn, 2. Aufl., 1994.
Kohler, Dayton. "Time in the Modern Novel". *College English* X, I (1948), 15–24.
Konersmann, Ralf. *Spiegel und Bild. Zur Metaphorik neuzeitlicher Subjektivität*. Würzburg: Königshausen & Neumann, 1988.
Konersmann, Ralf. *Der Schleier des Timanthes. Perspektiven der historischen Semantik*. Frankfurt am Main: Fischer, 1994.
Konersmann, Ralf. Hrsg. *Kritik des Sehens*. Leipzig: Reclam, 1999.
Krüger, Klaus. *Das Bild als Schleier des Unsichtbaren ästhetischer Illusion in der Kunst der frühen Neuzeit in Italien*. München: Fink, 2001.
Kuhlenkampff, Jens. "Spieglein, Spieglein and der Wand …". *Bild und Reflexion. Paradigmen und Perspektiven gegenwärtiger Ästhetik*. Hrsg. von Birgit Recki und Lambert Wiesing. München: Fink, 1997. 270–293.
Kumar, Shiv K. "Memory in Virginia Woolf and Bergson". *University Review* (Kansas City), XXVI (1960), 235–239.

Kurtz, Marilyn. *Virginia Woolf: Reflections and Reverberations*. New York et al.: Lang, 1990.
Lachmann, Renate. "Die 'Verfremdung' und das 'Neue Sehen' bei Vikor Šklovskij". *Poetica*, 3 (1970), 226–249.
Leavis, F.R. "After 'To the Lighthouse'. *Between the Acts* reviewed". *Scrutiny*, 10 (1942), 295–298.
Lee, Hermione. "The Burning Glass: Reflection in Virginia Woolf". *Virginia Woolf: A Centenary Perspective*. Ed. by Eric Warner and Quentin Bell. New York: St. Martin's Press, 1984. 12–27.
Lee, Hermione. *The Novels of Virginia Woolf*. London: Methuen, 1977.
Lee, Hermione. *Virginia Woolf*. New York: Vintage, 1999.
Lee, Hermione. *Virginia Woolf's Nose. Essays on Biography*. Princeton and Oxford: Princeton UP, 2005.
Levin, David M. *Modernity and the Hegemony of Vision*. Berkeley et al. U of California Press, 1993.
Levin, David M. Ed. *Sites of Vision. The Discursive Construction of Sight in the History of Philosophy*. Cambridge, Mass.: MIT Press, 1997.
Levin, David M. *The Philosopher's Gaze. Modernity in the Shadows of Enlightenment*. Berkeley: U of California Press, 1999.
Lobsien, Eckhard. "Bildlichkeit, Imagination, Wissen: Zur Phänomenologie der Vorstellungsbildung in literarischen Texten". *Bildlichkeit. Internationale Beiträge zur Poetik*. Hrsg. von Volker Bohn. Frankfurt am Main: Suhrkamp, 1990. 89–114.
Lobsien, Verena und Eckhard. *Die Unsichtbare Imagination. Literarisches Denken im 16. Jahrhundert*. München: Fink, 2004.
Lotman, Jurij. *The Structure of the Artistic Text*. Transl. from the Russian by Gail Lenhoff and Ronald Vroon. Ann Arbor: U of Michigan Press, 1977.
Lyons, Brenda. "Virginia Woolf and Plato: the Platonic Background of *Jacob's Room*". *Platonism and the English Imagination*. Ed. by Anna Baldwin and Sarah Hutton. Cambridge: CUP, 1994. 290–298.
Maag, Georg. "Ästhetische Erfahrung". *Ästhetische Grundbegriffe* Bd. 2. Hrsg. von Karlheinz Barck et al. Stuttgart: Metzler, 1997. 260–275.
Majumdar, Robin. *Virginia Woolf. An Annotated Bibliography of Criticism*. 1915–1974. London, N.Y.: Garland, 1976.
Majumdar, Robin and Allen McLaurin. Eds. *Virginia Woolf: The Critical Heritage*. London: Routledge & Kegan Paul, 1975.
Marcus, Jane. "'Britannia Rules *The Waves*'". *Decolonizing Tradition: New Views of Twentieth-Century 'British' Literary Canons*. Ed. by Karen Lawrence. Urbana: U of Illinois Press, 1992. 136–162.
Mares, Cheryl. "Woolf's Reading of Proust". *Reading Proust Now*. Ed. by Mary Anne Caws and Eugène Nicole. New York: Lang, 1990. 185–195.
Matz, Jesse. *Literary Impressionism and Modernist Aesthetics*. Cambridge: CUP, 2001.
Mayer, Verena. *Semantischer Holismus*. Berlin: Akademie, 1997.
McLaurin, Allen. *Virginia Woolf: The Echoes Enslaved*. Cambridge: CUP, 1973.
McNichol, Stella. *Virginia Woolf and the Poetry of Fiction*. London, New York: Routledge, 1990.
Meisel, Perry. *The Absent Father: Virginia Woolf and Walter Pater*. New Haven: Yale UP, 1980.
Menke, Christoph. "Wahrnehmung, Tätigkeit, Selbstreflexion: Zu Genese und Dialektik der Ästhetik". *Falsche Gegensätze: Zeitgenössische Positionen zur philosophischen Ästhetik*. Hrsg. von Andrea Kern und Ruth Sonderegger. Frankfurt am Main: Suhrkamp, 2002. 19–48.

Mergenthaler, Volker. *Sehen schreiben – Schreiben sehen. Literatur und visuelle Wahrnehmung im Zusammenspiel.* Tübingen: Niemeyer, 2002.
Merleau-Ponty, Maurice. *Phénoménologie de la perception.* Paris: Gallimard, 1945.
Middeke, Martin. Hrsg. *Zeit und Roman.* Würzburg: Königshausen & Neumann, 2002.
Miller, Hillis. "*Mrs. Dalloway*. Repetition as the Raising of the Dead". Hillis Miller. *Fiction and Repetition: Seven English Novels.* Cambridge: Harvard UP, 1982. 177–202.
Miller, Ruth. *Virginia Woolf: The Frames of Art and Life.* New York: St. Martin's Press, 1989.
Minow-Pinkney, Makiko. *Virginia Woolf and the Problem of the Subject.* Brighton: Harvester Press, 1987.
Minow-Pinkney, Makiko. "The Problem of the Subject in Mrs. Dalloway". *Clarissa Dalloway.* Ed. by Harold Bloom. New York, Philadelphia: Chelsea House Publishers, 1990. 183–192.
Mirzoeff, Nikolas. *An Introduction to Visual Culture.* London, New York: Routledge, 1999.
Mitchell, W.J.T. *Iconology. Image, Text, Ideology.* Chicago: U of Chicago Press, 1987.
Mitchell, W.J.T. *Picture Theory: Essays on Verbal and Visual Representation.* Chicago: U of Chicago Press, 1994.
Mitchell, W.J.T. "What Is Visual Culture?" *Meaning in the Visual Arts: Views from the Outside.* Ed. by Irving Lavin. Princeton: Institute for Advanced Study, 1995. 207–217.
Mitchell, W.J.T. "Was ist ein Bild?". *Bildlichkeit. Internationale Beiträge zur Poetik.* 17–69.
Mitchell, W.J.T. "Interdisciplinarity and Visual Culture", *Art Bulletin*, 77 (1995), 540–544.
Mitchell, W.J.T. "Über die Evolution von Bildern". *Der zweite Blick: Bildgeschichte und Bildreflexion.* Hrsg. von Hans Belting und Dietmar Kamper. München: Fink, 2000, 43–55.
Moog-Grünewald, Maria. "Der Sänger im Schild – oder: Über den Grund ekphrastischen Schreibens." *Behext von Bildern. Ursachen, Funktionen und Perspektiven der textuellen Faszination durch Bilder.* Hrsg. von Maria Moog-Grünewald und Heinz J. Drügh. Heidelberg: Winter, 1999. 1–21.
Mulligan, Kevin. "Perception". *The Cambridge Companion to Husserl.* Ed. by B. Smith and D.W. Smith. Cambridge: CUP, 1995.
Naremore, James. *The World without a Self. Virginia Woolf and the Novel.* New Haven, London: Yale UP, 1973.
Nünning, Vera. *Die Ästhetik Virginia Woolfs: eine Rekonstruktion ihrer philosophischen und ästhetischen Grundanschauungen auf der Basis ihrer nichtfiktionalen Schriften.* Frankfurt am Main et al.: Lang, 1990.
Nünning, Vera. "'Increasing the bounds of the moment': Die Vielschichtigkeit der Zeiterfahrungen und Zeitdimensionen in den Werken Virginia Woolfs". *Zeit und Roman*, 297–313.
Nünning, Vera und Ansgar. "The German Reception and Criticism of Virginia Woolf". *The Reception of Virginia Woolf in Europe.* Ed. by Mary Ann Caws and Nicola Luckhurst. London, New York: Continuum, 2002. 68–102.
Nugel, Bernfried. *The Just Design. Studien zu architektonischen Vorstellungsweisen in der neoklassischen Literaturtheorie am Beispiel Englands.* Berlin, New York: Lang, 1980.
Nussbaum, Martha C. "The Window: Knowledge of Other Minds in Virginia Woolf's *To the Lighthouse*". *New Literary History*, 26 (1995), 731–753.
Olejniczak, Verena. "Die Prosa Virginia Woolfs: Konzentration und Entgrenzung". *Die literarische Moderne in Europa, Bd. 1, Erscheinungsformen literarischer Prosa um die Jahrhundertwende.* Hrsg. von Hans Joachim Piechotta, Ralph-Rainer Wuthenow und Sabine Rothemann. Opladen: Westdeutscher Verlag, 1994. 219–242.
Olejniczak, Verena. *Wirkungsstrukturen in ausgewählten Texten T.S. Eliots und Virginia Woolfs: Eine Untersuchung zur Lesewirkung moderner englischer Literatur.* Hildesheim: Olms, 1987.

Olk, Claudia. "Virginia Woolf's 'Elizabethan Play': *Between the Acts* and *A Midsummer Night's Dream*". *Shakespeare Jahrbuch*, 146 (2010), 113–130.
Oster, Patricia. "Der Schleier zwischen religiöser und ästhetischer Erfahrung". *Schleier und Schwelle II. Geheimnis und Offenbarung*. Hrsg. von Aleida and Jan Assmann in Verbindung mit Theo Sundermeier (München: Fink, 1998). 233–252.
Oster, Patricia. *Der Schleier im Text. Funktionsgeschichte eines Bildes für die neuzeitliche Erfahrung des Imaginären*. München: Fink, 2002.
Panofsky, Erwin. "Die Perspektive als Symbolische Form". *Aufsätze zu Grundfragen der Kunstwissenschaft*. Hrsg. von Hariolf Oberer und Egon Verheyen. Berlin: Hessling, 1964.
Parks, Lisa. *Cultures in Orbit: Satellites and the Televisual*. Durham: Durham UP, 2005.
Pater, Walter. *The Renaissance. Studies in Art and Poetry*. London: Macmillan, 1912.
Pater, Walter. *Miscellaneous Studies. A Series of Essays*. London: Macmillan, 1924.
Pater, Walter. *Plato and Platonism. A Series of Lectures*. New York: Greenwood Press, 1969 [1925].
Pedersen, Glenn. "Vision in *To the Lighthouse*". *PMLA*, 73 (1958), 585–600.
Pensky, Max. "Tactics of Rememberance: Proust, Surrealism, and the Origin of the Passagenwerk". *Walter Benjamin and the Demands of History*. Ed. by Michael P. Steinberg. Ithaca: Cornell UP, 1996. 165–189.
Pound, Ezra. "A Few Don'ts by an Imagiste", *Poetry* I (March 1912), *Literary Essays of Ezra Pound*. Ed. by T. S. Eliot. London: Faber and Faber, 1968, 4.
Prudente, Teresa. *A Specially Tender Piece of Eternity: Virginia Woolf and the Experience of Time*. Lanham: Lexington Books, 2009.
Rawlinson, Mary C. "Perspectives and Horizons: Husserl on Seeing and Truth." *Sites of Vision. The Discursive Destruction of Sight in the History of Philosophy*. Ed. by David Michael Levin. Cambridge Mass., London: MIT Press, 1997. 265–292.
Reed, Christopher. "Through Formalism: Feminism and Virginia Woolf's Relation to Bloomsbury Aesthetics". *The Multiple Muses of Virginia Woolf*. 11–36.
Regino, Robert. "Virginia Woolf and the Technologies of Exploration: *Jacob's Room* as a Counter-Monument", *Woolf and the Art of Exploration. Selected Papers from the Fifteenth International Conference on Virginia Woolf*. Ed. by Helen Southworth and Elisa Kay Sparks. Clemson: Clemson University Digital Press, 2006. 86–94.
Richter, Harvena. "Hunting the Moth: Virginia Woolf and the Creative Imagination". *Virginia Woolf: Revaluation and Continuity*. Ed. by Ralph Freedmann. Berkeley: U of California Press, 1980. 13–28.
Richter, Harvena. *Virginia Woolf. The Inward Voyage*. Princeton: Princeton UP, 1970.
Ricœur, Paul. *Temps et récit*. I-III, Paris: Seuil, 1983–1985.
Rippl, Gabriele. *Beschreibungs-Kunst – Zur intermedialen Poetik angloamerikanischer Ikon-Texte (1880–2000)*. München: Fink, 2005.
Roe, Sue. "The Impact of Post-Impressionism". *The Cambridge Companion to Virginia Woolf*. Ed. by Sue Roe and Susan Sellers. Cambridge: CUP, 2000. 164–191.
Rogge-Wiest, Gudrun. *Wahrnehmung und Perspektivik in ausgewählten Romanen Virginia Woolfs*. Frankfurt am Main, Bern, New York: Lang, 1999.
Rogge-Wiest, Gudrun. "Multiperspektivisches Erzählen und Perspektivenstruktur in *Jacob's Room*, *Mrs. Dalloway* und *The Waves* von Virginia Woolf". *Multiperspektivisches Erzählen. Zur Theorie und Geschichte der Perspektivenstruktur im englischen Roman des 18. bis 20. Jahrhunderts*. Hrsg. von Vera und Ansgar Nünning. Trier: WVT, 2000. 225–243.
Rorty, Richard. *Philosophy and the Mirror of Nature*. Princeton: Princeton UP, 1979.

Rosenbaum, S. P. *Aspects of Bloomsbury: Studies in Modern English Literary and Intellectual History*. New York: St. Martin's Press, 1991.
Rubin, James. *Impressionism*. London: Phaidon, 2001.
Ruotolo, Lucio. *The Interrupted Moment. A View of Virginia Woolf's Novels*. Stanford: Stanford UP, 1986.
Ruotolo, Lucio. *Six Existential Heroes. The Politics of Faith*. Cambridge, Mass.: Harvard UP, 1973.
Russell, Bertrand. *The Problems of Philosophy*. London, 1912.
Russell, Bertrand. "On the Experience of Time". *The Monist*, 25 (1915), 212–233.
Schwab, Gabriele. *Entgrenzungen und Entgrenzungsmythen. Zur Subjektivität im modernen Roman: Daniel Defoe, Herman Melville, Virginia Woolf, James Joyce, Samuel Beckett, Thomas Pynchon*. Stuttgart: Steiner, 1987.
Schwank, Klaus. *Bildstruktur und Romanstruktur bei Virginia Woolf. Untersuchungen zum Problem der Symbolkonstitution in Jacob's Room, Mrs Dalloway und To the Lighthouse*. Heidelberg: Winter, 1975.
Seel, Martin. "Ästhetik und Aisthetik. Über einige Besonderheiten ästhetischer Wahrnehmung. Mit einem Anhang über den Zeitraum der Landschaft". *Ethisch-Ästhetische Studien*. Frankfurt am Main: Suhrkamp, 1996. 36–69.
Seel, Martin. *Ästhetik des Erscheinens*. Frankfurt am Main: Suhrkamp, 2003.
Seel, Martin. "Über die Reichweite Ästhetischer Erfahrung – Fünf Thesen". *Ästhetische Erfahrung im Zeichen der Entgrenzung der Künste. Epistemische, ästhetische und religiöse Formen von Erfahrung im Vergleich*. Hrsg. von Gert Mattenklott. Hamburg: Meiner, 2004. 73–83.
Seeley, Tracy. "Virginia Woolf's Poetics of Space: 'The Lady in the Looking-Glass: A Reflection'". *Woolf Studies Annual*, 2 (1996), 89–116.
Shone, Richard. *The Art of Bloomsbury, Roger Fry, Vanessa Bell, and Duncan Grant*. London: Tate Gallery Publishing, 1999.
Silver, Brenda. *Virginia Woolf's Reading Notebooks*. Princeton: Princeton UP, 1983.
Smith, Oates J. "Henry James and Virginia Woolf: The Art of Relationships". *Twentieth Century Literature*, 10 (1964), 119–129.
Smuda, Manfred. *Der Gegenstand in der bildenden Kunst und Literatur. Typologische Untersuchungen zur Theorie des ästhetischen Gegenstands*. München: Fink, 1979.
Spalding, Frances. *Roger Fry: Art and Life*. Berkeley: U of California Press, 1980.
Squier, Susan. "Mirroring and Mothering: Reflections on the Mirror Encounter Metaphor in Virginia Woolf's Works". *TCL*, 27 (1981), 272–288.
Stadtfeld, Frieder. "Virginia Woolfs letzter Roman: 'more quintessential than the others'". *Anglia*, 91 (1973), 56–76.
Stanzel, Franz. "Die Erzählsituation in Virginia Woolfs *Jacob's Room*, *Mrs. Dalloway* und *To the Lighthouse*". *Germanisch-Romanische Monatsschrift*, 35 (1954), 196–213.
Stanzel, Franz. *A Theory of Narrative*. Transl. by Charlotte Goedsche. Cambridge: CUP, 1984.
Starobinski, Jean. "Le voile de Poppée". *L'œil vivant* I. Paris: Gallimard, 1961. 1–27.
Steward, Jack. "Spatial Form and Color in *The Waves*." *TCL*, 28.1 (1982), 86–107.
Stierle, Karlheinz. *Ästhetische Rationalität. Kunstwerk und Werkbegriff*. München: Fink, 1996.
Tanger, Marilyn. "Looking at *The Waves* Through the Symbol of the Ring". *VWQ*, III. 4 (1974), 241–251.
Torgovnick, Marianna. *The Visual Arts. Pictorialism and the Novel*. Princeton: Princeton UP, 1985.
Uhlmann, Anthony, Helen Groth, Paul Sheehan, and Stephen McLaren (Eds.) *Literature and Sensation*. Newcastle upon Tyne: Cambridge Scholars, 2009.

Varty, Anne. "Flux, Rest and Number: Pater's Plato". *Platonism and the English Imagination*. Ed. by Anna Baldwin and Sarah Hutton. Cambridge: CUP, 1994. 257–267.

Volk-Birke, Sabine. "'Nothing is simply one thing.' Das Problem der Wahrnehmung in Virginia Woolfs Roman *To the Lighthouse*." *Literaturwissenschaftliches Jahrbuch*, 64 (1993), 115–130.

Wagner, Peter. Ed. *Icons – Texts – Iconotexts. Essays on Ekphrasis and Intermediality*. Berlin et al.: de Gruyter, 1996.

Wiesing, Lambert. *Die Sichtbarkeit des Bildes: Geschichte und Perspektiven der formalen Ästhetik*. Reinbek: Rowohlt: 1997.

Wiesing, Lambert. *Phänomene im Bild*. München: Fink, 2000.

Wiesing, Lambert. *Philosophie der Wahrnehmung. Modelle und Reflexionen*. Frankfurt am Main: Suhrkamp, 2002.

Wilson, James Southall. "Time and Virgina Woolf". *Virginia Quarterly Review*, XVIII (1942), 267–276.

Wittgenstein, Ludwig. *Philosophische Untersuchungen*. Frankfurt am Main: Suhrkamp, 1984.

Wittgenstein, Ludwig. "Wittgenstein's Lecture on Ethics". *The Philosophical Review*, 74 (1965), 3–26.

Wolfe, Linda. *Literary Gourmet: Menus for Masterpieces*. New York: Harmony Books, 1989.

Wolin, Richard. *Walter Benjamin: An Aesthetic of Redemption*. New York: Columbia UP, 1982.

Woolf, Leonard. "The Pageant of History". *Essays on Literature, History, Politics Etc*. New York: Harcourt, 1927. 125–148.

Wyatt, Jean. "The Celebration of Eros: Greek Concepts of Love and Beauty in *To the Lighthouse*." *Philosophy and Literature*, 2 (1978), 160–175.

Zwerdling, Alex. *Virginia Woolf and the Real World*. Berkeley, London: U of California Press, 1986.

Zwerdling, Alex. "'Mastering the Memoir': Woolf and the Family Legacy". *Modernism/Modernity*, 10 (2003), 165–188.

www.ingramcontent.com/pod-product-compliance
Lightning Source LLC
Chambersburg PA
CBHW070612170426
43200CB00012B/2662